Advancing Models of Mission

Other Books in the EMS Series

www.emsweb.org

The Evangelical Missiological Society is a professional organization with more than 400 members comprised of missiologists, mission administrators, reflective mission practitioners, teachers, pastors with strategic missiological interests, and students of missiology. EMS exists to advance the cause of world evangelization. We do this through study and evaluation of mission concepts and strategies from a biblical perspective with a view to commending sound mission theory and practice to churches, mission agencies, and schools of missionary training around the world. We hold an annual national conference and eight regional meetings in the United States and Canada.

Advancing Models of Mission

Evaluating the Past and Looking to the Future

Kenneth Nehrbass
Aminta Arrington
& Narry Santos
editors

Evangelical
Missiological
Society
Series

no. **29**

**WILLIAM
CAREY**
PUBLISHING

Published by William Carey Publishing
10 W. Dry Creek Cir
Littleton, CO 80120 | www.missionbooks.org

William Carey Publishing is a ministry of Frontier Ventures
Pasadena, CA 91104 | www.frontierventures.org

Cover and Interior Designer: Mike Riester
Cover image by Aaron Burson, unsplash.com
Copyeditor: Andy Sloan
Managing Editor: Melissa Hicks

ISBNs: 978-1-64508-407-5 (paperback)
        978-1-64508-410-5 (epub)

Printed Worldwide

25 24 23 22 21   1 2 3 4 5   IN

Library of Congress data on file with publishers.

Contents

Preface

As long as Christians have been engaging in missions, they have been reflecting on the best way to do missions. From China at the turn of the last century, Roland Allen critiqued the Anglican mission of which he was a part, believing that their mission station approach did not lead to the spontaneous expansion of the church. From India, Donald McGavran argued in his book *The Bridges of God* that church growth happens best through family and kinship ties. Based on his missionary experience among the Maasai in Tanzania, Vincent Donovan eschewed individual conversions in favor of community-wide statements of faith. Over the last few centuries of the missionary movement, strategies have been developed for indigenous church planting, Bible translation, orality, people movements, social justice, education, and chronological Bible storytelling.

The world is changing; strategies for discipling the nations must be regularly examined and updated to address those changes. The Evangelical Missiological Society (EMS), an academic organization committed to using research to "advance the cause of world evangelization,"[1] recognized this need for updating missionary methods and strategies. EMS determined that the theme for 2020 would be "The Past and Future of Evangelical Mission" and encouraged members to rethink long-held paradigms of missiology in preparation for the regional and national meetings. Dozens of professors of missions, mission leaders, and missiology students wrote papers for their regional EMS gatherings, on themes ranging from Business as Mission (BAM), to the C-Spectrum, to historical approaches toward women in missions, to the implications of missions for those with disabilities or mental health issues. Many of these authors were recommended to bring their presentations to the national conference in September of 2020—a conference that, as things turned out, could not have any in-person meetings.

The worldwide struggle with COVID-19 served as a poignant example that missiology must be flexible and responsive to the times. The fact that EMS was able to move the conference fully online offers encouraging evidence that evangelical stakeholders in missions do, in fact, listen to the needs of the day and respond with nimbleness.

Many of the presentations at the EMS conference on "The Past and Future of Evangelical Mission" also demonstrated ways in which missionaries are updating their paradigms and models of missions. As the editorial team, we compiled thirteen of those papers in this volume. We tried to capture a broad range of robust scholarly works that critically examine the past and reimagine the future of evangelical mission. Since the resulting compendium can introduce students

---

1 "Who is the Evangelical Missiological Society?" https://www.emsweb.org/about/who-is-ems/.

to a variety of missiological themes in the context of the twenty-first century, we believe it is an excellent resource for courses on missions.

Because missiology is so interdisciplinary, it is difficult to place these chapters neatly into unique categories. But we have ultimately settled on three main parts: models and missionaries from the past, revisiting models, and models for the future of missions.

In part 1, "Looking Back: Missionaries and Models from the Past," Matthew Winslow (chapter 1) reveals how the modernist/fundamentalist debate impacted missionary outreach in China: Those who maintained a high hermeneutic argued for the primacy of evangelism, whereas others believed that missions could serve the Chinese people without persuading them to convert. Emma Wild-Wood (chapter 2) provides social history of twentieth-century evangelicalism in East Africa, showing that the movement attempted to challenge inequalities of power, wealth, and influence that had become increasingly racialized. In chapters 3 and 4, Linda Saunders and Robert Gallagher describe how early Protestant missionaries (Rebekka Protten and Bartholomäus Ziegenbalg, respectively) paved the way for culturally contextualized missionary work. And Xenia Chan and Lisa Pak (chapter 5) trace how Confucian ideals have historically impacted views about women in mission.

Part 2, "Revisiting Long-Held Models," contains critiques of prominent missionary models. Ken Baker (chapter 6) contends that much of the debate about the unreached people groups (UPG) model can be settled if we conceptualize missions more as a role than as a task. Michael Crane (chapter 7) further deconstructs the UPG model, explaining that unreached peoples are also found in large cities, where they are not in enclaves but rather are integrated into heterogenous social groups. Rochelle Scheuermann (chapter 8) also touches on UPGs, suggesting that if we retain the model, we must update it to include other marginalized groups, such as people with disabilities. Martin Rodriguez (chapter 9) considers another seminal missiological model: critical contextualization. His application of identity theory and power dynamics points to dangers in Hiebert's model. And Allan Varghese (chapter 10) revisits the debate surrounding the role of social action in missions. He proposes (based on data from the work of Pandita Ramabai and Amy Carmichael) that providing social uplift serves as an *apologia* for the gospel.

Part 3 looks to the future. Annette Harrison (chapter 11) examines ways in which current trends will impact the who, what, where, when, why, and how of evangelism. Todd Johnson's analysis of demographic data (chapter 12) points to several aspects that future missionary work must address, including increasing conflict with other global religions, the importance of women in the Christian church, and the incorporation of leaders from around the globe.

The appendix surveys thirty milestones in missions over the past fifty years. Luis Bush and Tom Steffen have traced the history of these ideas, showing how each model or event reverberates in our missionary outreach even today.

Down the road there will undoubtedly be more scholarly examinations of the past and future of mission. This is appropriate. Missiologists serve the church by applying academic ideas to real challenges faced in the field.

Kenneth Nehrbass, Aminta Arrington, and Narry Santos

PART I

Looking Back
Missionaries and Models from the Past

CHAPTER 1

"How Shall They Hear?":
A History of the Use of Romans 10:14 Among Missionaries to China, as Seen in the *Chinese Recorder and Missionary Journal*, 1868 to 1938

MATTHEW STEVEN WINSLOW

In 1877, Rev. Dean Butcher preached a sermon in Shanghai that would later be published in *The Chinese Recorder and Missionary Journal*. In his reflections on Romans 10:14, the preacher echoed the thoughts of the majority of missionaries when he stated that "everywhere and always the plan of God seems to be 'how shall they hear without a preacher,' man shall be taught by man" (Butcher 1878, 295).

Indeed, in the late nineteenth century, missionary men and women who came to China from the West generally did so with the conviction that China needed to hear the gospel clearly preached. Romans 10:14 and the surrounding verses served as an important rallying cry for these missionaries—and for the entire nineteenth-century Protestant missionary movement. So, historian Andrew Walls notes that "the number of nineteenth-century missionary sermons and appeals based on Romans 10:14f. alone is beyond calculation" (Walls 1996, 55). Yet, in the waning years of that century and carrying forward through the dramatic changes of the early twentieth century, a debate began to take shape among missionaries to China regarding the importance of Romans 10 and the necessity of preaching the gospel to the "Chinese heathens."

Finally, in the late 1920s, when Pearl S. Buck burst onto the literary scene, views on Romans 10 and the necessity of preaching the gospel had considerably changed.[1] In this chapter I will look at these changes through the lens of *The Chinese Recorder and Missionary Journal*. By reading articles and letters to the editor, one sees a missionary community that slowly segregated into two different groups. The resulting modernist/fundamentalist divide was based on a number of issues, but of central importance was the spiritual condition of the Chinese people and the necessity—or futility—of preaching to them.

Within this debate, Romans 10:14 played a central role. In exploring the use of this text within a specific community of missionaries, in this chapter I will argue that the way Romans 10:14 was used, and its importance, shifted as worldviews and models of missions changed in the late nineteenth and early twentieth centuries. In many ways, this transformation mirrored the shift in the mainline Protestant church in America; yet in China there were some particularities to the debate, and missions texts like Romans 10:14 played a more prominent role in the arguments.

The Chinese Recorder and Missionary Journal

The Chinese Recorder and Missionary Journal was published from 1868 to 1941. During the years that it circulated, the *Recorder* was probably the most widely read journal within the missionary community in China. The journal published feature articles on topics of interest to the missionaries, as well as opinion pieces, letters to the editor, and mundane details, such as which missionaries had arrived and left the country each month, marriages, deaths, and important regional legislation or announcements. At its height, its distribution was only around three thousand copies,[2] but most missionaries in China read the journal. Generally, one missionary in each station would subscribe to it, and the monthly copies would be shared among everyone in a location (Lodwick 1986, vol. 1, xii).

The stated aim of the journal was "to appear before the public as the recognized advocate of the Missionary cause." Furthermore, the editors defined their purpose as giving a voice to "every shade of Christian teaching and shewing a readiness to give each side a fair hearing" (Introductory 1874, 2). The articles in the *Recorder* are thus fairly representative of the wide spectrum of views among missionaries across China, and they provide a window into that world. So, in the words of one reader, "I do not agree with a considerable portion of the opinions expressed, nor do I find value in all the ideas proposed. But I do contend that it is the

---

1 In 1932, Buck famously observed that she was "weary unto death with this incessant preaching" (Buck 1932b, 1437). Her comments, which were hotly debated in China and in much of the Christian world, are discussed below.

2 This is an estimate. No records for the journal exist; they were all destroyed when the Japanese took over in 1941.

function of the Recorder to keep me acquainted with all these diversified activities and opinions" (Hayes 1932, 316). I am using the diverse views expressed in the *Recorder* to examine how Romans 10:14 was used as a foundational principle of missions within China.

Early Missionary Views of Romans 10:14

In the mid-nineteenth century, in the wake of the Opium Wars, China was forced to open a series of port cities to foreigners. The reach of foreign powers gradually expanded; and as opium traders flooded into the country, so did missionaries. The majority of these missionaries came with the expectation that gospel preaching would play a central role in their activities. In an 1869 article, one observer noted that "it will be agreed, perhaps on all hands, that preaching claims a position of paramount importance" (S. A. 1869, 173). The author further reflected that while schools, hospitals, and other institutions have a place in missions, preaching is of the utmost concern to the missionary and should consume the majority of his time. He thus concluded, "It is not civilization that the Chinese want, not education, but true religion; and 'faith cometh by hearing'" (S. A. 1869, 175).

This appears to be the first allusion to Romans 10:14 in the *Recorder*, and it echoes the way that many others saw the verse. "Faith cometh by hearing" serves as a rallying cry to remind all true believers of the monumental task of preaching the gospel to those who do not believe.[3] This strong emphasis on preaching the gospel also leads to the maxim, "The soul first, then the body" (S. A. 1869, 174).

This idea is further supported by glancing through other articles in the 1869 and 1870 editions of the *Recorder*. The journal, for example, ran a nine-part series of feature articles, with a total of sixty pages, addressing the topic "On the Best Method of Presenting the Gospel." In those articles a missionary to Hong Kong explored several aspects of how the gospel was received and presented in China. Ultimately, he implores other missionaries to continue to think carefully about how to preach the gospel to the Chinese so that they can believe (Turner 1870).

In his 1877 sermon, Dean Butcher took Romans 10:14 as his text and then proceeded to explain how the whole Bible was a record of the missionary endeavor. For him, Romans 10:14 represents the theme of the entire narrative of God: Throughout history, God has been sending men and women to proclaim the gospel in order that all may be saved. Ultimately this continued proclamation

---

3 One should note that in this context preaching is not merely teaching Scripture; but rather, in the words of one evangelist, it is "The presentation of Christ as He is made known to us in the sacred scripture" (Muirhead 1893, 253.) So, as the rest of Muirhead's article on preaching makes clear, what he and others have in mind when they talk about gospel preaching (especially in the context of Romans 10:14) is a focused explanation of the doctrines of sin, repentance, and forgiveness as they relate to Christ. The expectation and hope of this kind of preaching is that those who hear will convert to Christianity.

of the gospel in all lands will lead to the triumph of Christ over all. "Therefore, though at times the task be hard and the deferrings of Hope often make the missionary's heart sad, still the ultimate triumph of Christianity is one of the very few things about which there cannot be a shadow of doubt" (Butcher 1878, 298).

Butcher concludes his sermon by reminding his hearers that the map of China is big and that each one is called to do what he can in his own station to proclaim the gospel, in spite of all hindrances, so that light will overcome darkness. For him, Romans 10:14 is foundational to any method of missions to China. This seems to be the general tenor of the early editions of the *Recorder* and presumably the China missionary community. As one reader of the *Recorder* put it, Romans 10:13–15 is Paul's missionary creed and should be the creed of every missionary following him (Editorial 1893, 92).

Debates around the State of the Heathen

By the late 1880s, however, certain questions, which would affect the direction of gospel preaching in China, were beginning to bubble to the surface. As early as 1882, an anonymous article acknowledged that passages such as Acts 10:35 and even Romans 10:12 were being quoted to imply that those who worship the gods of their respective countries would be saved in light of their sincerity. The author firmly declares that "these passages, taken according to their connection and the scope of their meaning, afford no support to any such opinion" (A Student 1882, 391).

Not everyone agreed with this, though. Influenced by modernist Bible interpreters in Europe, some among the missionary community began to wonder if the Chinese really needed to hear the gospel or if they were already seeking God in their own manner. In other words, was it not enough that they were seeking the truth through Confucianism or Buddhism?

In 1883, Rev. D. Z. Sheffield wrote an article seeking to address these growing concerns. In his argument, he acknowledged that other systems of religion do contain some elements of truth and are useful in certain ways to restrain evil and promote good deeds. Sheffield, however, made it clear that from a biblical worldview one must acknowledge that Christ is supreme and that apart from him no one can be saved (Sheffield 1883). In a similar vein, an anonymous article that same year declared that the way to transform China was not to find good teaching in Confucianism or any other system but rather "by returning to the Apostles [i.e., Apostles'] method 'by preaching Christ and him crucified'" (An Evangelist 1883, 280). Both authors viewed preaching the gospel as central to any model of missions.

Later, in 1887, the *Recorder* published a four-part, forty-four-page series in which Sheffield again tackled the issue of preaching the gospel to the Chinese. In the first article of the series, he outlined his firm belief that apart from the gospel, all people are separated from the one true God and are without hope in the world. Sheffield then quoted Romans 10:14, noting that "such teachings need no commentary to explain their meaning, and any man who propounds the doctrine that there are true worshippers of God in the heathen world, walking in the dim light of nature, is building up a theology upon his own speculations as to the moral government of God, and not upon the teachings of the great apostle to the Gentiles" (Sheffield 1887a, 96).

For Sheffield, Romans 10:14 and the surrounding context presented a clear message that applied directly to the needs of those in China: Apart from the true preaching of the gospel, the Chinese cannot hear, and apart from hearing they cannot believe. In the article, Sheffield proceeded to point out that some theologians, contrary to his views, were proposing a future "acceptation" or probation for the heathen.[4] He said that this view has no real scriptural support, but rather represents only the vague hopes of some younger thinkers. He went on to assert that this theology offers hope and relief to those Christians who don't want to go to foreign lands to preach to "the heathen." However, as he wryly observed, these hopes are false hopes (Sheffield 1887a, 98).

Sheffield concluded his series by imploring his readers to follow the plain direction of Scripture and faithfully proclaim the gospel to those who have not heard.

> There is a long, low wail of hopeless misery that is sounding forth from heathen lands, that breaks like the moaning ocean surge upon the shores of Christendom. Christianity is God's lifeboat which was prepared to save these perishing, immortal souls. Christian sailors, make haste to man the lifeboat. (Sheffield 1887b, 237)

For Sheffield, the misery of the unevangelized is remedied by the preaching of the gospel—the lifeboat of Christianity.

Responses to Sheffield's series were varied. The *Recorder* published several replies; and from what appears in the journal, it seems that many missionaries agreed with Sheffield's assertions and were still firmly committed to the ministry of preaching the gospel as the primary means to help the Chinese. Not everyone was so sanguine, though. A thirteen-page article from an anonymous German missionary argued passionately for "the doctrine of a future acceptance of the

---

4 The idea of the future probation of the heathen arose in the mid-nineteenth century and seems in many ways to be a mild form of universalism. Sheffield mentions Canon Farrar in his article, and probably had Farrar's two books on the topic (1879, 1881) in mind when he referred to this idea.

heathen, under certain conditions, as one of the undoubted verities of Christian faith" (A German Missionary 1887, 316). The writer reasoned that the more enlightened of "the heathen" are not totally condemned before God. To say that men like Socrates or Confucius are eternally damned is to accept uncritically "quasi-scriptural doctrines, handed down by the traditions of the church, and not the fruit of 'candid and critical' study of the Scriptures" (A German Missionary 1887, 308).

As one might expect, the German missionary's treatise elicited several replies from eager readers. One letter to the editor noted that while the article had some merit, the reader was not convinced that any of the biblical passages cited by the German were actually relevant to the state of "the heathen." Most of them seemed to be spoken about genuine believers (Moule 1887). Another submission suggested that perhaps it was best to say that the Bible made no definite statements about eternal time and thus the debate of the future of the heathen was unable to be resolved (Crossett 1887). Still another observer argued that while he agreed with the German's viewpoint, he felt that the author used strawman arguments, and the real issue rested on whether or not God's mercy was actually wider than we could imagine. Thus it would be folly to argue that God would not provide a way for those who had never heard the gospel to experience his grace and mercy ("Hopeful" 1888).

The debate continued throughout 1888, as the journal published several full-length articles and responses in regard to the issue. In March, a twelve-page response (Anonymous 1888) noted that the German missionary was obviously not reading the Bible in its full context.[5] The anonymous author pointed out that while the German missionary had cited a few verses in Roman 2 as proof for his theory, the whole point of Romans 1–3 was to argue clearly and repeatedly that apart from the gospel all were condemned.

The article went on to reason that Paul certainly knew about Socrates and Plato, and yet he still showed that everyone has sinned and no one is righteous. Furthermore, the author attacked the German's interpretation of Matthew 25, pointing out that to say the passage is talking only about a judgment of those who have never heard the full gospel "does violence to the plain words of Scripture and to the obvious meaning of a universal judgment" (Anonymous 1888, 114). The writer concluded with a string of verses related to faith and salvation and then argued that Romans 10 is "most important of all." After summarizing verses 8–12, he quoted verses 14–15 and then declared,

---

5 The March issue of the *Recorder* also included a response to the German missionary from Moule, in which he clarified that the overwhelming majority of commentators, both ancient and modern, were opposed to the German's view (Moule 1888).

Here is Paul's great argument for Foreign Missions; and he seems to have framed it especially to shut out the "acceptation" theory.... The whole work of Missions rests on this basis—the need of the Gospel for the heathen as their only means of salvation. (Anonymous 1888, 119)

In August, yet another missionary attempted to bring the debates to an end, stating, "We all believe that the heathen will be judged according to their light, and that those who live up to their light will be saved. But have any heathen ever done this?" (Woods 1888, 377). He then proceeded to note that the clear teaching of Scripture rests in humankind's need to hear the gospel and believe in order to be saved. Attempting again to bring the argument back to Romans, he noted,

Especially is there that passage in Romans x. which teaches that outside of the Gospel there is no hope for fallen man.... It is impossible for language to speak plainer. Salvation only by faith; faith only by hearing; hearing only by preaching. (Woods 1888, 378)

By the end of 1888, the back-and-forth debate in the *Recorder* over the position of "the heathen" seemed to be dying down. Judging from the number of articles and letters to the editor published in support of Sheffield's view, it would appear that most missionaries believed gospel preaching was the essential task of the missionary and the greatest need of the Chinese. For these missionaries, Romans 10:14 clearly played a central role and was the passage that most lucidly set forth God's plan of salvation.

In the last decade of the nineteenth century, discussions in the *Recorder* were increasingly filled with reports of violence toward foreigners and suggestions for how to best relate to the Chinese.[6] Even amid these concerns, though, the journal did publish several articles discussing "the state of the heathen" (Ashmore 1893; Genahr 1893; Schaub 1893; Muirhead 1893), most of them covering terrain similar to the previous decade. Romans 10:14 still played a vital role for those who believed that only through faith in Christ could one find eternal happiness. Thus, one missionary, in a letter to the editor, noted that "the wholesome principle" of Romans 10:14–15 should drive major decisions on the mission field (Pruitt 1898). For many, this "wholesome principle" formed the bedrock of missionary methods in China. The debate, however, was certainly not settled.

---

6 In retrospect, these events were an obvious foreshadowing of the Boxer Uprising and the other anti-foreign protests of the early twentieth century.

Changing Attitudes Toward Mission and Romans 10:14

In 1904, longtime missionary to China J. Percy Bruce noted that "'faith cometh by hearing,' and 'How shall they hear?' is the problem of evangelization in every age and in every country. How shall those who need the gospel be brought into contact with those who have it?" (Bruce 1904, 503). Indeed, for thousands of nineteenth-century missionaries, this question had been the driving force behind their actions. However, that mindset was quickly changing. As David Hollinger has noted, when early missionaries went out from America they had a clear purpose and understanding for what their task was and where their motivation came from. In the early twentieth century, the children of those missionaries were beginning to question those motives and methods (Hollinger 2017, 59). Verses like Romans 10:14, which many missionaries had seen as "the wholesome principle" behind missions and which had provided such a strong missionary impulse throughout the nineteenth century, no longer seemed quite as relevant.

What changed? Within the pages of the *Chinese Recorder*, one notices an increasing focus on the social gospel and the impacts of social change on China. For example, in the twenty years from 1910 to 1929, the journal published over one hundred full-length articles on different aspects of the social gospel (an average of about five a year).[7] Clearly this became an issue of importance on the field. Although Pearl Buck only published a few articles in the *Recorder*, her life and writings demonstrate these changes.

Pearl S. Buck and Changing Attitudes

Born in 1892, Pearl Buck grew up in China as the daughter of longtime Presbyterian missionaries. She attended university in the US, but upon graduating she returned to China as a missionary herself. In 1917, she married fellow missionary, J. Lossing Buck. Her early views seem to have been decidedly evangelical in outlook; and after marrying her husband, she evidently was involved with him in arranging Bible studies and evangelistic campaigns for the Chinese (Wacker 2003, 857–58). But by the 1920s her outlook began to shift.

In 1923, Buck published her first article in the *Recorder*, a piece entitled "The Conflict of Viewpoints." There she argued that "everything does depend upon your point of view. There are as many viewpoints as there 'are people in the world" (Buck 1923, 537). The article then proceeded to gently admonish missionaries for thinking that they know everything and that they could possibly

---

7 Some of this was no doubt due to Frank Rawlinson's leadership as editor, from 1913 onward. While the journal remained broadly ecumenical under his leadership, Rawlinson himself was liberal in his outlook; and critics who saw him moving the journal in that direction probably had some justification. At the same time, the rise in the number of articles on the social gospel is also surely a reflection of an issue that was relevant and very pertinent to the missionary task of the early twentieth century.

Buck's deep fear was that
the vision she, her parents,
and thousands of other
missionaries had been striving
for, was an immoral hoax.

tell others what to believe. Her theme verse was Micah 6:8, which she set forth as a motto for missionaries to adopt. She encouraged them to walk humbly and to be mindful that others have different points of view and that the Chinese point of view is not necessarily wrong.[8]

In the article, Buck was not overly critical of the older missionaries; and her main theme was humility. However, throughout the 1920s and 30s she became increasingly antagonistic toward what she eventually came to see as a paternalistic, condescending attitude that most missionaries had toward the Chinese.

In 1927, Buck published a piece which accurately depicted her own shifting feelings, as well as those of many of her younger colleagues.

> More insidious in its pessimism is that spirit which creeps into the missionary's heart, the spirit which really has silver wings, if one could but see them. It is that struggling idea, fundamentally ethical in its content; born of these times when internationalism is only beginning to be dimly understood in all its moral importance; the question of whether or not anyone has the right to impress upon another the forms of his own civilization, whether those forms be religious or not. Here is the real crux... . Has his life been a mistake? Is the thing for which he has lived really a subtle form of imperialism? It is this which shakes him, the possible immorality of the missionary idea. (Buck 1927, 104)

Buck's deep fear was that the vision she, her parents, and thousands of other missionaries had been striving for, was an immoral hoax. In the article she brings up many valid points, noting that missionaries have unconsciously brought both the gospel and a form of cultural imperialism to China. In doing this, they have angered the Chinese and failed to represent Christ. Although she doesn't mention any specific Bible verses, she talks about "the ideal vision" (Buck 1927, 105) of the missionary; and with that phrase she certainly has in mind the "wholesome principle" of Romans 10:14–15 that earlier missionaries held so dear. For Buck (and many others), the answer to the deep problems that missionaries were having was to abandon this old "wholesome principle" of missions and to adopt a new model based on service to the poor, rather than on preaching. Thus, China needed "a fresh vision of what humanity, and that includes ourselves, needs. No more sermons which leave the hungry souls unfed" (Buck 1927, 108).

---

8 Buck certainly wasn't the first to have this sentiment; her words echo many other liberal thinkers in America and Europe. Even within the *Recorder*, many had begun to call for tolerance in language and viewpoints. For example, one Chinese reader declared that "everybody has the right to be conservative or liberal as he chooses, but no one has the right to condemn the other, because he happens not to have the same point of view" (Hsu 1921, 823).

Buck concluded her article with a rousing cry for men and women to take up the vision of a Christ who loved and served the people. She called foreign missionaries to strive to live out the ideals of Christ rather than to just preach meaningless words. Buck was obviously tired of the missionary emphasis on preaching the gospel, and she wanted to radically shift the focus to social action. She made this even clearer in 1932 when she wrote, "Above all do I wish to protest against that arid and sterile preaching of the mere word of the gospel.... . Mere preaching of the word, mere sermons and churches and such organization as depends upon them, can offer nothing to China today" (Buck 1932a, 451–52).[9]

The Social Gospel and Romans 10:14

Buck certainly was not alone in her feelings about preaching and the need for social action. As one native worker put it, "Evangelism as now understood is no longer needed in China" (Rees 1933, 34). Indeed, many in China began to feel that the old emphasis on preaching was overdone and it neglected more important social work.

Not everyone went quite as far as Buck did with her condemnation of preaching. In fact, in the minds of most proponents of the social gospel, preaching was not the problem so much as the lack of other social supports. Thus, when George Sherwood Eddy surveyed the China scene in 1923, he suggested that the country needed both an individual as well as a social gospel.[10] He observed that "we are facing today a deep human need and a challenging opportunity. We believe that the Church in China will rise to its high calling with a whole gospel, individual and social, applied to the whole of life" (Eddy 1923, 89).

Likewise, other articles published in the *Recorder* in the 20s and 30s called not for an end to preaching but an amendment to it with the social gospel. Sentiments such as those expressed at a conference on evangelism were common. "Is there anywhere that our conversion can stop ... short of all relationships that go to make the systems of men, social, economic and political?" (Rees 1933, 32).

Still, even with more moderate calls to add social elements to the message of repentance, the effect was to reduce actual gospel preaching as missionaries focused on other tasks. In regard to biblical texts, these missionaries of the social gospel tended to emphasize Jesus' call to feed the poor and on Old Testament passages about taking care of the outcasts. Passages like Romans 10 were seldom mentioned. In one case in which Romans 10:14 did seem to be in view, a Chinese churchman pondered,

---

9 In the same year, back in the US, Buck declared in the *Christian Century*, "I am weary unto death with this incessant preaching" (Buck 1932b, 1437).

10 Brian Stanley refers to Eddy as "one of the most influential Protestant mission leaders of the twentieth century" and a "prophet of the social gospel" (Stanley 2000, 128).

Let us see what this emphasis of the Chinese church on "preaching" and "hearing" has accomplished during the past century or more.... The result of these long years of preaching done by the church is tragically meagre. (Lew 1937, 103)

The remedy to this, he suggested, was to join with the YMCA in emphasizing the social gospel and the social reconstruction of all of China. As Lew's words show, the impact of the social gospel on the "wholesome principle" of Romans 10:14 was to minimize it and to replace it with an emphasis on other aspects of the Christian message.

Responses to Buck and the Social Gospel

By 1920 it was becoming apparent to everyone that the missionary community was sharply divided along modernist/fundamentalist lines.[11] So, unsurprisingly, the *Recorder* was filled with fierce arguments both for and against the new ideas. In response to Pearl Buck's call for an end to preaching, one minister noted, "[When] I read over criticisms like this, therefore, they leave me gasping with astonishment" (Moncrieff 1935, 337). He went on to say that what China needed was a thousand more genuine preachers of the gospel. Another critic of the social gospel stated, "I believe there is a danger in our day of overemphasizing the social message of the church.... Christianity will fulfill the needs of this great people about us in so far as we stress the spiritual life through regeneration and justification" (Swenson 1924, 195–96).

Interestingly, even among critics of the social gospel, Romans 10:14 was seldom used as a rallying cry.[12] It seems that in the face of other concerns fundamentalist missionaries felt the need to carefully explain and draw out their motives rather than just refer to one passage as the "wholesome principle" of missions.[13]

---

11 It should be noted that while conservative missionaries of the 1920s generally embraced the label of fundamentalists, those on the opposing side of the debate were less likely to appreciate the term "modernist" and instead saw themselves as simply faithful Christians. Note, for example, the manifesto in the *Bulletin of the Bible Union of China*, stating, "Fundamentalists, that is exactly what we are" ("Fundamentalists" 1922).

12 Of course, some missionaries did still see Romans 10:14–15 as a clear directive for the missionary life. Thus, a 1921 article on preaching concluded by quoting the verses as a clarion cry for the missionary (E. M. P., Jr. 1921, 192). See also Scott (1938).

13 Increasingly, if conservative Christians did look to one text as the clarion call for missions, it became Matthew 28:18–20. The Great Commission perhaps better encompassed the full view of missions that conservatives wanted to emphasize in the face of liberal criticisms which suggested that they only cared about one aspect of the person.

The Use of Romans 10:14 and Shifting Missionary Models

With the penultimate issue of the *Chinese Recorder*,[14] Roderick Scott attempted to sum up the state of preaching in China by noting, "Even in the best missionary circles—or perhaps not in the very best—there is much confusion about evangelism" (Scott 1938, 573). Indeed, during the course of the *Recorder's* publication a change occurred in the way the community viewed evangelism. In the nineteenth century, Romans 10:14 and the surrounding verses served as a central motivation and rallying cry for the missionary cause. In debates about the status of non-Christians or the work of missions, the verse was frequently referenced as the ultimate argument for the urgency and supremacy of preaching the gospel to unreached peoples. However, by the 1930s, missionaries like Pearl Buck were derogatively referring to the "incessant preaching" of the earlier generation, and texts like Romans 10:14 were no longer the focus of missions. Instead, attention shifted to other passages and broader motivations. Even fundamentalist missionaries of the 1930s no longer seemed to refer to Romans 10:14 as the final authority for their work.

Interestingly, part of the shift in missionary models that occurred in the 1920s and 30s sprung from a shift in focus from one biblical text to another. George Ridout noted that "they have put more emphasis on Amos than on the Apostle Paul" (Ridout 1929, 106). Clearly, this critic of the social gospel believed that the emphasis on Amos over Paul was an inversion of the proper order. And most nineteenth-century missionaries would have agreed that while all Scripture is God-breathed, in the task of missions Romans 10:14 is more germane than the social justice passages in Amos.

The pages of the *Recorder* were silent on exactly how one decides which texts should be the most important, but the debates in the 1920s and 30s centered in part around which set of verses should be determinative in the task of missions. Buck and others wanted passages like Micah 6, Amos 5, and Matthew 25 to guide the missionary task, while fundamentalists argued that Romans 10 and Matthew 28 should set the missionary agenda.[15] Both sides were proof-texting, and the debates within the *Recorder* rarely went into extensive exegesis of the passages. Perhaps all parties assumed that their points were obvious, and that the extensive exegesis had already been done by others.

---

14 The journal actually ceased publication in 1941, but in 1939 it merged with *The Educational Review*, changed its name to *The Chinese Recorder and Educational Review*, and slightly shifted its focus for the last three years of its publication.

15 Many liberals rejected Romans 10:14-15, the Great Commission, and other passages that emphasized gospel preaching. Grant Wacker makes a convincing argument that this disregard for these traditional missions texts led liberals first to alter their mission strategy and then to eventually abandon missions altogether (Wacker 1990).

For the modern Bible interpreter, this debate brings to the forefront the difficult task of building a theology that is biblically balanced and faithful to God. How should missionaries handle these different emphases of Scripture, and how can they faithfully apply Romans 10:14 in light of other scriptural themes? Furthermore, in the context of missions today, how does one decide where to allocate limited resources in light of pressing needs in a variety of areas? If resources allow only one focus, which is more important, gospel preaching or social justice? These questions have no easy answers, and thus require godly wisdom.

Conclusion

In his commentary on the book of Romans, F. F. Bruce noted,

> There is no telling what may happen when people begin to read the Epistle to the Romans. What happened to Augustine, Luther, Wesley and Barth launched great spiritual movements which have left their mark in world history. But similar things have happened, much more frequently, to very ordinary people as the words of this Epistle came home to them with power. (1985, 67–68).

This is indeed what happened to thousands of missionaries as they read Romans 10:14. Paul's questions, "How can they believe in the one they have not heard? And how can they hear unless someone preaches to them?" inspired men and women to leave their homeland in order to share the gospel with unreached peoples. For a period of time, it formed the bedrock of a model of missions to China which focused on preaching the gospel at all cost. Nineteenth-century missionaries to China used the verse as a "wholesome principle" of missions. It served as a bedrock to anchor views of other religions and to focus the task of missions.

That use, however, changed over the course of the 1920s and 30s. As proponents of the social gospel grew in number, they minimized the importance of verses like Romans 10:14 and elevated passages such as Micah 6:8 and Amos 5. The resulting division within the missionary community left no distinct theology of mission and entrenched fundamentalists and modernists in separate camps, clinging to different biblical texts as their guiding principles of mission. It also forced fundamentalists to rethink their model of missions. Was Romans 10:14 still the "wholesome principle" of missions, or did other elements need to be added? In the century since then, conservatives have continued to wrestle with this issue. Still, in 1938 Romans 10:14 remained an important impetus for a robust model of missions for many conservative missionaries in China. Thus, in the words of one evangelist, "God comes to man through men. The evangelist is the initiator, the instrument, the channel. 'How shall they hear without a preacher?'" (Scott 1938, 575)

References Cited

A German Missionary. 1887. "The Condition and Hope of the Heathen." *The Chinese Recorder and Missionary Journal* 18 (8): 305–17.

A Student. 1882. Correspondence. *The Chinese Recorder and Missionary Journal* 13 (5): 390–92.

An Evangelist. 1883. "The Apostolic Method of Preaching the Gospel as Presented in the Acts of the Apostles and in the Epistles." *The Chinese Recorder and Missionary Journal* 14 (4): 261–80.

Anonymous. 1888. "Can the Heathen Be Saved without the Gospel?" *The Chinese Recorder and Missionary Journal* 19 (3): 110–21.

Ashmore, William. 1893. "God's Own Estimate of Heathenism". *The Chinese Recorder and Missionary Journal* 24 (1): 21–22.

Bruce, F. F. 1985. *Romans.* Rev. 2nd ed. Tyndale New Testament Commentaries. Downers Grove, IL: InterVarsity Press.

Bruce, J. Percy. 1904. "Our China Missions, Chi-Nan-Fu: An Appeal for Special Work in the Provincial Capital of Shantung." *The Chinese Recorder and Missionary Journal* 35 (10): 500–507.

Buck, Pearl S. 1923. "The Conflict of Viewpoints." *The Chinese Recorder and Missionary Journal* 54 (9): 537–44.

———. 1927. "Is There a Place for the Foreign Missionary." *The Chinese Recorder and Missionary Journal* 58 (2): 100–110.

———. 1932a. "Give China the Whole Christ." *The Chinese Recorder and Missionary Journal* 63 (7): 450–52.

———. 1932b. "The Laymen's Mission Report." *The Christian Century,* November: 1434–37.

Butcher, Dean. 1878. "The Bible in Its Missionary Aspect." *The Chinese Recorder and Missionary Journal* 9 (4): 295–99.

Crossett, J. 1887. "The Condition and Hope and the Heathen." *The Chinese Recorder and Missionary Journal* 18 (11): 443–44.

E. M. P., Jr. 1921. Little Parables of Chinese Life. *The Chinese Recorder and Missionary Journal* 52 (3): 191–92.

Eddy, George Sherwood. 1923. "The Social Gospel in China." *The Chinese Recorder and Missionary Journal* 54 (2): 77–89.

Editorial. 1893. *The Chinese Recorder and Missionary Journal* 24 (2): 91–92.

Farrar, Frederic William. 1879. *Eternal Hope: Five Sermons Preached in Westminster Abbey, November and December, 1877.* London: Macmillan and Co.

———. 1881. *Mercy and Judgment: A Few Last Words on Christian Eschatology, with Reference to Dr. Pusey's "What Is of Faith?"* London: Macmillan and Co.

"Fundamentalists." 1922. *The Bulletin of the Bible Union of China* 9 (October): 1.

Genahr, Imanuel. 1893. "God's Own Estimate of Heathenism." *The Chinese Recorder and Missionary Journal* 24 (10): 484–86.

Hayes, Paul G. 1932. "The Service of the *Recorder.*" *The Chinese Recorder and Missionary Journal* 63 (5): 315–17.

Hollinger, David A. 2017. *Protestants Abroad: How Missionaries Tried to Change the World but Changed America.* Princeton, NJ: Princeton University Press.

"Hopeful." 1888. "Christ the Light of the World." *The Chinese Recorder and Missionary Journal* 19 (5): 223–25.

Hsu, P. C. 1921. What the Chinese Are Thinking about Christianity: The Prospect of Christianity in China.: *The Chinese Recorder and Missionary Journal* 52 (12): 818–25.

Introductory. 1874. *The Chinese Recorder and Missionary Journal* 5 (1): 1–2.

Lew, T. T. 1937. What the Young Men's Christian Association Has Contributed to the Chinese Church. *The Chinese Recorder and Missionary Journal* 68 (2): 102–8.

Lodwick, Kathleen L. 1986. *The Chinese Recorder Index: A Guide to Christian Missions in Asia, 1867–1941.* Vol. 1, 2 vols. Wilmington, DE: Scholarly Resources Inc.

Moncrieff, Hope. 1935. "This Incessant Preaching!" *The Chinese Recorder and Missionary Journal* 66 (6): 337–40.

Moule, G. E. 1887. "Condition and Hope of the Heathen." *The Chinese Recorder and Missionary Journal* 18 (9): 358.

———. 1888. "An Additional Remark." *The Chinese Recorder and Missionary Journal* 19 (3): 131–32.

Muirhead, W. 1893. "How to Preach to the Heathen." *The Chinese Recorder and Missionary Journal* 6 (June): 253–59.

Pruitt, C. W. 1898. Correspondence on "Philanthropy and Christian Missions." *The Chinese Recorder and Missionary Journal* 29 (3): 136.

Rees, R. D. 1933. "Evangelism in China." *The Chinese Recorder and Missionary Journal* 64 (1): 31–36.

Ridout, George W. 1929. "The Christian Message for the China of Today." *The Chinese Recorder and Missionary Journal* 60 (2): 103–9.

S. A. 1869. "On Preaching to the Chinese Public." *The Chinese Recorder and Missionary Journal* 2 (1): 173–75.

Schaub, Martin. 1893. "Heathenism: A Scriptural Study." *The Chinese Recorder and Missionary Journal* 24 (8): 353–61.

Scott, Roderick. 1938. "Evangelism: An Inquiry." *The Chinese Recorder and Missionary Journal* 69 (11): 572–79.

Sheffield, D. Z. 1883. "The Relation Between Christianity and Heathen Systems of Religion." *The Chinese Recorder and Missionary Journal* 14 (2): 93–107.

———. 1887a. "The Condition and Hope of the Heathen." *The Chinese Recorder and Missionary Journal* 18 (3): 89–98.

———. 1887b. "The Condition and Hope of the Heathen." *The Chinese Recorder and Missionary Journal* 18 (6): 228–37.

Stanley, Brian. 2000. "The Legacy of George Sherwood Eddy." *International Bulletin of Missionary Research* 24 (3): 128–31.

Swenson, Victor E. 1924. "What Place Shall We Give the Social Gospel?" *The Chinese Recorder and Missionary Journal* 55 (3): 195–96.

Turner, F. S. 1870. "On the Best Method of Presenting the Gospel to the Chinese." *The Chinese Recorder and Missionary Journal* 2 (11): 300–305.

Wacker, Grant. 1990. "Second Thoughts on the Great Commission: Liberal Protestants and Foreign Missions, 1890–1940." In *Earthen Vessels: American Evangelicals and Foreign Missions 1880–1980*, edited by Wilbert R. Shenk and Joel A. Carpenter, 281–300. Grand Rapids: William B. Eerdmans Publishing.

———. 2003. "Pearl S. Buck and the Waning of the Missionary Impulse." *Church History* 72 (4): 852–74.

Walls, Andrew. 1996. *The Missionary Movement in Christian History: Studies in the Transmission of Faith*. Maryknoll, NY: Orbis Books.

Woods, H. M. 1888. "The Gospel, the Only Hope of the Heathen." *The Chinese Recorder and Missionary Journal* 19 (8): 376–81.

CHAPTER 2

Evangelicalism:
A Transnational Movement in East Africa during the Twentieth Century

EMMA WILD-WOOD

In 2010, the largest of the four conferences held to commemorate the centenary of the World Missionary Conference in Edinburgh was held on the African continent. Cape Town 2010, the third Lausanne Congress, was seen by many as evidence of a new dynamism of international evangelicalism and a sign of the vibrancy and maturity of the evangelical movement in Africa and the Global South (Yeh 2016, 122–24). The confident "all nations" transnationalism displayed at Cape Town 2010 was partially rooted in the history of evangelicalism in twentieth-century East Africa.

The Cape Town conference brought together from across the globe 4,500 delegates who subscribed to an evangelical understanding of Christianity. Central to the conference was an expectation of repentance, a focus on evangelism and mission, a high regard for the Bible and the centrality of Christ's sacrifice on the cross (Bebbington 1989, 2–3), and a broad acceptance of charismatic spirituality as a sign of renewal (Stanley 2013b, 209). A joyful, multicultural cosmopolitanism marked the event, with prominent African speakers sharing the platform with leaders from across the globe. The Cape Town Commitment generated from the conference indicated a desire to honor cultural differences, while expecting consensus in formulations of belief and practice. Although the influence of the Western world was apparent, the unity and diversity of a worldwide evangelical movement was visible and audible.

Cape Town 2010 took place in Africa, but whether it was *of* Africa was a question asked by organizers, delegates, and observers.[1] This question reaches the heart of evangelicalism, which has, for good and ill, been particularly attentive to the conundrum of how to be *in* the world, but not *of* the world. Evangelicalism cannot be properly studied in one location alone, because it is always on the move—expanding across the globe, convinced of the unity of human nature and keen to overcome human differences. Yet the regional dynamics of evangelicalism are important, where conformity is encouraged to maintain global coherence and local community (Freston 2008, 28).

In this chapter, I will provide an overview of the social history of twentieth-century evangelicalism in East Africa in three chronologically organized sections. I will examine a stream of evangelicalism that had greater asceticism and less pronounced attention to the Holy Spirit than has become the case in the Pentecostal-charismatic movement. This stream of African evangelicalism has appeared unexciting to scholarly outsiders who are looking for either distinct forms of cultural or political theology or a lived experience that appeared "indigenous." I will argue that evangelicalism maintained a transnational outlook and retained its distinctive characteristics in East Africa, while giving those characteristics new meaning in a particular regional context. I will focus particularly on the conundrum of being "not of the world" that expressed itself in an "all nations" transnationalism and in a critical or counter-cultural approach to the local, customary, ethnic, and political. These evangelical attributes produced a commitment to overcome human differences, even if there was sometimes failure to acknowledge how harmful these differences can be.

East Africa 1900–1930

Conversion was prompted by early African adopters of Christianity who evangelized their own communities and traveled to neighboring polities with the gospel. In the process of transmission, African Christians made the movement their own and applied its tenets to their own social-political contexts. By 1900, evangelicalism, propelled by the Protestant modern missionary movement, had begun to influence inland communities. East Africa saw a surge in interest spreading from the kingdom of Buganda and Zanzibar and from the Kenyan coast. Civil wars in Central Uganda brought a Protestant party into power in 1893.

---

1 Prior to Cape Town 2010, African Enterprise organized twenty-one evangelistic campaigns, called "Mission Africa," to spread the benefits of the conference across the continent. Songe Chibambo and Scott Lenning. "The Power of Partnership," in *Cape Town 2010: New and Insights from The Third Lausanne Congress on World Evangelization*, 14, https://www.lausanne.org/wp-content/uploads/2010/12/English_comm.pdf.

By the 1890s, most independent polities in Africa had fallen under European political control. By the 1930s, systems of taxes, industry, and infrastructure were under colonial authority. Education and medicine, introduced by Anglican, Presbyterian, and Lutheran evangelical missions, were now often a joint endeavor with the colonial state. The Africa Inland Mission, a faith mission critical of modernism and secularism, began to gain influence in the second decade of the century.

Evangelism was carried out largely by African Christians. Eternal life with Christ was presented as a radically new possibility to sections of society who questioned the power of spirits and ancestors to respond to contemporary challenges of well-being and to those who doubted the wisdom of male elders. Their heavenly hope was entangled in the earthly learning of new skills and reordering of social relations that appeared to offer well-being in a period of great social change.

African Christians propagated their membership in a worldwide community of Christians by using the language of "a family of all nations." There were a number of ways in which this evangelical kinship was made manifest in East Africa. Biblical teaching with a crucicentric focus, worship, behavioral change, and new relationships were part of this process.

In disseminating a vision for "all nations," one such missionary, Apolo Kivebulaya, traversed the region and crossed colonial boundaries (Wild-Wood 2020, 13–22). Kivebulaya preached, "The Lord loves us all… . The Messiah died for us all… . God gives life to us all… . We are brothers and sisters with Jesus." His diary presents us with his peripatetic itinerary and short summaries of his sermons. He taught that books give better protection in life than spears. The Bible, he said, was the "Key of Heaven," and it also provided appropriate advice for every part of life. The Bible became the primary agent in creating a sense of belonging and a pattern of behavior that crossed time and space. Christians grafted themselves into a transnational memory of a sacred past.

The evangelical insistence on translation into the "heart languages," or vernacular tongues, of people encouraged literacy and access to a wider cosmopolitan community with brothers and sisters across the world. Evangelicalism in East Africa was no longer majority English-speaking. This meant that Bible translation also became a vehicle for identity-formation into nations and ethnicities, an approach which often dimmed the transnational vision. Christian rulers of different ethnic groups insisted on the Bible in their own language as they jostled for equal recognition in the colonial sphere (Wild-Wood 2020, 188–93). Translation was as likely to inculcate pride in a particular language and ethnic group as it was to create transnational sensibilities. For many readers of the Bible in their own language, ethnic pride and transnationalism were intermingled—something evangelicals would later criticize.

Evangelical expectations changed behavior as people became Christians. Church services were supplemented by corporate Bible study and prayer, such as regular missionary meetings to pray and plan "for spreading the gospel to the nations." Participants at prayer meetings shared news of local and worldwide missionary activity. The information was repeated in intercessory prayer, which operated on both a vertical and horizontal plane of communication. Intercessors sought God's will and requested that God intervene for success in particular activities of evangelism.

The practice of intercessory prayer encouraged an imaginative, empathetic connection with colleagues and with people for whom they prayed but would never meet, thus inculcating a sense of fellowship among participants (Wild-Wood 2020, 247). Temperance registers signaled a particular commitment to the church and created a communal Christian bond. Teetotalism became a sign of Christian kinship, analogous to regional food prohibitions that signaled clan allegiance. Alcohol became the totem of Christians: abstainers could inherit the kingdom of God. Sobriety demonstrated a new form of belonging, kinship, and inheritance (Wild-Wood 2020, 183–84).

Cross-cultural friendships with European missionaries demonstrated the veracity of the claim of access of "all nations" to the kingdom of God. The opportunities for such relationships remained limited. Even at the height of the missionary movement, European missionaries remained small in number relative to the African population. In 1896, Archdeacon Robert Walker of the Church Missionary Society (CMS) remarked upon "the close intimacy that exists between the European teachers and the native converts." Baganda Christians assumed protective seniority over European missionaries. "They truly stand to us in the relationship of brothers. In fact, their mode of address to us, '*Mwana watu*,' is one of endearment which would be used to a younger brother" (Annual Report 1897, 118).[2]

Kivebulaya had companionate oversight over European missionary colleagues, as a traveling companion, and a chaperon to female missionaries. These friendships were built on a shared aim of preaching the gospel and on common approaches to the task (Robert 2011, 100–107). However, cross-cultural friendships were vulnerable to attitudes of racial superiority, and this increased as the colonial regime became more entrenched. By the late 1920s, many Western missionaries had become more distant from their African counterparts—indeed, they ceased

---

2 R. H. Walker, quoted in *The Annual Report: Ninety-Eighth Year* (London, 1897), 118.

to see them as counterparts, as fellow missionaries. The early evangelical belief that it was salvation through Jesus that brought human equality was undermined in Western missionaries by a soft form of racism and compliance with colonial structures. From the 1930s, African evangelicals brought to account white Christians for their attitudes of racial superiority, as well as their fellow Africans for their competitive ethno-nationalism.

East Africa 1930–1965

By the 1930s, much of the international evangelical missionary movement in Africa had made what it understood to be necessary compromises with the colonial order. The attention to inward holiness that distanced itself from contemporary politics was often accompanied by a tacit acceptance of racial hierarchies and imperialism. Optimism for societal equality through Christian conversion had dimmed. Social theories of race influenced Christian theologies, missiology, and action (Stanley 2010; Kidd 2006). The relative gender and racial inclusiveness of the church in East Africa was compared favorably—but somewhat complacently—with South Africa (Willis 1930, 465). Even Westerners who advocated for African leadership saw themselves as vital conduits of "wider Christendom" (Willis 1930b, 83). This attempt to maintain a cosmopolitan Christian vision of human unity actually placed the church under significant strain, because it accepted political inequalities. Missionaries increasingly became "interlocutors between empire and indigenous peoples," overriding Africans' desire to speak for themselves (Stuart 2011, 193). A new generation of East Africans felt that missionaries possessed a superior attitude and were unwilling to relinquish power (Willis 1930b, viii). African missionaries like Kivebulaya, who held on to a desire for racial reconciliation, seemed to be sycophantic toward European missionaries.

As movements for African independence grew in the 1950s, Western missionaries, with some notable exceptions, appeared to be more concerned about communism and the renewal of paganism than the equality and self-determination of African peoples. For nationalist leaders, many of whom had been educated in Christian schools, this was a betrayal of Africans and of the Christian message of liberation, which had so inspired freed slaves and other disenfranchised peoples in the nineteenth century. The East African Revival offered a critical and peculiarly evangelical response to this situation.

The revival began in Uganda (1920s) and Rwanda (1933) in the Anglican Church, and spread through organized itinerant preaching and conventions into Kenya (1937), Tanzania, (1939), South Sudan, Burundi, and Eastern Congo through a number of Protestant denominations. Following the previous generation of itinerant evangelists and missionaries, revivalists placed the story of Uganda's conversion and eventual revival within a global renewal history

From the 1930s, African evangelicals brought to account white Christians for their attitudes of racial superiority, as well as their fellow Africans for their competitive ethno-nationalism.

(Katarikawe 2015, 13). They focused upon rigorous examination of self, "at the foot of the cross," and developed a strong sense of affiliation with the worldwide church that encouraged regular itineration around East Africa and beyond. A visit to the British Isles and Switzerland in 1947 by William Nagenda and Yosiya Kinuka was the first of many international evangelistic tours taken by revivalists.

A number of Western missionaries working in East Africa joined the revival movement and took its teaching back to the US, Australia, and Europe (MacMaster, with Jacobs 2006, 78). Other Western missionaries rejected the movement. Revivalists renounced clan and ethnic affiliation, questioned political communities, and were connected regionally and globally with similar movements (Wild-Wood 2012b). Adapting the tools of international evangelicalism, such as conventions and mission programs, revivalists intended to impact the East African societies—convert by convert.

Revivalists organized fellowship groups as antidotes to the institutionalization and formal worship of the church and as places for prayer and organization for evangelism (Katarikawe, 2015, 28–29). Revivalists were actively engaged—ideally, several times a week—in evangelistic preaching in public places, promoting the need for repentance and a change of life through a focus on the centrality of Christ's sacrifice on the cross and close attention to the Bible. Spiritual relations overrode the quotidian claims to land or governance along national or ethnic lines. The revivalists' rejection of indigenous religious practices and criticism of nominal Christianity prompted arguments with ethno-nationalists about civic duties, kinship obligations, and social relations.

The East African Revival also altered female agency. Women were applauded when their challenge to traditional customs fitted with dominant revivalist teaching, like rejecting of polygamy and preaching alongside of "saved" Christian husbands (Larsson 2012; Mombo 2012; Onyango 2019). However, where women's ecstatic forms of worship appeared uncontrollable, their practices were censured (Peterson 2017). Women had an equal right to preach the gospel only when they conformed to familiar ways of doing so.

Revivalists scrutinized their relationships with white missionaries. Desirous of revival, they called for a transcending of racial difference rooted in a Christian fellowship of equals (Ward 2012, 18). Christ's crucifixion, as the means by which humans are first reconciled to God and—only then—to each other, proposed a moral economy of global kinship in Christianity. Revivalists confronted white missionaries with the need to confess their superior attitude (MacMaster, with Jacobs 2006, 41). They called missionaries to change here-and-now because they were in conflict with their spiritual kin, with whom they would live eternally.

In taking this line of critique to obtain reconciliation, revivalists appeared to undermine the colonial construction of a "grammar of difference" between Africans and Europeans (Stoler and Cooper 1997, 3–4). Colonists (with missionaries among them) had created notions of race, ethnicity, and gender roles that bolstered their belief in European superiority and excluded the possibility of African autonomy. Many African associations learned to rebut this racial superiority by developing their nationalist pride and common cause with which to counter the racial superiority of white people. The public performance of a revivalist lifestyle by Africans and Europeans included a strict code of practice that marked a fictive kinship of "brothers and sisters in Christ." Race, ethnicity, and gender were not to be understood as markers of difference but as insignificant distinctions among family members. The East African Revival provided its members with a grammar of similarity, which had some success in providing strategies for common belonging to evangelical Christianity.

Some white missionaries confessed, and called upon others to do the same, as a way of combatting the "color bar." Some considered the revivalists impudent or ungrateful for calling them to account. Others worried about revivalist behavior. The patterns of public confession in fellowship meetings and vibrant forms of worship were sometimes closer to regional healing cult practices than they were to the more subdued or earnest piety of their Western missionary counterparts.

Some Western missionaries were unsure that the movement was "sound." Could a true evangelical articulation of the gospel come in such a loud, robust, and bodily form? Such concerns about what constituted proper evangelical behavior and how behavior reflected proper belief were shared by East African revivalists. They checked on each other. The rigorous self-discipline and conformity to evangelical beliefs performed through certain practices meant that those who deviated from one form of revivalist behavior could be considered outside the fellowship. There were few allowances for contextual responses that did not fit the orthodoxy they had established (Wild-Wood 2012b).

Even as revivalists translated their preaching and pamphlets into local languages, they scrutinized cultural and linguistic differences for erosions of evangelical orthodoxy and established a strict code of self-discipline. Fissures in the movement also occurred when regional groups outdid each other in zeal. Although they disagreed among themselves, revivalists were unequivocal in their opinion on ethno-nationalist resistance to colonial rule.

In the 1950s, the revival provided an alternative view of the colonial regime. This view was most starkly apparent in Kenya. The Kikuyu people had had their land taken by British settlers and their way of life disrupted by urban migrant labor. The Mau Mau rebellion was a movement that sought to return to older standards of social discipline and to resist the increasingly violent British rule by forming a guerrilla group to undermine British forces. During the state of emergency in Kenya (1952–60), Mau Mau who were captured were interred in appalling conditions. Many Christians joined the Mau Mau, but the revivalists refused to take the Mau Mau oath of allegiance, saying that they had no need of goat's blood since they had been washed in the blood of Jesus (Stoker 1994). Their "grammar of similarity" caused them to eschew violent protest and the Kikuyu customs to which the Mau Mau wished to return.

In 1969, revivalists protested against Jomo Kenyatta's attempts to consolidate Kikuyu nationalism against Luo and Luyia discontent. Because they refused to enter into ethnically charged politics, revivalists have often been regarded as politically acquiescent. Revivalists considered that they promoted unity by preaching the importance of breaking down mistrust between different ethnic groups and races. They refused to equate the kingdom of God with any existing or possible political scenario.

East Africa 1965–2000

During the last thirty-five years of the twentieth century there was an efflorescence of Christianity on the African continent. Many scholars anticipated that as African countries gained their independence and European states relinquished political control, the commitment to religious forms introduced by Europeans, such as evangelicalism, would also wane. But instead there was an *increase* in conversion to Christianity and of its influence on all aspects of social life. In much of the continent, the embedding of Christian institutions and cultures was a postcolonial phenomenon. Evangelicalism had inserted itself into a range of social contexts, and as a result its approach to those issues was altered. By the early 1990s, the growth of the East African Revival movement was decreasing. Its impact on public life was being replaced by rapidly growing Pentecostal-charismatic churches (Mugambi 2020).

Nevertheless, the revival inculcated into Protestant churches in East Africa a particular evangelical spirituality in the face of difficulty that critiqued dominant cultural and social trends and resisted the more flamboyant style of worship and taste for extravagant consumption as signs of blessing from God that accompanied the rise of Pentecostal churches. Revivalists had established an austere lifestyle that valued education, discipline, and public service and was uneasy with ostentation

(Ward 2015). During the 1980s, as HIV/AIDS spread across East Africa, revivalists preached temperance and faithfulness in heterosexual marriage to avoid disease spread. This moral judgement was supported by international evangelical groups who wished to uphold "family values" and condemned by international public health organizations who wanted to avoid stigmatizing those who had contracted the disease. Revivalists continued to preach interethnic unity and cooperation, but after the Rwandan genocide in 1994 there was much internal reflection about the ability of their personalized message of repentance to prevent widespread violence.

In the post-independence years, church leaders influenced by the East African Revival influenced global discussions on mission and evangelism; they engaged in international ecumenical relations and rejected the otherworldly ethic that kept aloof of politics. It is to these elements of leadership to which we turn now. Although it is not possible to examine these elements in depth, a brief overview will show that evangelical leaders in East Africa were developing their own responses to regional and international issues as a result of maintaining an "all nations" view.

Evangelical leaders in East Africa were self-conscious internationalists. The formation of regional organizations, like African Enterprise, Scripture Union, the Association of Evangelicals of Africa and Madagascar and its national counterparts, the International Fellowship of Evangelical Mission Theologians, and InterVarsity Fellowship were conduits for the exchange of ideas and personnel across the globe and provided mechanisms for maintaining orthodoxy. Revivalist-influenced responses led some African church leaders to conclusions that surprised Western evangelicals, with whom they were otherwise close.

The revivalist cosmopolitan confidence could mount a critique to the way in which Western evangelicals thought their movement should be run. Rev. Dr. John Gatu, general secretary of the Presbyterian Church of East Africa, was unusual in the extent of his criticism, but he demonstrates the rationale of evangelicalism as it had developed in East Africa in the independence era. He was a revivalist who had renounced his involvement in the Mau Mau uprising in 1950 but had remained committed to African independence. In 1971, at the Milwaukee Mission festival, and in 1974, at the All Africa Council of Churches (AACC) in Lusaka, Zambia, and the Lausanne International Congress on World Evangelization, where Billy Graham condemned his call for a moratorium, Gatu called for a temporary moratorium on Western missionary work to give time for a reassessment of the working relationship between missionary organizations and the churches they had planted (Reese 2014; Stanley 2013a). He criticized the status quo as prohibiting the possibility of Kenyan churches participating in global missions in any meaningful way. His call was related to social and political liberation: If the African church were to liberate and reconcile the African people, and support economic and social independence, then Gatu believed that a moratorium on external assistance in money and personnel had to be a matter of policy. He considered that inequalities in wealth and decision-making and a belief in the superiority of the Western world reduced the ability of Christian people to relate as brothers and sisters in Christ regardless of ethnic or racial affiliation, and therefore reduced the impact of the gospel (Gatu 2006, 2016).

Gatu's ideas were modified in the Lausanne Covenant, a document which was to influence global evangelical relations for the rest of the century. Clause 9 reads, "A reduction of foreign missionaries and money in an evangelized country may sometimes be necessary to facilitate the national church's growth in self-reliance and to release resources for unevangelized areas." Yet the sentence that follows not only recalls an "all nations" evangelicalism, but also demands an appropriate attitude from foreign missionaries: "Missionaries should flow even more freely from and to all six continents in a spirit of humble service" (Lausanne Movement, 1974).

Gatu found ecumenists to be more ready to listen to these ideas than evangelicals. Some Western mission societies seriously pondered a moratorium on missions; others expressed alarm and hurt. Some were hostile because Gatu had spoken before the AACC, an ecumenical body connected with the World Council of Churches, about whom some evangelicals were deeply suspicious. Generally speaking, African evangelicals did not support the moratorium. They thought it risked the interdependency of the church and were concerned about maintaining good relationships with international partners. However, like Gatu, many of the East African church leaders formed in the revival were equally involved in ecumenical discussions as they were in evangelical fora. Since many evangelicals in the East African Revival were also members of mainline Protestant denominations, they had structures which made this more likely.

Josiah Kibera (1925–88), for example, was a bishop in the Lutheran church in Tanzania and a member of the Faith and Order Commission of the World Council of Churches and president of the Lutheran World Federation (1977–84). Kibera was also the most prominent revival theologian. His book, *Church, Clan and the World* (1974), developed into social ethic and ecclesiology the notion that Christians were a "clan." Kibera also used the rite of blood brotherhood, practiced in many African societies to bring nonkin into close relationship, as a metaphor for the reconciliation of hostile people and humanity to God through the blood of Christ, while eschewing the actual practice of the rite.

Festo Olang', archbishop of the Anglican Church of Kenya (1970–80), was also an evangelical ecumenist. He hosted the Anglican Consultative Council in

1971, the Pan-African Christian Assembly in 1974, and the Partners in Mission Consultation in Nairobi in 1975. He also participated in the World Council of Churches and the All Africa Council of Churches. In his autobiography, he says that these international gatherings were an opportunity "to consult one another, draw on one another's wisdom and, more than that, marvel at the worldwide fellowship of which the church is part" (Olang' 1991, 56).

Ecumenical relations allowed revivalists an expansive view of the fellowship of all nations that complemented the evangelical networks of which they were a part. Ecumenical fora also encouraged forms of contextual theology, which allowed reflection on what cultural material might enable the translation of the gospel message into regionally accessible thought forms.

The East African Revival discouraged its members from engaging in politics. Apolo Nsibambi (1940–2017), son of Simeon Nsibambi, an instigator of the revival, left the revival movement in which he was raised to become a political scientist and eventually chancellor of Makerere University in Uganda. Beginning in 1999, he served as prime minister of Uganda for twelve years. He was recognized as being an honest and committed public servant, but he could not maintain the strict ascetic discipline of the revivalists and their ambivalence toward politics while holding such posts. He returned to the revival fellowship only after retiring from public office (Interview 30th June 2015). During his lifetime, however, a number of church leaders who had been nurtured within the revival were challenging the assumption that evangelical Christians could not engage publicly in the political sphere. Although Archbishop Janani Luwum lost his life in 1977 after he criticized President Idi Amin of Uganda, and Bishop Festo Kivengere had to flee Uganda in 1973 because of his public stance, such challenges were exceptions to the rule. However, beginning in the 1980s, church leaders in Africa began to play a significant role in shaping and criticizing the state (Freston 2001; Ranger 2006).

In what has been called a "second liberation" that challenged the immediate postindependence political order, church leaders came to the fore in constitutional conferences which sought a new approach to the governance of African states (Gifford 1998; 2009). Prominent among them in East Africa was Archbishop David Gitari of Kenya, who was part of the East African Revival. Gitari used the pulpit to criticize the authoritarianism and corruption of the government of Daniel arap Moi (himself a member of the African Inland Church) (Sabar 2009, 124). Gitari's bold leadership of the National Council of Churches of Kenya helped in the reconciliation of ethnic division, criticizing the Kenyan government's approach and providing practical aid to those made homeless by ethnic violence (Klopp 2009, 196). Gitari led the Kenyan churches in prompting national discussions on democracy and human rights, challenging those who put their ethnic, national, or cultural loyalties before that of their commitment to Christ. Kenyan churches attempted to provide a prophetic voice in the national discussions on democracy and human rights. Nevertheless, trenchant challenges from the pulpit often failed to provide concrete alternatives to poor governance and the co-option of churches into state apparatus and ethnically charged politics.

Almost forty years after Gatu's call for a mission moratorium and 110 years after Kivebulaya's first missionary work in Western Uganda, and while Kenya was still reeling from the ethnic violence after the elections of 2007, Henry Orombi, archbishop of the Church of Uganda and a revivalist, addressed the Cape Town conference. He *still* had to remind people that "We in Africa and the Global South must begin to see ourselves differently. No longer are we only the receivers of missionaries from the West." And yet he was also able to remind the world of the history of "seeing ourselves differently." He said, "When the East African Revival swept through Uganda, it brought deep and lasting changes in families and societies" (Orombi 2010, 16). For Orombi, the revival was a contribution to the prophetic work of evangelical mission in the world.

Conclusion

In the summer of 2020 the Western world was once again forced to reckon with its violence against and marginalization of peoples of color—specifically, people of African heritage. During the colonial period in Africa, when a small number of white Europeans governed African populations, there were a number of movements which tried to reverse or challenge the political domination of Europeans. The evangelical European and American modern missionary movement was, as a whole, not among them. Its attentions for the most part lay in debates elsewhere. The evangelical movement in East Africa *did* attempt to challenge inequalities of power, wealth, and influence that had become increasingly racialized—but it did not enter the political arena. This movement rejected the vision of communities of belonging that were either ethnocentric or nationalist and embraced a global vision of a community in which true Christians were equal in the sight of God, an aspiration which ran through the evangelical movement since its Moravian antecedents and which was celebrated in Cape Town 2010.

The transnationalism of African evangelicalism has often appeared to its critics to place too much emphasis on the transcendent message of the gospel and not enough on the incarnational aspect. The story of God's salvific breaking into history was overwhelmingly focused on the crucifixion and the rupture from the "old man" that conversion entailed. It required the curating of beliefs and behaviors deemed to be properly Christian in such a way that they could also be shared across the globe. Thus, goes the critique, attention to localized forms of expression was underdeveloped, the opportunity to identify God at work in the lives of Africans before the arrival of the Christian gospel was lost, and, instead, African evangelicalism was a copy of the Western missionary tradition. Furthermore, it failed to offer direct critique to political regimes and their policies and offered instead a transcendent and cosmopolitan vision.

Using East Africa as an example, this presentation has provided a more nuanced view. The confident "all nations" transnationalism of East African evangelicalism responded to the grounded issues of its time. On the issue of racial superiority and ethnic division, it was emphatic: Ethnic background or the color of one's skin was irrelevant to accepting Christ crucified as Savior, and entering into kinship "in Christ." The conviction that human divisions were irrelevant when recognizing one's sinful nature provided a powerful message of equal belonging to the Christian church, and allowed revivalists to renounce the priority of kinship, clan, ethnicity, nationality, and race and critique the ways in which they created barriers among humanity.

Nevertheless, revivalists erected their own barriers between those who were evangelically Christian and those who fell short of their high standards. Their grammar of similarity had its own rules of exclusion. Furthermore, identifying ethnicity, nationality, and race as "irrelevant" and focusing on evangelical similarity sometimes prevented evangelicals from seeing how pernicious are the systems of injustice that operate to the detriment *even* of members of the movement. The Evangelical movement in East Africa did bring lasting change. One of those changes was a particular way of critiquing, in their own context, the human problem of disparaging the differences of others.

References Cited

Annual Report. 1897. Church Missionary Society, Ninety-Eighth Year. London.

Bebbington, David. 1989. *Evangelicalism in Modern Britain: A History from the 1730s to the 1980s*. London: Unwin Hyman.

Freston, Paul. 2001. *Evangelicals and Politics in Asia, Africa and Latin America*. Cambridge: Cambridge University Press.

———. 2008. "Globalization, Religion and Evangelical Christianity." In *Interpreting Contemporary Christianity: Global Processes and Local Identities*, edited by Ogbu Kalu and Alaine Low, 24–51. Grand Rapids: Eerdmans.

Gatu, John. 2006. *Joyfully Christian + Truly African*. Nairobi: Acton Press.

———. 2012. "Jesus Christ, The 'Truthful Mirror.'" In *The East African Revival: History and Legacies*, edited by Kevin Ward and Emma Wild-Wood, 33–41. Surrey, UK: Ashgate.

———. 2016. *Fan into Flame*. Nairobi: Moran Publishers.

Gifford, Paul. 1998. *African Christianity: Its Public Role*. Bloomington, IN: Indiana University Press.

———. 2009. *Christianity, Politics and Public Life in Kenya*. New York: Columbia University Press.

Katarikawe, James. 2015. *The East African Revival*, n.p.

Kidd, Colin. 2006. *The Forging of Races: Race and Scripture in the Protestant Atlantic World, 1600–2000*. Cambridge: Cambridge University Press.

Klopp, Jaqueline. 2009. "The NCCK and the Struggle against 'Ethnic Clashes' in Kenya." In *Religion and Politics in Kenya: Essays in Honor of a Meddlesome Priest*, edited by Benjamin Knighton, 183–99. New York: Palgrave Macmillan.

Knighton, Benjamin, ed. 2009. *Religion and Politics in Kenya: Essays in Honor of a Meddlesome Priest*. New York: Palgrave Macmillan.

Larsson, Birgitta. 2012. "Haya Women's Response to Revival." In *The East African Revival: History and Legacies*, edited by Kevin Ward and Emma Wild-Wood, 119–28. Surrey, UK: Ashgate.

Lausanne Movement. 1974. "The Lausanne Covenant." https://www.lausanne.org/content/covenant/lausanne-covenant#cov.

Lausanne Movement. 2010a. "Cape Town 2010." https://www.lausanne.org/gatherings/congress/cape-town-2010-3.

Lausanne Movement. 2010b. "The Cape Town Commitment." https://www.lausanne.org/content/ctcommitment#capetown.

MacMaster, Richard K., with Donald R. Jacobs. 2006. *A Gentle Wind of God: The Influence of the East Africa Revival*. Scottdale, PA: Herald Press.

Mombo, Esther. 2012. "The Revival Testimony of Second Wives." In *The East African Revival: History and Legacies*, edited by Kevin Ward and Emma Wild-Wood, 153–62. Surrey, UK: Ashgate.

Mugambi, Kyama. 2020. *A Spirit of Revitalization*. Waco, TX: Baylor University Press.

Olang', Festo. 1991. *An Autobiography*. Nairobi: Uzima Press.

Onyango, Emily. 2019. "Gender Equality in the East African Revival Movement." *African Multidisciplinary Journal of Research* 4 (1): 21–40.

Orombi, Henry. 2010. "Cape Town and the Future." In *Cape Town 2010: News and Insights from The Third Lausanne Congress on World Evangelization*. https://www.lausanne.org/wp-content/uploads/2010/12/English_comm.pdf.

Peel, J. D. Y. 2000. *Religious Encounter and the Making of the Yoruba*. Bloomington, IN: Indiana University Press.

Peterson, Derek R. 2017. "The East African Revival." In *The Oxford History of Anglicanism Volume V: Global Anglicanism c. 1910–2000*, edited ny William L. Sachs, 211–31. Oxford: Oxford University Press.

Ranger, Terrance. O., ed. 2006. *Evangelical Christianity and Democracy in Africa*. Oxford: Oxford University Press.

Reese, Robert. 2014. "John Gatu and the Moratorium on Missionaries." *Missiology* 42 (3): 245–56.

Robert, Dana. 2011. "Cross-cultural Friendship in the Creation of Twentieth-century World Christianity." *International Bulletin of Missionary Research* 35 (2): 100–107.

Sabar, Galia. 2009. "'Was There No Naboth to Say No?' Using the Pulpit in the Struggle for Democracy: The Anglican Church, Bishop Gitari, and Kenyan Politics." In *Religion and Politics in Kenya: Essays in Honor of a Meddlesome Priest*, edited by Benjamin Knighton, 123–49. New York: Palgrave Macmillan.

Stanley, Brian. 2010. From 'The Poor Heathen' to 'The Glory and Honour of All Nations': Vocabularies of Race and Custom in Protestant Missions, 1844–1928." *International Bulletin of Missionary Research* 34 (1): 3–10.

———.2013a. "Lausanne 1974, the Challenge from the Majority World to Northern Hemisphere Evangelicalism." *Journal of Ecclesiastical History* 64 (93): 533–51.

———. 2013b. *The Global Diffusion of Evangelicalism: The Age of Billy Graham and John Stott.* Nottingham, UK: IVP.

Stoker, Dorothy. 1994. *Ambushed by Love: God's Triumph in Kenya's Terror.* Fort Washington, PA: Christian Literature Crusade.

Stoler, Ann, and Frederick Cooper. 1997." Between Netropole and Colony: Rethinking a Research Agenda." In *Tensions of Empire: Colonial Cultures in a Bourgeois World*, edited by Frederick Cooper and Ann Laura Stoler, 1–58. Berkeley, CA: University of California Press.

Stuart, John. 2011. *British Missionaries and the End of Empire: East, Central and Southern Africa, 1936–64.* Grand Rapids: Eerdmans.

Ward, Kevin. 2012. "Revival, Mission and Church in Kigezi, Rwanda and Burundi." In *The East African Revival*, edited by Kevin Ward and Emma Wild-Wood, 11–31. Surrey, UK: Ashgate.

———. 2015. "The Role of the Anglican and Catholic Churches in Uganda in Public Discourse on Homosexuality and Ethics. *Journal of Eastern African Studies* 9 (1): 132–35.

Wild-Wood, Emma. 2012a. "Chosen Evangelical Revival on the Northern Congo-Uganda Border." In *The East African Revival*, edited by Kevin Ward and Emma Wild-Wood, 129–41. Surrey, UK: Ashgate.

———. 2012b. "The East African Revival in the Study of African Christianity." In *The East African Revival*, edited by Kevin Ward and Emma Wild-Wood, 201–12. Surrey, UK: Ashgate.

———. 2020. *The Mission of Apolo Kivebulaya: Religious Encounter & Social Change in the Great Lakes c. 1865-1935.* Woodbridge, UK: James Currey.

Willis, J. J. 1930a. "Synod of the Native Anglican Church of Uganda." *Uganda Church Review* (17).

———. 1930b. "The Relationship of the Younger and Older Churches." *Uganda Church Review* (19).

Yeh, Allen. 2016. *Polycentric Missiology: Twenty-First-Century Mission from Everyone to Everywhere.* Downers Grove, IL: InterVarsity Press.

CHAPTER 3

The Future of the Evangelical Missionary Movement Must Include an Accurate Portrayal of Her Past

LINDA P. SAUNDERS

The Protestant missionary movement began amid a world of religious persecution. Those who sought religious freedom and separation from the Roman Catholic Church envisioned carrying the gospel to "heathen" lands. This group of protestors were soon called Protestants, and their quest to reach the world with the gospel message began a missionary movement that took the world by storm. Roman Catholic missionaries were already evangelizing the continents of Africa and Asia, and Black missionaries were known to be among their ranks. The missionary history the Catholic Church, however, is outside the scope of this chapter, which focuses on the Protestant missionary movement and a people group who pioneered that movement. Blacks, though rarely, if ever, mentioned and never properly credited for their role in this movement, are unsung heroes of the modern Protestant missionary movement. In this chapter I will argue that Rebekka Protten—a woman of African descent—is the mother of the Protestant missionary movement, and that an accurate portrayal of the evangelical missionary movement must include her vignette. The writing of this chapter was inspired by my PhD research study and includes an excerpt from my dissertation (Saunders 2020).

> Blacks, though rarely, if ever, mentioned and never properly credited for their role in this movement, are unsung heroes of the modern Protestant missionary movement.

In this chapter I will examine the Protestant missionary movement by exploring the Moravian Brethren and their missionary exploits. While Rebekka Protten had already begun an amazing missionary endeavor on the island of St. Thomas, the Moravian missionaries called her out of obscurity and gave her a platform that would forever change the trajectory of the modern missionary movement. For this reason, Rebekka Protten's vignette cannot be told in its entirety without highlighting the role the Moravian Brethren played on the stage of the modern Protestant missionary movement. Once the historical backdrop has been chronicled, I will focus on Rebekka Protten's personal vignette, as well as her threefold missiological strategy. This threefold strategy includes linguistic acquisition, cultural contextualization, and a contextualized delivery of the gospel—all of which are still practiced today. Finally, I will examine Protten's missional theology and praxis and take a brief glimpse at her lasting legacy.

Historical Backdrop: The Moravian Missionary Movement

It is imperative for this chapter to situate Rebekka Protten within her proper historical context, therefore, a brief chronicle about the Moravians and their missionary movement is an appropriate place to commence. The Moravian Brethren, their self-ascribed name, began a missionary movement that Protestant missionaries mark as the commencement of the Protestant missionary movement. The Moravians, as they came to be known, were originally known as the *Unitas Fratrum* ("Unity of the Brethren"). The Thirty Years' War practically destroyed this group, causing them to scatter in search of religious freedom and refuge in other parts of the world. The resuscitation of *Unitas Fratrum* resulted in the formation of the Moravian Brethren, who traveled the world spreading the good news of Jesus Christ (Hamilton and Hamilton 1900, 13–14).

In 1722, a great exodus ensued as Bohemians and Moravians fled their countries in hopes of preserving their religious heritage. Many of the Bohemians and Moravians arrived at Berthelsdorf, Germany, the home of Count Ludwig von Zinzendorf, and found the haven which they so desperately sought. Beginning in the late 1720s and continuing for decades, the Moravian Brethren made an indelible impression on the stage of global missions—an impression whose ideology and methodology still reverberates within the corridors of missiology.

At the outset of this missionary movement, Count Zinzendorf sent men to London, the West Indies, and the British colonies in America. As the Moravians began to take the good news throughout the known world, at first not even Count Zinzendorf had "fully recognized that by the logic of events the Brethren's Church constituted a distinct ecclesiastical body" ready to engage in global evangelization (Hamilton and Hamilton 1967, 88). From such beginnings, the Protestant missionary movement was birthed. Now we will explore how the Brethren's influence—on the island of St. Thomas—catapulted a young woman of color onto the pages of missions history.

The Moravian Missionary Movement

It is prudent to commence this historical chronicle with the Moravian missionaries and their missionary endeavors, beginning in the eighteenth century, because this is where Rebekka Protten's story beg. The Moravian missionaries, also known as the Moravian Brethren, in Berthelsdorf, Germany, at the estate of Count Nicolaus Ludwig von Zinzendorf. Historians, missiologists, and missionaries are familiar with the Moravian missionary movement and how Count Zinzendorf's reception of a man called Christian David ignited a worldwide evangelical missionary movement. Persecuted Christians began to arrive at the count's estate, and soon a community of believers was thriving. This community—*Herrn Hut*—received their missionary vision from their leader, Count Zinzendorf, and missionaries were soon commissioned to take the gospel around the world. The slave population in the West Indies—specifically the island of St. Thomas—was one of their first missionary endeavors (Hamilton and Hamilton 1900, 13–15, 23, 34–49).

Count Zinzendorf's Passion to Reach the Negroes in St. Thomas

The count's missionary zeal began long before Christian David arrived at Berthelsdorf. As a young child living in his grandmother's castle, the young count encountered the missionary adventures of the Pietist Philipp Spener. Zinzendorf, overcome with a desire to pursue a like passion, never forgot the spiritual instructions and the countless renderings of Spener's missionary adventures (Hutton 1923, 4–5, 8). Years later, Zinzendorf encountered a West Indian Negro from the island of St. Thomas called Anton. Anton shared with the count and other Moravian Brethren how he longed to learn about the doctrine and precepts of Christianity and how he prayed for an intimate relationship with the God of Christianity.[1] The count was so moved by Anton's lament that he was compelled to send missionaries to the island immediately; this was not possible, so he presented the matter to the Brethren at Herrn Hut (Oldendorp 1987, 270–71, 276).

The Brethren at Herrn Hut were also convinced and soon arranged to send missionaries to the island of St. Thomas. The Moravian Brethren believed wholeheartedly:

---

1 By the time the Moravian Brethren arrived in St. Thomas, Anton had recanted his request. Not to be deterred, the Moravian missionaries began their labor among the slave population.

Following the wise dispensation of our Lord and Savior, it was the heathen Negroes serving as slaves in the West Indian islands of St. Thomas, St. Croix, and St. John who were to be the first to experience the blessings of a concern for their salvation that had been implanted in the hearts of the Brethren by God Himself. (Oldendorp 1987, 270)

Upon their arrival at St. Thomas, the Moravians would soon encounter a young mulatto girl, barely twenty years of age, who was already engaged in a missionary enterprise that would astound the Moravians.

The history of the Moravian missionary movement is well documented. Count Zinzendorf's diaries and journals are well-preserved, along with letters written by many Moravian missionaries, documenting their global missions endeavors. William Carey, the renowned father of the modern missionary movement, credits the Moravian Brethren for their missionary exploits. In Carey's *An Enquiry into the Obligations of Christians to Use Means for the Conversion of the Heathens*, he credits the Moravian Brethren for his missionary inspiration (Carey 1791; Carey 1792 [1967], ix, 71). While the history of the Moravian missionary movement is commonly rehearsed, there is a well-hidden, or forgotten, piece to this historiography: the labors of Rebekka Protten, the Moravian missionary of color.

Rebekka Protten: Mother of the Modern Missionary Movement

The biography of Rebekka Protten is set in motion on the island of Antigua, where she was born to an African mother and a Danish father and given the name Shelly, circa 1718.[2] According to Rebekka's personal testimony, she was abducted as a young girl, sold into slavery and taken to the island of St. Thomas. On the island of St. Thomas, Shelly was purchased by Lucas van Beverhout, a wealthy planter and slaveowner, and raised in his household (Oldendorp 1987, 314; Sensbach 2005, 35–37).

The Beverhout family belonged to the Reformed Church, thus Shelly's early introduction to Christianity was from a Reformed Church perspective. The Beverhout family and Shelly were regular congregants at the Reformed Church in St. Thomas. The Beverhout family is credited with Shelly's early biblical and spiritual formation. Shelly was also educated while living in the Beverhout household. Evinced by the spiritual nourishment and the opportunity for educational pursuits Shelly received while living in the Beverhout household, historians surmise the Beverhout family held Shelly in high esteem, an unusual

---

2 C. G. A. Oldendorp's ethnographic work, originally published in 1770, is an invaluable resource for gleaning biographical information about Rebekka Protten, as well as the missionary endeavors of the Moravian Brethren on the Island of St. Thomas. Additionally, letters and diaries written by Count Zinzendorf and other Moravian missionaries and letters written by Rebekka Protten collaborate her contribution to the Protestant global missions endeavors during its nascent years.

position for a slave girl (Sensbach 2005, 35–37). While it is unclear whether Shelly's education led her to pursue Christianity or if her interaction with Christianity ignited her desire to learn to read and write, it is clear that Shelly acquired both spiritual guidance and a secondary education while living among the Beverhout family.

Surviving documents demonstrate that Shelly was a gifted linguist. She undoubtedly spoke English or an African creole of English in her early years in Antigua, and then she acquired her fluency in Dutch when she lived in the Beverhout house. Later, her communication with the Moravians indicated she had obtained a fluency in German. And her interaction with the St. Thomas slave population demonstrates her skill and fluency in the slaves' language of Dutch-Creole.

While still living in the Beverhout house, Shelly encountered a Catholic priest whom she heard had baptized Negroes; so Shelly sought out the priest to receive the sacrament of baptism. The unusual circumstances surrounding this event is the fact Negroes were thought to be less than human and unworthy of baptism or any part of Christianity, yet Shelly longed to be baptized. When the priest baptized her, he gave her a new name—Rebekka. From that time forward, Rebekka embraced her new name as well as her new identity in Christ (Oldendorp 1987, 314; Sensbach 2005, 38–39).

Another gift Rebekka received from the Beverhout family was her manumission from slavery. As per the custom on the West Indies islands, White Europeans who fathered mulatto children secured the child's emancipation through their written wills. When Lucas van Beverhout died, his son—Adrian van Beverhout—granted Rebekka her emancipation from slavery. While the details enveloping her freedom are not known, historical records indicate Rebekka was a free mulatto woman. With her freedom, Rebekka reached out to the slave community to provide them an opportunity to learn the tenets of Christianity and the chance to receive an education. Her lessons to the slave population began with the slaves in the Beverhout household soon Rebekka was reaching the slave population around the island of St. Thomas (Sensbach 2005, 38).

When the Moravian missionaries arrived in St. Thomas, they joined forces with Negro slaves who were already engaged in reaching lost souls for the sake of the kingdom. The first Moravian Brethren to arrive were considered courageous because they sought to forge relationships with Negro slaves, which could mean "social ostracism … or worse" (Hamilton and Hamilton 1900, 47–48). During the early eighteenth century, Negroes were considered little more than dogs or soulless creatures, to be abused by their masters. Association with a Negro slave beyond a master/slave relationship was rare, placing the Moravian missionaries in a precarious position from a social context perspective (Hamilton and Hamilton 1900, 47–48).

Upon their arrival, the Moravian Brethren also noticed a young mulatto girl who was transforming the island through her missionary endeavors. This young girl was Rebekka (Oldendorp 1987, 314; Sensbach 2005, 46). Sixty years before William Carey penned his *Enquiry*, Count Zinzendorf recognized a woman of African descent who had accomplished great missionary exploits. In amazement, the count acknowledged that St. Thomas was a "greater wonder" than what he had witnessed in Herrn Hut (Hamilton and Hamilton 1900, 49–50). To fully appreciate Rebekka's work among the slaves on the island of St. Thomas and the reason she is worthy of the title "Mother of the Protestant Missionary Movement," it is necessary to examine her missionary strategy to illustrate how she orchestrated a missionary movement William Carey would later use as his inspiration to ignite what missiologists, historians, and Christians call the modern Protestant missionary movement.

Rebekka Protten's Missionary Journey: The Path

The path was a well-worn conduit around the island of St. Thomas, a customary route everyone on the island traversed, both Black and White (Sensbach 2005, 70–73). For slaves, however, this passageway posed imminent dangers. Because slave curfew laws were strictly enforced, to be caught without one's traveling pass could culminate in deadly consequences. Therefore, for safety reasons slaves were often forced to veer off the island's major artery onto the rugged mountainous terrain of St. Thomas. Nonetheless, neither Rebekka nor her missionary apprentices were dissuaded by these encumbrances. Additionally, due to curfew times and a myriad of other codes imposed upon slaves regarding gathering times, the "traveling gospel" became the best means by which to spread the good news (Sensbach 2005, 70–74). What Rebekka accomplished on the path was a contextualized delivery of the gospel. She adapted the methodology, the style, and the means by which the slaves on the island of St. Thomas could receive the message of salvation.

Rebekka's fervor for spreading the gospel led to her encounter with Friedrich Martin, a Moravian missionary stationed on the Danish Islands in the Americas (Sensbach 2005, 46; Oldendorp 1987, 314, 330). Rebekka's zeal for Christ, her passion to spread the good news, and her knowledge of God's Word forged an immediate kinship between herself and Martin. From the outset, Martin recognized that Rebekka could serve as an impetus for the Moravian Brethren's missionary endeavors. One prerequisite Martin deemed necessary though, was that Rebekka needed a husband. He arranged for Matthäus Freundlich—with mutual consent—to marry Rebekka (Oldendorp 1987, 338–39).

Rebekka Protten's Missionary Journey: Imprisonment

Soon, the Freundliches became a missionary duo on the island of St. Thomas. They ministered together, they cared for orphaned children together, and they were jailed together. Later Count Zinzendorf would choose them as candidates for further training and education among the Moravians in Herrn Hut, the Moravian headquarters at the time. The count was keenly aware of Rebekka's work among the Negro slaves. He witnessed her missionary strategy firsthand and praised her for the missionary enterprise she had created on the island of St. Thomas. His letters and diaries evidence his support for her work and his admiration for her mission's passion.

In January of 1740, Count Zinzendorf's visit to St. Thomas proved to be both providential and beneficial for Rebekka, her husband, and Friedrich Martin, who at the time were imprisoned based on false charges. Troubles began for the missionaries when their ordinations were brought into question by the authorities. Another Moravian brother, Timotheus Fiedler, was accused of theft. And finally, Rebekka and Matthäus Freundlich's marriage was questioned. The pending charges brought against the missionaries culminated in their arrest, and soon they faced fines that became insurmountable obstacles. The count's arrival to the island and his influence was enough to secure freedom for the trio (Oldendorp 1987, 345–52, 357–59).

When Count Zinzendorf created a new post in St. Thomas, Rebekka was one of the chosen leaders. Zinzendorf appointed Rebekka and Maria—another prominent Black female leader in the Moravian Church—to be ordained, creating a watershed event in Christendom. It was highly unusual for women to be ordained during the eighteenth century, notwithstanding that ordaining Black women was unprecedented in the Americas (Oldendorp 1987, 360; Sensbach 2005, 188).[3] During the mid-eighteenth century, men and women in the Brethren church were spiritual equals, though. This meant that as an ordained Moravian missionary or minister, Rebekka would have the freedom not just to teach, but to hold a position as a spiritual leader (Oldendorp 1987, 333, 360). This elevation gave Rebekka the authority to administer the sacraments to White European women.

The Moravian Church was standing on the cusp of a historical and religious revolution. Before the count left St. Thomas, he instructed Rebekka and the leaders to gather the slaves and he imparted words of wisdom and blessings on them. Although Zinzendorf insisted obedience to their masters was in their best interest, he praised Rebekka and the Negro missionaries and ministers who labored among the slaves (Oldendorp 1987, 360–62; Weinlick 1956, 143–46).[4]

---

3 According to Sensbach, it is possible that Rebekka and Maria were the first Black women ordained in Western Christianity.

4 Count Zinzendorf acquiesced to the ideology of his era, while most Moravian missionaries promoted racial equality. This serves to emphasize the dichotomy which existed in the global missionary movement from the outset.

Rebekka Protten's Missionary Journey: Leadership Appointment

Count Zinzendorf, impressed with the missionary zeal and labor of Rebekka and Matthäus Freundlich, appointed them to go to Herrn Hut for further missionary training. Unfortunately, Matthäus Freundlich never arrived for their appointment he died shortly after their arrival in Amsterdam (Oldendorp 1987, 343–52, 357, 398–99). After Matthäus Freundlich's death, Rebekka and their daughter Anna Marie remained in Herrn Hut. Rebekka's passion for teaching and prayer, along with her missionary zeal, won the hearts of those among whom she labored.

In Herrn Hut, once again the Moravian Brethren deemed it necessary for Rebekka to take on a husband. This time, the union would not be considered interracial, rather, as a union with a man who appeared to be compatible with Rebekka's ethnic heritage. Christian Jacob Protten was born on Africa's Gold Coast to an African mother and a Danish father, identical to Rebekka's ethnic heritage (Sensbach 2005, 162). As a young child, Christian Protten was chosen by the Danish preacher Schwane to go to Copenhagen for missionary training. Schwane, a Moravian minister, envisioned training the young Protten to later send him back to Africa to minister among his own people (Sensbach 2005, 164).[5] Protten was among the first Africans who were educated in Europe expressly to be sent back to Africa as missionaries to their own people (Oldendorp 1987, 167–70).

When the Prottens completed their training at Herrn Hut, eventually the Brethren sent Christian and Rebekka to Africa to serve as missionaries. Rebekka continued to reach cultural others with the good news through spiritual tutelage and rudimentary educational training. Although her time in Africa was replete with hardships, Rebekka Protten left an indelible mark on the Protestant missionary movement as a Moravian missionary of color.

Rebekka's missionary model can be further comprehended by examining her missional approach for reaching the slaves on the island of St. Thomas. As identified in her correspondence to the king of Denmark and the Moravian Brethren, Rebekka contended education for slaves was crucial to their Christian growth.[6] Furthermore, discipleship was the paramount goal of her missionary vision. Her passion to reach the slave population with the good news of Christ compelled Rebekka to give her all in service for the kingdom.

Rebekka Protten: A Missionary Strategy

Rebekka established a missions training model that incorporated three key tenets for global missions: linguistic acquisition, cultural contextualization, and a contextualized delivery of the gospel. The linguistic aspect for missionary

---

5 The idea of training Africans as missionaries, then sending them back to Africa was a Eurocentric worldview, although there were a few Africans who envisioned such a plan.

6 See the letter on page 44.

training incorporates language acquisition, Bible translation, and the transference of the spoken Word into a culturally comprehensive adaptation. Rebekka's fluency in several languages, as well as her ability to adapt to the linguistic context in which she ministered, illustrates this point. She spoke fluently with the slaves to whom she ministered. She may have acquired her fluency in Dutch-Creole prior to moving into the Beverhout house; however, it is more likely she acquired it as a result of living in the Beverhout household, because she lived and worked with other slaves. Her fluency in German and other languages—evidenced by her letters which survived—allowed her to mediate between Friedrich Martin, Count Zinzendorf, and the slaves of St. Thomas with regard to the Moravian Brethren's island ministry (Oldendorp 1987, 314–15, 330, 357–66).

Rebekka understood not just the slaves' spoken language, Dutch-Creole, but she had an intimate familiarity with their cultural worldview. Without doubt, Rebekka's ministry among the slaves in the Beverhout household strengthened this familiarity. From a cultural context, Rebekka related to the slaves' spoken language and many of the slaves' cultural traditions. Because of her upbringing in the Beverhout household, she understood Dutch from a linguistic, cultural, and religious perspective. Finally, evidenced by the Brethren's acceptance of her as their equal, Rebekka adapted to their culture as well. She learned the importance of cultural contextualization and the necessity for a contextualized delivery of the gospel. Unequivocally, Rebekka possessed a high cultural intelligence, which enabled her to move fluidly between the various ethnolinguistic, cultural, and religious settings that were intermingled on the island of St. Thomas.

Rebekka's model also included a strategy for discipleship which incorporated an educational and training paradigm—key elements necessary to teach the newly converted slave. Likewise, Rebekka intimated that social equality for all should be practiced among those who embraced Christianity. Her missionary discipleship methodology included a plan to teach others to reach the lost. The education and training paradigm placed the missionary focus on proper contextualization of the gospel as well as a properly contextualized delivery of the gospel. As Rebekka demonstrated, educating the slave was key to advancing the gospel on the island of St. Thomas. The letter which she and other Negro leaders wrote—addressed to the King of Denmark—serve to highlight Rebekka's influence on the slave community and her success in spreading the gospel among the St. Thomas slave population (Protten n.d.).

The Letter

A Letter of the Awakened Negroes in St Thomas wrote to His Majesty the King of D. in ye year 1739

Most gracious King

We are in good hopes your Majesty will give Order yt we may continue to Learn to know the Lord Jesus. We stand unmoveably hither as our Lord God pleases, tho' we are oppressed very much by every one, yea beaten & struck with ye Sword when being assembled to learn of ye Lord Jesus. Yea they burn our Books & call our Baptism Dogs Baptism & ye Bretrn Beasts, saying ye that must not be quiet & that a Baptized Negro is worse to burn in Hell Fire & have for 3 months together put in Prison out of ... ye Lord has made use of amongst us especially our dear Mr Martins who is the only one that is left of 20 when all the rest ... & they will Banish our Bretrn from ye Country, & when they Appeal to ye King, then they say that Thou hadst forbid it that the Negroes might learn to know our Lord & that thou soon will turn out Mr Martins. But we Pray let us learn & abide with ye Church of ye Bretrn for we will go with them to our dear Savr we will be Obedient to our Masters in all things, for before we have robbed them & have run away from them & have been Lazy & have cheated them of their Fruits &c. And now all that is otherwise with us, which also our Masters themselves know well enough. Many Negroes have had their

Hands & feet cut off because of their Malice
So we are now willing for ye Lord's Church
sake to lay down our Head under ye Axe for ye
Lord Jesus sake as our Masters have a mind
to kill us, & will say God bless our Lord &
King a 1000 times. St Thomas Feb. 15. 1739

In the Name of above 650 Black
Scholars of Jesus Christ whom Mr Martin
instructs but especially in the Name of them
who have already been Baptised by Mr Martin   Signed by the Elders of the Church
in St Thomas.

Peter   Magdalene
Mingo   Abraham   Rebecca
Andrew   _____   Ann Maria
              ____ (Christ ____ Deb?) ____ ____

A Letter of the Eldress of the Chr
of the Negroes at St Thomas to
her Majesty ye ~~Queen~~ of D. 1739
Great ~~Britain~~ Queen.   _____

      + During ye time I have
been in Popo I have served ye Son of God
now I have come among ye ~~Dutch~~ they will
not suffer me to serve him tho' now I have
more ground to serve him than before I had
in my Heart I am grieved in my Heart
that the Poor Negro Women in St Thomas
~~will~~ have (can) not serve ye Lord Jesus. The Blank

· 45 ·

In Rebekka's methodology, two core elements are identified as essential components for an effective missions training model: bicultural intelligence and spiritual sensitivity grounded in biblical precepts (Aiyedogbon 2010, 34–38).[7] The slave population on the island of St. Thomas during the mid-eighteenth century was quite diverse. There were both African-born and Caribbean-born, representing a plethora of tribes, dialects, and languages. How would Rebekka evangelize such a diverse group of people? More than a century before Henry Venn and Rufus Anderson diagramed a three-self model, Rebekka and the Moravian missionaries had already successfully navigated this principle. Rebekka discipled individuals who were taught to disciple others. Once their training was complete, they were placed in charge of other slaves, whom they in turn discipled. These groups were organized among the slaves, allowing them to have full autonomy and leadership roles. The slaves were then equipped to traverse the island as disciples of Christ, birthing new disciples (Oldendorp 1987, 317–20).

Moreover, Rebekka taught Christian principles by translating biblical principles into broad African or Caribbean terms. Most Africans were familiar with blood sacrifice, so to translate the concept of Christ as the blood atonement for sin was not a difficult concept to bridge. While Rebekka did not promote syncretism, neither did she denigrate the Africans' traditions or customs (Sensbach 2005, 84–89; Oldendorp 1987, 198–206, 318–28). Rebekka utilized Christ's example, discipling a small group who could in turn disciple others. On the island of St. Thomas, Rebekka's traveling teams of disciple-makers were effective.

The traveling gospel was a direct response to curfew laws that restricted the slaves' free travel, which means Rebekka created an avenue to reach the "unreachable." Because Rebekka observed the culture, she learned from cultural others; and she developed a missions training system to teach members of the slave community to do likewise, hence enabling the spread of the gospel among the slave population. In essence, Rebekka bridged the cultural gap between the Negro slaves and their plantation owners, who desired that they become Christian—in both doctrine and culture (Emerson and Smith 2000, 22).

Rebekka Protten: Missional Theology and Praxis

Looking through the lens of C. G. A. Oldendorp's early eighteenth-century ethnographic research provides a glimpse of Rebekka's missional theology and praxis. Oldendorp's ethnographic studies provide a thorough depiction of how African customs were interwoven into the lifestyle of West Indies slaves. Oldendorp studied the Negroes' religious practice, moral constitution, language acquisition, and cultural worldview regarding marriages, births, and baptisms, as well as funeral and burial ceremonial practices (Oldendorp 1987, 171–265).

---

7 Aiyedogbon's research addresses the importance of bicultural competency.

It is Oldendorp's ethnography of the eighteenth-century West Indies slave population that provides a backdrop for comprehending Rebekka's missiological training model.

During the eighteenth century, polygamy, as well as men marrying child brides, were accepted customs on the continent of Africa—with the exception of the Congo people. Punishable crimes included—but were not limited to—murder, adultery, and theft. Most African tribes buried their dead and were extremely spiritual and ritualistic regarding burials, prayers, and offerings (Oldendorp 1987, 171, 177, 183, 190–91). Tribal differences existed, but Oldendorp identified the previously mentioned practices as universal among Africans. Rebekka's familiarity with various African tribal practices induced a sensitivity for how she presented the gospel in word and practice.

Rebekka and the Moravians practiced monogamy and taught spirituality from a biblical perspective. Their familiarity with sacrificial offerings provided an avenue to introduce Christ as the supreme sacrifice. Since all Africans believed in a higher deity, the concept of an all-knowing God was not an impossible leap for the African slaves. Prayers and offerings demonstrated their dependence on God; thus, the God of the Bible was more familiar than the land to which they had been transported (Oldendorp 1987, 192–94, 200–202). Biblical lessons were juxtaposed against tribal religion to demonstrate appropriate similarities and denounce inappropriate religious practices, thereby reducing the tendency toward syncretism. Moreover, many African nations were already familiar with the concept of Christianity, as evidenced by Christian doctrine that had intermingled with tribal religions (Oldendorp 1987, 165). Because the European view of the African slave contributed to the demoralizing and negative portrayal of enslaved Blacks, Rebekka avoided teaching biblical principles based upon a "White" man's God (Oldendorp 1987, 245–49; Rowlandson 1682, 77, 85).

Instead, Rebekka approached biblical teaching from the standpoint of spiritual identity with Christ. The transatlantic voyage had stripped Africans of their cultural identity, thereby rendering them less than human and without moral or spiritual value from a Eurocentric viewpoint, and sometimes from their own personal viewpoint (Oldendorp 1987, 214–19). Rebekka's audacious attempt to insist on dignity for the slave community set the Negro converts on the same plane as the White missionary. Thus, it can be argued, the gospel was placed in an appropriate setting—contextualized—because slaves were allowed to embrace a new temporal identity and they found a new spiritual identity in Christ.

Her legacy reminds missionaries how a young woman of color challenged the status quo of her era and by so doing ignited a missionary movement that continues three centuries later.

Rebekka Protten: A Lasting Legacy

The preservation of Rebekka Protten's legacy is owed to the Moravians, but her missionary legacy is owed to the fortitude and tenacity of the Negro slaves on the island of St. Thomas who exercised a courageous avidity to spread the good news of Christ. Sold into slavery as a young girl and introduced to Christianity by her slaveowner, Rebekka then courageously introduced Christianity to the slave population on the island of St. Thomas.

More importantly, the Moravian Brethren acknowledged her accomplishments along the "path," as she unashamedly and courageously led lost souls—slave souls—to Christ. Rebekka did not just introduce Christ and Christianity to the enslaved peoples of St. Thomas, she dared them to hope by offering them education and humanitarian equality with their masters.

Rebekka leaves a legacy of transformation and hope. She leaves a legacy for people of color and for women to recognize that their identity in Christ means that there is equality in the body of Christ. Her legacy reminds missionaries how a young woman of color challenged the status quo of her era and by so doing ignited a missionary movement that continues three centuries later. And as Jon Sensbach contends, "Rebecca was in fact celebrated in print during her lifetime" (Sensbach 2005, 235). As the Moravians began to pen their story, they could not deny the legacy of one who pioneered the Protestant missionary movement.

Conclusion

Historian C. G. A. Oldendorp attributes the missionary success on the island of St. Thomas to the Negroes. "In addition to the many blessed means employed in the [Moravian's] missionary efforts to extend the work of God among the Negroes, the major contribution came from the Negroes themselves" (Oldendorp 1987, 319). However, Rebekka Protten is a woman of color who has not been given her rightful place in the annals of missions history. Rebekka created an avenue by which to reach the slave population on the island of St. Thomas. She followed biblical principles to encourage and influence godly discipleship. Finally, she contextualized the delivery of the gospel, as well as the gospel message itself, in a fashion so as not to offend cultural others, yet not to incite syncretism.

A careful and thorough examination of the history of the Moravian Brethren, as well as Oldendorp's ethnographic study of the islands of Antigua and St. Thomas, provides ample information regarding Rebekka Protten and her missionary enterprise on the island of St. Thomas. Yet her biography has been omitted from the historical annals of the evangelical missionary movement. To properly situate the historical accounts of the evangelical missionary movement, it is imperative to include the contributions of all pioneers.

Rebekka Protten is not the only missionary of color whose missionary exploits have been omitted or erased from the historical chronicles of global missions endeavors. The future of the evangelical missionary movement must include an accurate portrait of its missional past, which means the inclusion of all missionary pioneers and their contribution to the Protestant missionary movement. William Carey praised the Moravian missionaries, and the leader of the Moravian missionaries—Count Zinzendorf—lauded Rebekka Protten. So now it is time to do likewise. As the evangelical missionary movement contemplates its future, it is imperative to include—in its entirety—the rich historical missionary legacy of its past.

References Cited

Aiyedogbon, Kola. 2010. "The Challenges of Missionary Training in the 21st Century: A Manual for Training of Missionaries." DMin diss., Liberty University Baptist Theological Seminary.

Carey, William. 1792 [1961]. *An Enquiry into the Obligations of Christians, to Use Means for the Conversion of the Heathens.* London: The Carey Kingsgate Press Limited. http://www.gutenberg.org/files/11449/11449-h/11449-h.htm.

Emerson, Michael O., and Christian Smith. 2000. *Divided by Faith: Evangelical Religion and the Problem of Race in America.* New York: Oxford University Press.

Hamilton, J. Taylor, and Kenneth G. Hamilton. 1900. *A History of the Church Known as the Moravian Church, or the Unitas Fratrum, or the Unity of the Brethren, During the Eighteenth and Nineteenth Centuries.* Bethlehem, PA: Times Publishing Company.

Hutton, Joseph E. 1923. *A History of Moravian Missions.* London: Moravian Publication Office. https://archive.org/stream/historyofmoravia00huttuoft#page/n7/mode/2up.

Oldendorp, Christian Georg Andreas. 1987. *C. G. A. Oldendorp's History of the Mission of the Evangelical Brethren on the Caribbean Islands of St. Thomas, St. Croix, and St. John.* Edited by Johann Jakob Bossard. Ann Arbor, MI: Karoma Publishers, Inc.

Protten, Rebekka. n.d. A Letter of the Awakened Negroes in St. Thomas.

Rowlandson, Mary White. 1682. *The Sovereignty and Goodness of God Together, with the Faithfulness of His Promises Displayed Being a Narrative of the Captivity and Restoration of Mrs. Mary Rowlandson.* Cambridge, MA: Samuel Green.

Saunders, Linda P. 2020. "Laying an Historical Foundation to Examine the African-American Church's Relationship to 21st Century Global Missions to Create a Contextualized Missions Training Model for Future Generations of African-American Missionaries." PhD diss., Columbia International University.

Sensbach, Jon F. 2005. *Rebecca's Revival: Creating Black Christianity in the Atlantic World.* Cambridge: Harvard University Press.

Weinlick, John R. 1956. *Count Zinzendorf.* New York: Abingdon Press.

CHAPTER 4

Bartholomäus Ziegenbalg Models Holistic Missions:

Pietism in Eighteenth-Century Southern India

ROBERT L. GALLAGHER

In the early eighteenth century, a Danish king sent a young German student to a distant land to spread the gospel. The consequences of his missionary ventures sent reverberations through the European courts of ecclesiastical and political power. E. Arno Lehmann (1956, 109–11) and Hans-Werner Genischen (1957, 835) view his mission strategy as a model and source of inspiration for early Western Protestant missions. Daniel Jeyaraj asserts that he is "the true father of modern Protestant mission movements" (2006, 9). In this chapter I will tell the unfeigned story of Bartholomäus Ziegenbalg, the first Protestant missionary to India, complete with unexpected twists, ironic turns, and surprising pathways. It is a story that models the way of contemporary holistic missions.

Bartholomäus Ziegenbalg, a German Pietist missionary to India in the early eighteenth century, developed a missional strategy of education, translation, mutual respect, discipleship, and indigenous leadership that—revolutionary for its time—still informs mission movements today. His work in translation, collection of indigenous religious writings, and correspondence with fellow missionaries provides a valuable insight into the historic Pietist mission movement and international holistic outreach.

Influences of Pietism

Bartholomäus Ziegenbalg was born to pious Lutheran parents in 1682 in the Saxon farm village of Pulsnitz, near Dresden, Germany. In the years leading up to his birth, the Thirty Years' War (1618–48) and a plague (1680) and a severe fire through his village altered the cultural landscape. While still a child, he lost both parents and two sisters. No wonder he gave great thought to death, heaven, and hell. At the age of ten, Ziegenbalg left home to attend Latin school at Kamenz, Saxony, and to seek answers to his theological questions (Jeyaraj 2006, 54). Two years later, he moved to the gymnasium (high school) in Görlitz, Saxony, where the rector of the school remarked that he was weak in body and mind. At eighteen, in the midst of nine months of wrestling with questions of God's purpose for his life, he found comfort in Christ's saving grace. For teenage Ziegenbalg, God became the greatest, loveliest, best, sweetest, and wisest—of all treasures, the noblest.

Following this spiritual liberation, Ziegenbalg wrote to August Hermann Francke at Halle University, Saxony, seeking new direction for his Christ-committed life. The biblical scholar advised the young Saxon to enroll at the Friedrich-Werderschen Gymnasium near Berlin in 1702, under the tutelage of Joachim Lange, a controversial Pietist educator. Philipp Jakob Spener (also mentioned in chapter 3), the venerated theologian of Pietism and provost of St. Nicholas Church in Berlin, provided a letter of recommendation; and Baron von Canstein, founder of the Canstein Bible Society, supplied a financial scholarship (Jeyaraj 2006, 54). Recurring anxiety and academic overload caused periods of chronic stomach disorders, forcing Ziegenbalg to interrupt his studies and not complete his final examinations (Beyreuther 1955, 7–21; Scherer 1999, 487).

At Francke's invitation, in 1703 Ziegenbalg enrolled at the University of Halle, where he thrived in its academically rigorous program, which included Latin, Hebrew, and Greek. His studies in pietistic convictions and values confirmed his beliefs in personal conversion, faith, study, and witness. He joined a group of students who met daily for Scripture exegesis, prayer, and singing, and whose members were pledged to the pietistic ideal of religious devotion and Christian service. At this time, the young Lutheran declared his life's direction:

> For this reason we are made Christians, that we should be more bent upon the life to come, than upon the present. This is my daily memorandum, lest I should perhaps forget, entirely to consecrate my life and actions to an invisible eternity, minding little the world either in its glory and smiles, or in its frowns and afflictions. (Beach 1904, 163)

Ziegenbalg continued to battle physical ailments and depression, so after one semester he temporarily withdrew from Halle to become a family tutor in Merseburg, and later in Erfurt. In both locations, he organized pietistic meetings and witnessed about Christ. Despite his own doubts and feelings of inadequacy, he retained his interest in missions through the influence of Pietist leaders, including Joachim Justus Breithaupt, a friend of both Spener and Francke (Zorn 1933, 27–30). While at Merseburg, Ziegenbalg made a vow with a friend that foreshadowed his future vocation in southeast India.

> We two will seek nothing in this world but the glorification of the name of God, the extension of his Kingdom, the spread of the divine truth, the salvation of our fellow-men, and the continued sanctification of our souls, in whatever part of the world we may be, and no matter what amount of cross and affliction may befall us on account of it. (Zorn 1933, 31)

Missions in India

At the beginning of the eighteenth century, Muslim overlords governed the southern peninsula of India. These overlords appointed local Hindu kings as their regional governors (*poligars*), each with his own monetary organization and army. Under this oppressive system, the impoverished lower castes suffered immense social injustices. The major people groups in the region were Armenians, Jews, Muslims, Portuguese, Tamils, and Thomas-Christians; and the main languages included Gujarathi, Marathi, Portuguese, Sanskrit, Tamil, and Telugu (Jeyaraj 2008, 26). This was a time of rapid social change within the Hindu society of South India, and the scattered Portuguese, French, Dutch, English, and Danish trading settlements added to the turbulent socioeconomic milieu.

In 1620, Denmark obtained the town and surrounding territory of Tarangambâdi, or Tranquebar, on the east coast of southern India, from Rakunaāta Nāyak, the Rajah of Tanjore (Jeyaraj 2006, 262–65). Eighty-five years later, the king of Denmark, Frederick IV (under the influence of his Pietist wife, Louise of Mecklenburg-Güstrow), commissioned Franz Julius Lütkens, the king's German Pietist court chaplain, to find missionaries for his colonies. Lütkens, through Pietist friends in Berlin, contacted Lange, who suggested his theological students, Ziegenbalg and Heinrich Plütschau (1677–1746) of Mechlenburg, Germany, as worthy candidates (Jeyaraj 2006, 28).

Ziegenbalg received the invitation with reservation. He knew he lacked experience, suffered poor health, and had not completed his university studies or the ordination process. Lange forwarded their names to Lütkens in Copenhagen even though neither young man had formally accepted. The Danish king approved the choice, allocated the finances, and commanded that the missionaries report to the capital for ordination and final instructions. Lütkens first proposed that their objective would be the Danish West Indies, and then suggested the West African "slave coast" of Guinea. Ultimately, the king altered the missionaries' destination to southern India.

After a dangerous seven-month voyage on the *Princessa Sophia Hedwiga*, on July 9, 1706, Ziegenbalg and his companion arrived at the Danish Crown Colony of Tranquebar on the Coromandel Coast. At that time, Tranquebar comprised fifteen square miles, twenty small villages, and between eighteen thousand and thirty thousand inhabitants (Zorn 1933, 34; Jeyaraj 2006, 13). The two university students were to become the first Protestant missionaries to India for the express purpose of evangelizing the indigenous people. Drawing on the principles and teachings of the universities at Berlin and Halle, they sought to share the Scripture with cultural awareness. Their message was a blend of Lutheran theology and pietistic relevance: They believed the Word of God was efficacious and powerful for personal conversion and holiness.

The German missionaries immediately met opposition from Johann Hassel, the Tranquebar Danish chaplain; local Hindu leaders and Brahmins; the Danish East India Company; and the hostile Johan Sigismund Hassius, the Danish governor. Despite Ziegenbalg's success in outreach to the governor's household, Hassius later imprisoned Ziegenbalg for four months (1708–09) for "rebellion against [his] authority" (Jeyaraj 2006, 287). Rather than being connected to political issues, the imprisonment was associated with Protestant-Catholic religious tensions, such as the local Catholic practice of separate churches for high and low castes and an accusation concerning the Catholics' limited knowledge of the Christian faith. Even though the two Lutherans were Royal Danish missionaries receiving salaries from the Danish crown, they were Germans working in a Danish colony and had no interest in gaining a political or territorial advantage over the local people. The Pietists were seemingly without racism or imperialism, which aggravated the European colonialists. Records of their work challenge the popular contemporary view that all missionaries in India participated in colonialism (Beyreuther 1955, 22–30; Scherer 1999, 489–91).

Five Missional Principles

The Royal Danish Mission grew through Ziegenbalg's vision and skill, which he heavily supported by intensive prayer and extensive correspondence. Stephen Neill, the Anglican Bishop of Tirunelveli (1939–44) in southern India claimed, "At point after point, with hardly any precedent to guide him, Ziegenbalg made the right decision, and showed the way that has been followed ever since by the best and most successful among the Protestant missions" (1964, 194).

Below, I will expand upon the five missional principles that Neill recognized as characteristic of the Royal Danish Mission in South India (195–96).

1. *Church and school are to go together. Missionaries need to link the propagation of the Christian faith with education, since they need to train children to read the Word of God.*

To this end, a year after the two Pietists arrived, they began day schools for the Portuguese and Danish workers. Following the Francke Foundations' model, a revolutionary innovation was made when they started a day school for girls—India's first—in 1707. (Jeyaraj 2006, 70). The Halle missionaries adapted Francke's pedagogical principles (for example, children divided by age), and taught in the vernacular, with the Bible and Lutheran catechism as their core texts. They believed it was critical to teach children the Scriptures before they grew hardened to spiritual truth (Lehmann 1956, 103). Their curriculum included astronomy, cooking, geography, mathematics, medicine, poetry, reading, rhetoric, and writing—using European clocks, globes, and world maps (Jeyaraj 2008, 25).

Concerning the connection between church and school, Ziegenbalg wrote,

> It is a thing known to all persons of understanding that the general good of any country or nation depends upon a Christian and careful training of children in schools, with due care and diligence in this matter, producing wise governors in the State, faithful ministers of the gospel in the church, and good members of the commonwealth in families. (Sabiers 1944, 10)

Although Tamil society had a rich history in the arts and sciences—astronomy, cosmology, mathematics, medicine, moral teaching, music, physics, poetry, surgery, and writing—education was restricted to the high-caste Brahmins. In 1715, the cross-cultural workers founded a Tamil "free-charity" boarding school and an orphanage, where indigenous communities entrusted poor children to the care of house parents. The start of a seminary twelve months later (with eight senior Tamil students) to train teachers, catechists, and pastors looked forward to a time when missionaries would no longer be needed.

The Lutheran missionaries were opposed to Westernizing the Indian Christians. They diligently taught the Tamil schoolchildren their own language and customs, using free-Tamil church members. Some of the Tamils involved in the teaching were Andreas (Ziegenbalg's former cook, originally named Cepprumāl), Johann Almede, and Rāyappan (alias Petrus). In addition, teachers such as Otto Friedrich, Ole Ollussen Thoren, and Manuel de Coste (the Portuguese catechist) also taught the children a European curriculum (Jeyaraj 2006, 278–81).

2. *If Christians are to read the Word of God, it must be available to them in their own language. Scripture needs to be available in the vernacular to build a native church and facilitate a non-colonialist approach to missions.*

During the voyage to India, the two Germans studied Danish, not realizing that the trade language of Tranquebar was Portuguese. Upon arriving, Ziegenbalg studied the Tamil language, while Plütschau learned Portuguese. Gifted in learning languages, Ziegenbalg quickly mastered colloquial and written Tamil (Jeyaraj 2006, 66).

In learning the language, Ziegenbalg built upon the Tamil dictionaries of the Jesuit missionaries (Henrique Henriques [1520–1600], Roberto de Nobili [1577–1656], and Constantino Giuseppe Beschi [1680–1747]). In addition, he devoted himself to the study of Tamil literature. Ziegenbalg explained, "I chose such books as I should wish to imitate, both in speaking and writing, and had such authors read to me a hundred times that there might not be a word or expression which I did not know, or could not imitate" (Holcomb 1901, 21).

In Tranquebar, there were two dialects of Tamil—Shen and Kodun—so Ziegenbalg learned both by hiring indigenous tutors, such as Ellappar, a high-caste Hindu. Although Shen was the dialect of the Brahmins, together with sacred literature and scholarship, it had ceased to be intelligible to the common people. Thus the missionaries chose the ordinary dialect of Kodun for their pamphlets, books, and translations (Singh 1999, 65–66). Within eight months, the German preached his first sermon, exclaiming, "With God's grace I was able to read, write, and speak in this very difficult language, and even understand the conversation of others" (Lehmann 1956, 24).

By 1708, Ziegenbalg had compiled a forty-thousand-word Malabar (Tamil) dictionary, *Grammatica Damulica* (published at Halle eight years later), and a dictionary of poetical terms of some seventeen thousand words (*Lexicon Poeticum*). This enabled him to write, print, and promote Tamil literature. Ziegenbalg, with the help of Johann Ernest Gründler (a former schoolteacher at the Francke Foundations), had translated the entire New Testament into Tamil less than five years after his arrival in Tranquebar. This was the first translation of the Bible in any Indian language. Following this accomplishment was a Tamil translation of *Luther's Small Catechism* (printed in 1713). In that same year, Plütschau returned to Germany due to ill health and became a Lutheran country pastor at Beyenflieth in Holstein in northern Germany. Accompanying the missionary to Europe was Timothy, a Tamil Christian from Tranquebar, who provoked missionary interest at Halle, and remained there to teach the Tamil language at the Collegium Orientale Theologicum.

An English printing press and paper arrived at Madras in 1712, but the printer, Jonas Fink, had fallen overboard and drowned during the voyage. Ziegenbalg subsequently recruited a German soldier, Johann Heinrich Schloricke, who printed the first book in the Portuguese language in India (Jeyaraj 2006, 186–87). By 1715, a printer named Johanne Gottlieb Adler, using Halle-manufactured Tamil typefaces, printed the first Tamil New Testament. The Tranquebar Tamil press was now in business to print studies of the Tamil language and culture. The outcomes of this breakthrough were the spread of the gospel, a uniformity of script for the Tamil writing system, and the indigenous people's increased desire to read.

3. *Missionaries need to base the preaching of the gospel on an accurate knowledge of the mind of the people. That is, they need to understand the worldview of the indigenous inhabitants in order to share the gospel with them.*

Ziegenbalg was aware of the importance of understanding the Hindu customs of the people of southern India, with whom he was sharing the gospel. He set out to study the belief systems and lifestyle of the Bhakti religion by analyzing the social and religious thought in order to present a meaningful message. He asserted, "Hardly an hour passes that I do not have an opportunity to speak with the heathen on the way," as he visited villages and towns (Lehmann 1956, 31). For instance, he asked Kanabadi, a Tamil poet, to translate some Christian literature; and upon his subsequent conversion, the local artist wrote poems using Christian themes in place of Hindu legends, which the workers then used to teach the schoolchildren.

The Halle missionary wrote about his cultural discoveries of the Tamil society in a number of monographs. Two significant publications were the 1711 *Malabarian Gods*, which quoted 176 passages from Tamil literature to introduce Europe to the Tamil worldview, and the 1713 *Genealogy of the Malabar (South-Indian) Gods*, a detailed study of Savaite and Vaishnavite beliefs, using 145 letters written by Tamil scholars, allowing the people to speak for themselves. On receiving this material, Francke wrote critically to Ziegenbalg. Francke concluded that such studies were unimportant, since the Danish king had sent the missionaries to extirpate heathenism in India, not to spread heathenish ideas in Europe. Consequently, the Halle director deliberately hid the ethnographies in the archives of the university. This material remained concealed for over 150 years until the scholar Wilhelm Germann (Leipsic Missionary Society) discovered and published the manuscripts in both German and English (1869, xv).

4. *The aim must be definite and personal conversion. The spread of Christianity should focus on individuals rather than on mass movements.*

The Pietist missionaries in southern India avoided mass conversions, in contrast to Catholic missions, and prayed for individual transformation. Within the first few months of their arrival, the Europeans assembled the Malabar slaves of the settlement two hours every day for religious instruction in the fundamentals of the Christian faith. One year after their arrival, the missionaries publicly examined multiple slaves on the Lutheran Articles of the Christian Faith, and then baptized them; and they also erected the "Jerusalem Church" in 1707 to conduct Tamil services (Jeyaraj 2006, 66–67).

Church membership gradually grew. Eleven years later, the church building became too small, so the members built an expanded "New Jerusalem Church." As the Indian Christians moved from the Danish protectorate in search of work, most bore faithful witness, which resulted in church growth elsewhere in South India. In contrast, the missionaries were mainly restricted to the Tranquebar colony (Singh 1999, 25). Ziegenbalg and Plütschau endeavored to work not only with the indigenous people, but also with the German and Portuguese inhabitants employed by the Danish monarchy; and thus, they started church services especially for them in the local Danish church.

In addition to these accomplishments, Ziegenbalg and Plütschau held interreligious dialogues with Hindu priests, doctors, and poets. From these meetings, Ziegenbalg wrote three collections of conversations in which he argued the truth of Christianity. In 1719, Mr. Phillip made an English translation of Ziegenbalg's and Gründler's *Thirty-Four Conferences between the Danish Missionaries and the Malabarian Bramans (or Heathen Priests) in the East Indies, Concerning the Truth of the Christian Religion*, which was published in London— an account of the German Lutheran missionaries' religious discussions with Hindus in Tranquebar.

The missionaries founded stations in Srirangam, Tanjore, Madura, Kanchi, Chidambram, and Tirupathi; and upon traveling through the region, they established contacts with Brahmins and held fifty-four conversations with them. From 1715 onwards, the administration at Halle published these recorded dialogues that were sent to Saxony. In addition, Ziegenbalg sent a large number of letters with different questions to a selection of Hindu Brahmins and non-Brahmins. He then translated into German the answers to these questions and forwarded the results to Halle.

Genischen summarizes these evangelistic efforts:

> Every phase of Ziegenbalg's conversations reveals that, notwithstanding his untiring attempts to meet the Hindus on their own level, the uncompromising proclamation of the free-saving grace of God in Jesus Christ was the heart and center of his evangelism" (1957, 841).

5. *The dissemination of Christianity must result in an indigenous church with indigenous leadership.*

Ziegenbalg insisted on developing a Tamil church of Lutheran faith and worship with Indian characteristics. Rather than follow a Danish or German pattern of church life and administration, he adopted aspects of the Malabar culture. For example, men and women sat together on the floor (emphasizing the equality of women and men), and wedding and funeral services, together with music and meals, followed Tamil customs.

Ziegenbalg insisted on developing a Tamil church of Lutheran faith and worship with Indian characteristics.

Even more insightful was the realization that Christian theological concepts needed to be clothed in Hindu thought. Hence, Ziegenbalg used indigenous metaphors and parables in his preaching. Further, the Lutheran Pietist arranged hymns using German chorales and Tamilian melodies and lyrics for corporate worship, instructed children in the catechism, and introduced the singing of Psalms. In 1715, Ziegenbalg published his first Tamil hymnal, which contained forty-eight hymns (Lehmann 1956, 26; Jeyaraj 2006, 285). "The converts were encouraged simultaneously to be faithful Tamils and sincere Christians," writes Singh (1999, 25).

The Society for Promoting Christian Knowledge (SPCK) in England supported the Christian education of Indian children from Madras to Calcutta. In Tranquebar, a number of the young men became followers of Christ through these schools and mentored by Ziegenbalg, developed into valuable teachers and preachers. In a letter, he writes of the relationship between the mission church and school:

> We try to deeply plant in these young minds … the true Christian doctrine. We pay special attention in the daily instruction to catechization. We have several catechists who go from house to house and catechize our people…. We are not satisfied merely with an outer appearance of the Christian religion, but press for a real change of heart, and an implicit obedience of faith, and we look not so much for large numbers, but that all who accept our religion should attain a living knowledge of the truth unto godliness and … the true way of Christianity. (Lehmann 1956, 109)

Three years after Ziegenbalg's arrival, he petitioned the Danish authorities to ordain a native believer so that Europeans would not dominate the clerical ministry. Only partly realized were Ziegenbalg's convictions of a fully indigenous church. Aaron, an Indian catechist of fifteen years, eventually became the first Protestant Indian pastor in 1733 (fourteen years after Ziegenbalg's death) and was pastorally responsible for several congregations in the Māyāvaram area until his death in 1745. His assistance helped ease cultural awkwardness in administering the Holy Sacrament and the feast days of Easter, Pentecost, and Christmas.

Even though only fourteen pastors were ordained in the mission's first one hundred years, they were carefully chosen, and "there were few failures" (Neill 1964, 197). Extreme caution prevailed, however. The Tamil Evangelical Lutheran Church finally consecrated R. B. Manickam as their first Indian bishop at Tranquebar in 1956, the 250th anniversary of Ziegenbalg's arrival. The racial prejudice and belief in personal superiority of European Pietists influenced their strong reluctance to accept the notion of equality between a German missionary and an Indian pastor. Irony heightens this prejudice when we compare the Tamils' intense dislike of the Europeans' "evil lifestyle" to that of the Tamil views on cultural piety and simple living.

James A. Scherer summarizes Neill's final missional tenet: "From the beginning, Ziegenbalg appears to have grasped the principle of enculturation, developing an indigenous church with Indian characteristics in architecture, music, caste, and customs. Here also he was clearly ahead of his time" (1999, 493).

Missionary Statesman

In addition to Neill's five principles of the first Protestant missionaries in India (1964), Ziegenbalg and Plütschau's efforts mark the importance of an ethos of communication. Upon commissioning the missionaries, Frederick IV instructed them to send letters concerning the work, development, and plans of the Royal Danish Mission whenever a ship returned to Denmark (Fenger 1863, 238). Subsequently, Ziegenbalg diligently wrote and sent descriptions of their work. Pietists circulated these letters in the *Halle Reports* (the first German Lutheran missionary magazine) and later published them in Berlin in a book entitled *Notable News* (1708). Anton Wilhelm Böhme (the German Pietist chaplain at St. James' Palace, London) translated these descriptions into English in London for the SPCK (1709). Publishers renamed the letters *Propagation of the Gospel in the East* for distribution to Pietist communities in Germany, Denmark, and England (Zorn 1933, 101, 103).

This compilation of letters reached the royal courts of Denmark and England. In addition, they were read by John Wake (the archbishop of Canterbury), Cotton Mather (an influential Puritan in the New England colonies), and Suzanna Wesley (the mother of John and Charles), to name a few, and served as a catalyst to encourage financial giving and sending to the mission field. By 1712, the mission in southern India supported twenty-two workers.

Prince George, the Danish husband of Queen Anne of England, along with Böhme, his Lutheran chaplain, had a strong interest in the Danish Tranquebar mission. Böhme suggested to the SPCK that they should send a printing press to India for the service of the mission to translate the Scriptures into the languages of southern India. This resulted in an ecumenical partnership whereby a German Lutheran (in the service of a Danish sovereign) translated the New Testament into Tamil, which was then printed by Indian workers on an English press funded by an Anglican missions' society.

Owing to pressures from the Danish governor, Hassius, Ziegenbalg returned to Europe for a promotional tour (1714–16), whereupon he married Maria Dorothea Salzmann (Holcomb 1901, 32). During his home leave, he visited Plütschau in Holstein, King Frederick IV of Denmark, and Prince George of

England. He also founded both the Royal College of Missions, in Copenhagen, and a student-missionary society at Halle University—the Order of the Grain of Mustard Seed—which influenced Nikolaus Ludwig von Zinzendorf, the founder of the Moravian missions movement.

Ziegenbalg's Death and Legacy

Thirteen years after arriving in India, the model missionary died at Tranquebar in 1719, at the age of thirty-six. Ziegenbalg's sudden death may have been due to his intense workaholism over a long period, together with continued stress due to policy disputes with Christopher Wendt, the opinionated secretary of the Copenhagen Mission Society, who criticized the German for financially sustaining the poor Christians.

Daniel Jeyaraj explains Ziegenbalg's relationship with the secretary:

> Wendt lived in Copenhagen, and did not have any idea of personally engaging in a cross-cultural missionary work. His unrealistic views were so insensitive and hurtful that the missionaries never recovered from their psychological wounds. (2006, 116–17)

Wendt wanted a self-supporting Indian church where the missionaries only preached and were not involved in social action. Following the Francke pattern of Halle, the young Saxon did not merely speak words of love, but demonstrated that "the service of the soul" and "the service of the body" were connected—Christian ministry could not be effective without social action. In a letter to Wendt, Ziegenbalg wrote:

> As the body is bound to the soul, so precisely is the service of the body connected with the service of the soul, and these cannot be separated from each other. This work [the Tranquebar Mission] demands the service of the whole [person]. If I deny such service, I deny that in which the Scripture places the proper manner of faith and love.... The more one devotes to the service of [neighbors], and gladly helps in bodily and spiritual needs, the stronger one must be in Christianity. (Lehmann 1956, 87)

The missionary pioneer's immediate legacy was two hundred and fifty members in the church, studies of the Hindu religion and culture that aided future missionaries, two church buildings and a seminary for the training of national leaders, and the New Testament and Genesis through Ruth translated into the Tamil language. Both the New Testament Tamil translation of 1715 and the church building constructed in 1718 are still in use today by the Tamil Evangelical Lutheran Church. On Ziegenbalg's death, Gründler wrote a grieving letter to Francke, who in turn read the letter to Halle's theological students—moving many of them to become missionaries to India. During the existence of the Royal Danish Mission (1706–1845), European missionaries (forty-nine

Following the Francke pattern of Halle, the young Saxon did not merely speak words of love, but demonstrated that "the service of the soul" and "the service of the body" were connected—Christian ministry could not be effective without social action.

Germans, six Danes, and one Swede) worked in India, mostly following Ziegenbalg's missionary methods. In 1727, the forerunner's successor, Benjamin Schultze, completed the Tamil translation of the Old Testament; and in turn, his heir, Johann Philipp Fabricius, finalized a revised translation of the whole Bible and the Apocrypha (1777–82).

Ziegenbalg's reputation for excellence and his blameless lifestyle added to his effectiveness in India. During an age in which colonization and prejudice were normal, his respect and empathy for the host culture caused him to focus on the people over the task and gave him an ability to maintain flexibility. With love for the Indian people, he shared God's message wherever he could at festivals, work, and play. The German had publicly criticized some members of the Brahmin caste for their disregard of the lower castes in Hindu society (for example, the outcaste Pariahs). Nevertheless, "his impressive knowledge of Hinduism, high regard for Hindus as human beings, desire to preserve the integrity of the Tamil language and culture as he presented Christianity, and the lack of racist attitudes coupled with his repudiation of the racism of other Europeans towards Indians" gained him commendable respect from many Hindus (Singh 1999, 22–23).

Conclusion

In final consideration of the missionary Bartholomäus Ziegenbalg, I would deduce that even though he endured feelings of inadequacy, depression, and physical maladies throughout his life, he pioneered the Western study of South Indian culture, society, and religion, and in the process modeled a holistic ministry philosophy to generations of Pietist missionaries who followed his path. In demonstrating how to bring an uncompromised gospel to the marginalized of Asia, he confirmed Christian care and concern for the indigenous people and brought awareness of the importance of global missions to Protestant Europe. Furthermore, the Tranquebar Mission's influence extended to emerging missions movements, such as Zinzendorf's Moravian missionaries, the Leipzig Evangelical Lutheran Mission, and the Copenhagen Mission Society—the latter of which sponsored the Greenland missions begun by Hans and Gertrud Egede. In reflecting on Ziegenbalg's heritage, Neill concludes, "A new epoch in the history of the Christian missions had begun" (1985, 28).

References Cited

Beach, H. P. 1904. *India and Christian Opportunity.* New York: Student Volunteer Movement for Foreign Missions.

Beyreuther, E. 1955. *Bartholomäus Ziegenbalg, Bahnbrecher der Weltmission.* Stuttgart: Evangelischer Missionsverlag.

Fenger, J. F. 1863. *History of the Tranquebar Mission—Worked Out from the Original Papers.* Published in Danish and translated into English from the German of Emil Francke—compared with the Danish original. Madras: M.E. Press.

Genischen, H. 1957. "Imitating the Wisdom of the Almighty: Ziegenbalg's Program of Evangelism." *Concordia Theological Monthly* 28, no. 11: 835–43.

Germann, W. 1869. Preface. In *Genealogy of the Malabar (South-Indian) Gods,* i–xvi. Madras: Higginbotham and Company.

Holcomb, H. 1901. *Men of Might in Indian Missions: The Leaders and Their Epochs (1706–1899).* London: Oliphant, Anderson, and Ferrier.

Jeyaraj, D. 2006. *Bartholomäus Ziegenbalg: The Father of Modern Protestant Mission—an Indian Assessment.* New Delhi, India: The Indian Society for Promoting Christian Knowledge, and Chennai, India: The Gurukul Lutheran Theological College and Research Institute.

———. 2008. "Mission Reports from South India and Their Impact on the Western Mind: The Tranquebar Mission of the Eighteenth Century." In *Converting Colonialism: Visions and Realities in Mission History, 1706–1914,* edited by Dana L. Robert, 21–42. Grand Rapids: Eerdmans.

Lehmann, E. A. 1956. *It Began at Tranquebar: The Story of the Tranquebar Mission and the Beginnings of Protestant Christianity in India.* Translated by M. J. Lutz. Madras: The Christian Literature Society.

Neill, S. 1964. *A History of Christian Missions.* 2nd ed. New York: Penguin Books.

———. 1985. *A History of Christianity in India: 1707–1858.* New York: Cambridge University Press.

Sabiers, K. G. 1944. *Little Biographies of Great Missionaries.* Los Angeles: Robertson Publishing.

Scherer, J. A. 1999. "Bartholomew Ziegenbalg." *Missiology: An International Review* 27, no. 4: 487–94.

Singh, B. 1999. *The First Protestant Missionary in India: Bartholomaeus Ziegenbalg.* New Delhi: Oxford University Press.

Zorn, H. M. 1933. "Bartholomaeus Ziegenbalg." In *Men and Missions,* edited by L. Fuerbringer. St. Louis: Concordia Publishing House.

CHAPTER 5

The Proper Place for a Woman

XENIA L. CHAN AND LISA H. PAK

The issue of women in ministry, particularly in leadership positions, continues to be contentious in many churches and denominations. While some doors have been opening for women in ministry and leadership, many non-Western women remain restricted because of cultural values and norms. This is the lived experience of many current women ministers in Chinese and Korean church cultures.[1] This chapter will provide an overview of Confucian philosophy and its influence on gender roles and dynamics. Then it will present a historical-theological survey of the place of Asian women—specifically, Chinese and Korean women—in God's kingdom. Last, it will apply a suitable appropriation to the current Chinese and Korean Canadian context.

The Influence of Confucian Philosophy

Both Chinese and Korean cultures are greatly influenced by Confucian philosophy, so much so that subtle elements even in modern society harken back to deeply embedded Confucian principles. Confucianism, to a large degree, is the invisible weave that sets the societal norms and values by which people abide. Interestingly, Confucius seldom referred to women. In the *Analects*, Confucius writes that "Women and servants are hard to deal with" (*Analects*, 17.25). This particular passage clearly implies that Confucius understood women to be in a different, and inferior, social class than men.

---

1 To be fair, there are a growing number of women leaders in Asian churches. Still, many Korean and Chinese churches follow—consciously or otherwise—Confucian gender ideology.

In another passage, Confucius writes about a woman among the king's ministers and then willfully ignores her as he recounts the flourishing of the king's court (*Analects*, 8.20). He depicts the woman's role primarily in the context of the relationship to the male figure—daughter, sister, wife, mother, sister-in-law, mother-in-law, and grandmother. Confucius' *Book of Rites* 禮記 (*Liji*) emphasized the separation of women from men even within the home: the outer section belonged to the men, and the women stayed within the inner section (*Liji*, 10.12). In the *Book of Documents* 書經 (*Shujing*), a stronger statement illuminates that a wayward woman had the potential to destroy the family: "The hen does not announce the morning. The crowing of a hen in the morning (indicates) the subversion of the family" (*Shujing*, 2.2). And Mencius, a pupil of Confucius, writes that the worst of a woman's unfilial acts is the failure to continue the ancestral line (Mencius, 4A.26).[2]

In subsequent centuries, the discussion on gender would revolve around the dynamic of *yin-yang*. The *Book of Changes* 易經 (*Yijing*), formalized as part of the Five Classics in the second century BCE, depicts the woman's role as follows:

> The proper place for the woman is inside 內 (*nei*) the family, and the proper place for the man is outside 外 (*wai*) the family. When both man and woman are in their proper place, this is the great appropriateness 義 (*yi*) of heaven 天 (*tian*) and earth 地 (*di*). (Wang 2000, 41)

The *Book of Changes* strongly correlates physical space with the *yin-yang* cosmology.[3] Harmony, therefore, is achieved only when everyone assumes their rightful place in the hierarchy, recognizing that this is simply a natural order of the universe. Robin Wang observes that

> women's function is commonly understood as operating within the inner sphere (*nei*) of family. Teaching the children and helping the husband are woman's [*sp*] ultimate mandate and responsibility. (Wang 2006, 95)

Further defining Confucian gender ideology, Liu Xiang, a prominent Han Confucian scholar, compiled 125 biographies of women "to evoke and commemorate an ideal of womanhood" in the *Lienüzhuan* (Wang 2006, 93). Through these biographies, Liu concludes that there are six desirable virtues: maternal rectitude (母儀), sagely intelligence (賢明), benevolent wisdom (仁智), chaste obedience (貞順), pure righteousness (節義), and rhetorical competence (辯通) (Wang 2006, 94).[4] By the end of the Han period, the Confucian vocabulary regarding women was largely established, and though there would

---

2 Hence, the Asian focus on the male progenitor and the importance of firstborn sons.

3 Though these are understood contextually. For instance, before puberty boys are free to be in the *nei* and girls are free to be in the *wai*.

4 Interestingly, the *Lienüzhuan* says nothing about women and household chores.

be some diversity in activities undertaken in subsequent dynasties, much of this language and these attitudes still prevails, to a large extent, in the current context.

Chinese culture had always influenced the Korean peninsula, but it was not until the Choson Dynasty (1392–1910) that Confucianism became a "ruling principle" in Korean society (Kim 1996, 5).[5] Education in Chinese script and the classics was so integral that "if a young man had not received instruction in Chinese, it was considered tantamount to having no education at all" (Choi 2009, 108). "Good order in the family" meant security and stability in society, and "gender roles and status were clearly defined for the purpose of maintaining order in [the social values of marriage and family]" (Kim 1996, 6). A telling example is the common words used for wife: "ah-nae" (아내) or "ahn-sa-ram" (안사람). The first refers to the person who is inside in the domestic sphere, and the second literally means "inside/inner sphere person."[6] Confucian hierarchy and gender ideology undoubtedly shaped the Korean worldview and remains a significant influence in contemporary society.

Nineteenth- and Twentieth-Century Korea

In the late 1800s, American missionaries, many of whom were women, came to the Korean peninsula to bring "light to the presumed darkness of Korea"; and they were seen to be ushering in the world in which a new woman could emerge from under the "hierarchical Confucian gender relations in which women had been regarded as inferior to men" (Choi 2009, 2). The arrival of these missionaries and the contemporary socio-political backdrop is significant in Korea's attempt to reject the Chinese influence of Confucianism and accept the liberty of Western values. In particular, Confucian gender ideology secluded women in the home, prohibited education, forced them into early marriage, and exposed them to the abuses of the concubine system (Choi 2009, 33–34). Western culture brought new ideas and new possibilities.

Western missionaries and their criticism of Confucian gender ideology, however, neither resulted in domestic emancipation nor established gender equality—perhaps because gender discrimination existed, though more veiled, in the American presentation of Christianity. It was rightly observed that Christian women "assumed unequal, subordinate positions within the larger church organizations" (Choi 2009, 3). The missionaries had not divorced themselves from Victorian norms, and so Korean women essentially traded one form of gender ideology for another under the guise of liberation, education, and enlightenment.

5 When the Choson Dynasty was established, the ruling Yi family essentially replaced Buddhism with Confucianism.

6 Another common word to denote "wife" is "bu-in" 부인 (夫人), which has Chinese roots, literally meaning "husband-person."

> The missionaries had not divorced themselves from Victorian norms, and so Korean women essentially traded one form of gender ideology for another under the guise of liberation, education, and enlightenment.

This "women's rights but not fully" approach presented by Western missionaries influenced Korean intellectuals, who expressed their "enlightened" thoughts in newspaper editorials, writing that "women are equal but as the weaker sex needed to be protected," thus merging Confucianism with Christianity (Choi 2009, 34–37).[7]

In response to this rhetoric, a circulation of the *Yohhakkyo Solsi Tongmun* in September 1898 stands as the first public demand for equal rights *for* Korean women *by* Korean women (Choi 2009, 38–39). This was a cry from Korean women for equality, and particularly the right to be educated; and many point to the establishment of girls' mission schools as evidence of how Christianity positively impacted women's liberation and women's rights (Choi 2009, 3). One outstanding example is Mary Fitch Scranton, an American Methodist missionary who founded Korea's first school for women, *Ewha Hakdang,* in 1886 (Kim 1996, 13–14). This was a monumental achievement in a culture in which even women of nobility were limited in education.

Still, these social advances proved to be a double-edged sword. While the promise of girls' and women's education was so appealing that the king himself named the school, there was concern that Western education might cause Korean women to reject Korean traditions and desire the liberal Western lifestyle (Choi 2009, 97–100). The missionaries recognized that if they were perceived to be overthrowing Korean tradition, all their gospel work on the peninsula could come to an end. Hence, in an effort to alleviate public concern and prevent misconception, the "missionaries strategically emphasized that they trained girls not to become Westernized ladies but rather to become better Koreans and model housewives"—which meant recognizing, at the core of their curriculum, that a woman's place was in the domestic sphere (Choi 2009, 99).[8] This was also consistent with the Victorian ideals of womanhood (Kim 1996, 16).

---

7 Young J. Allen was known for his very progressive views on gender equality, including women's education and suffrage. Warren Candler, on the other hand, supported women's education but stood against women's suffrage and women's right to vote. Also, "Korean intellectuals" refers only to men. The *Tongnip Sinmun* (*The Independent*) was founded in 1896 and was the first Korean newspaper with an English edition. So Chae-Pil intended the paper to be the voice of the most disenfranchised of Korean society, including women.

8 One *Ewha* teacher explained, "Whatever may be the private opinion of anyone concerning woman's sphere and proper occupation, we must, for the present, at least act under the supposition that in Korea domestic life is her sphere and destiny... . They must learn to prepare food; cut, make, and repair their clothing; keep themselves and their rooms neat ... "

Thus, despite the establishment of mission schools for women, the most meaningful reforms in education affected men. Kim writes, "In retrospect, early Christianity and modern education in Korea failed to challenge, but rather confirmed the traditional self-images of Korean women, even as they introduced modern knowledge to those women" (Kim 1996, 13–15). In the end, the purpose of missionary school education for girls and women was to make them "good wives and wise mothers" (Choi 2009, 101–3). This educational philosophy was eagerly adopted and further perpetuated by native Koreans. Male scholars from the intellectual class "urged" educators to teach girls how to prepare a creative dinner table using a variety of ingredients (Choi 2009, 102). Thus, while Korean leaders encouraged and even welcomed change across the country—new ideas, cultural exchange, and avant-garde technologies that promised exciting possibilities for future generations—these opportunities were limited only to the men. Women were, yet again, relegated to the domestic sphere.

Nineteenth- and Twentieth-Century China[9]

Western incursions into China were met with hostility. The end of the Opium Wars left China humiliated, and the Taiping Revolution only accelerated tensions (Leung 2001, 141). From the Opium Wars until 1949, the gospel in China was "proclaimed in the context of power" (Noll and Nystrom 2011, 195).[10] Westerners did not separate Christianity from Western culture, viewing Chinese culture as heathen (Leung 2001, 142).[11] Hudson Taylor, while making significant effort to adapt to Chinese culture, did so out of strategic necessity rather than cultural respect. Still, his effort to learn Chinese culture showed him how the influence of Confucianism had prevented women from having access to the gospel. Taylor championed female missionaries, who were integral to the movement and whose work included reforms in education and health care.

Westerners also gave the Chinese a new perspective on family structures and the role of women (Spence 1990, 208–9). Where women were previously restricted to the home, their worth deriving from their kinship to the male figure (son, husband, or father), they were now free to enter society as individuals and could pursue careers previously inaccessible to them. Chinese women responded

---

9 There is evidence of Christianity arriving in China as early as the seventh century. However, the scope of this chapter is limited to only the Protestant missionary efforts of the nineteenth century onward.

10 One tangible consequence of the Opium Wars was that Chinese people who converted to Christianity were no longer seen as Chinese, because the terms dictated at the end of the Opium Wars made provisions for them (Leung, 141).

11 Foreigners were not the only ones who thought that these practices were abhorrent. Early Chinese feminist Qiu Jin 秋瑾 (1875–1907) wrote that "China's women still remain in the dark and gloom, mired in the lowest of all the levels of hell's prisons." 「我的二萬萬女同胞，還依然黑暗沈淪在十八層地獄°」.

to these missionary efforts, and by 1921 women represented about 37 percent of the Christian population (Kwok 1992, 1).

By the 1860s, female missionaries were recruiting Chinese women ("Bible women") to evangelize their own people (Chow 2018). By the 1880s, "Bible women" were teaching, publicly evangelizing, and preaching to mixed-gender groups—without the direct supervision of foreign female missionaries. Other women trained as doctors, both in China and overseas, to push the mission forward.[12]

The stories of Chinese women in ministry during this time show that these women often went to places—sometimes to their detriment and even death—where men were unwilling to go (eL 2017). This prompted questions about formal female leadership. After the May Fourth Movement, there was an increasing push for women to be raised up in the church as much as they had been liberated in broader society (Kwok 1992, 83–84). Others appealed to the work of the Spirit, enabling women to prophesy and appealing to female leadership within the Scriptures. Opposing this were missionaries influenced by Victorian ideals and locals influenced by Confucian ideals, arguing that women should not be in formal leadership but instead should assume their traditional roles in the home—although they were happy to accept the informal leadership of women, because such ministries pertained to the kitchens, children, and women (Kwok 1992, 83).

By the 1930s, the impact of women in the story of Christianity became largely superseded by male evangelists' narratives (Wu 2002, 86).

Current Experiences of Korean and Chinese Women in Ministry[13]

While the Korean and Chinese contexts in regard to women in ministry are different, there are enough similarities and common themes between these two demographics to make the following observations. First, women's roles within the home are directly transferred into the local expression of the church, producing a sense of second-class citizenship. Second, the women-in-ministry question is largely viewed as a Western construct. Third, women who question the system are viewed as arrogant, power-hungry, overly ambitious, and disruptive. Fourth, women continue to face gender-based violence and harassment, even in their ministries. Lastly, the rise in popularity of neo-Calvinist norms has revived a sentiment opposed to women in ministry.

---

12 Examples include Dora Yu Cidu, Mary Stone (Shi Meiyu), and Victoria Cheng (who was born in Canada).

13 In this section, Korean, Korean American, and Korean Canadian experiences of women in ministry will be discussed. As for the Chinese experience, Hong Kong and Hong Kong Canadian diaspora will be examined, due to the limits of this paper. Some key scholars in this area are Frederick Fällman and Mary Li Ma.

The assumptions of modern Christian womanhood, stemming from old-world Confucian gender ideology, reinforced by Victorian Christian values, is deep-seated in the Chinese and Korean churches.[14] One such assumption is that women should remain in the home. While this is not often taken literally, it often translates into women being relegated to women's ministries, caring ministries, and children's ministries. Some have been ordained in these positions, while others are merely given a token title, such as "pastor," "minister," or "intern." Many are disallowed from formal leadership and decision-making positions. Wai-Lin Lau recounts being placed consistently at the bottom of the hierarchy, even below a new seminary graduate (Lau 1999, 2). Rank and position in Asian culture is significant and indicates one's place or lack thereof. Congregants often mistake female pastors for office staff because the respect given to male pastors is not extended to female pastors (Lau 1999, 2).

One experienced woman pastor was, according to denominational requirements, eligible for ordination. However, she was told that her junior male colleague would be pursuing ordination first. When she persisted, the senior pastor finally told her that she was not eligible for ordination in his church because she was a woman. Unfairly, while church leaders may appreciate the work of women pastors, they withhold full recognition and acknowledgement of their calling, theological and pastoral training, and years of service (Law 1982, 64). In the 1970s, the Chinese Congress on World Evangelization (CCOWE) noted that the majority of seminarians in Hong Kong were women, but made a point of enquiring about ministry options—for instance, pastors' wives, volunteers, lay leaders, and missionaries—and tentatively proposed that the option for female ministerial workers was an "issue to be pondered" (Law 1982, 64).[15] Many more women have heard the call of ministry on their lives since then.

Christine Hong shares an experience that further illustrates the cultural challenges for women pastors in the Asian church (2015, 58–62). Hong had looked to church leaders and mentors to help discern and affirm her call to ministry. The responses she received, however, ranged from "You aren't practical enough for ministry" to "Isn't what you really feel a call to be is a pastor's wife?" (58).[16] Still, she was certain of her calling and had the courage to continue. After graduating from seminary and returning to her Korean American roots, what she experienced was, in her own words, "bizarre" (58). They would ask about her age, whether or not her parents were "OK with this," if she liked playing the piano, if she liked children, and if she was planning for marriage. Hong also recalls,

---

14 There are cases of Chinese and Korean churches where women are empowered, but this is largely not the case, as there are a number of assumptions which cause difficulties for women in vocational church ministry.

15 Churches associated with CCOWE in North America have since ordained women.

16 Hong later understood that being "practical" meant being male.

When I asked why they posed these questions, their response was, "Well, women follow their husbands when they get married, so you wouldn't stay here long." One interview ended with an elderly Korean American pastor giving me a paternalistic pat on my rear end as I left his office. He handed me a hundred-dollar bill, saying, "Go have something good to eat." (58–59)

These interview questions clearly indicate the undergirding Confucian gender ideology that has oppressed Asian women for centuries. The expectation of women to be "good wives and wise mothers," reinforced by the Victorian Christian values of the American missionaries, transferred all too easily into the sphere of ministry and lingers there even today. In short, women called to ministry were assumed to be called to the church equivalent of the domestic sphere.

The assumption is that because the father is the head of the household, in both the Christian complementarian and Confucian ideal, *he* is therefore suitable to be a pastor (Lau 1999, 158). Even in the churches where women are allowed to be pastors or even ordained, only men can be senior pastors. In other words, a "bamboo ceiling" of sorts still exists, and is reinforced by both men and women. Lau confesses that she thought that the administrative assistant, as a fellow woman, would support her effort to be recognized as a pastor in the church. Unexpectedly, she reported Lau to the senior pastor as a troublemaker (Lau 1999, 222–23).[17]

Similarly, Hong (2015) shares an experience that forced her to reckon with her own bamboo ceiling.

The worst was when one interviewer asked if I had any ambitions to become a senior minister someday. Initially, I thought that this was a prodding encouragement, as if to say that I *should* be thinking about such things. However, I realized that he was checking to see if I would fall in line. He was checking to see if I would try to reach beyond the boundaries set for me. (59)

In the same way that women were relegated to the private, domestic sphere in old-world Confucianism, women in the church have boundaries and are passive-aggressively "encouraged" to fall in line. Men belong in the public sphere, and therefore positions of senior leadership are expected to be filled by men. Women should not presume to reach too far or too high. Just like the walled homes of Confucian Korea, a woman should know her proper place in the church (Hong 2015, 59).[18]

When women do seek to be formally recognized in leadership, they are seen as being power-hungry, disruptive, attention-seeking, prideful, and overreaching (Lau 1999, 168). The onus of asking for ordination, even in denominations that ordain women, is often placed on the woman. In one case, at a Chinese diaspora

---

17 Other women pastors have reported that they thought they were unable to be senior pastors because women are too emotional and not rational enough.

18 The relief in all this, if one can even put it this way, is that Hong, despite the humiliation she endured, held fast to her calling, and trusted that God would guide her to the right ministry and equip her accordingly.

In the same way that women were relegated to the private, domestic sphere in old-world Confucianism, women in the church have boundaries and are passive-aggressively "encouraged" to fall in line.

church, a female pastor was asked to take over as acting senior pastor during the senior pastor's leave. Given the inconveniences of trying to accomplish her responsibilities without being given the proper credentials, she applied for ordination, but was accused of overstepping and of coveting the senior pastor's position (Lau 1999, 143).[19]

For Hong (2015), even when she found her place in ministry, there were other challenges that she had to overcome. For instance, she was not allowed to drive a van and had to find a man to drive in her place (60). The assumption was that a van was too "manly" of a vehicle for her to drive. She was also told to "cut her hair shorter," "wear less makeup," and "dress more modestly." Hong confesses that these comments stung the most because they were given by "well-meaning women who claimed they saw me as a daughter and they would not want their daughter running around that way" (60).

Hong's ordeal with her ordination as a woman pastor in the Korean American church reveals the deeply enculturated mindset of Korean church leadership. When she and another female minister approached the senior pastor about ordination, not only did he seem aggravated, but he suggested that they have a twenty-minute ordination service on a day when many people would be away (Hong 2015, 60). When Hong gently countered by expressing her desire to celebrate her well-earned ordination and her spiritual journey with her mother, grandmother, youth, teachers, and mentors, the senior pastor dismissed her, saying, "Go somewhere else! If you want to make this a show, go somewhere else. Rent out a gym or a room somewhere, but don't invite anyone from the church. No one will come" (62).

The effects of these words were deeply personal. Hong confesses that a series of questions, fueled by such exchanges, flooded her mind—questions like, Was a pastor's first call always like this—humiliating, belittling, frightening? Did this response come because I was a woman and did not fit into the preconceived mold of Korean American femininity? Did my male counterparts go through this? (Hong 2015, 61–62). Confucian gender ideology reinforced by culture and Christian doctrine has deeply damaging and humiliating consequences (60).[20]

---

19 In another case, in Toronto, the senior pastor supported a woman pastor's ordination. He even advocated for her, only to have his efforts stymied by the deacons. It took almost a decade for her to be ordained.

20 Members of the congregation had heard about her desire to seek ordination and rallied behind her. Mentors, teachers, and teammates from the past were in attendance, as were current colleagues and the youth under her care. Her spiritual advisor gave her the charge, and her mother and grandmother placed the sacred vestments upon her. Hong gave her first benediction—without getting her hand slapped. Previously, she had literally gotten her hand slapped because she spoke a blessing over her youth students that too closely resembled a benediction in the eyes of the church leadership.

Moreover, gender-based violence and harassment pervade the church as well. When forty-nine women in ministry in Hong Kong or Vancouver (or those who had significant crossover between the two cities) were surveyed, forty-eight of them answered that they had experienced sexual harassment from both colleagues and congregation members (Lau 1999, 214).[21] Lau's statement that "a mature woman in seminary should be taught by mature clergywomen how to cope firmly, but graciously, with minor verbal abuse and unwelcome joking relationships" exemplifies the normalization of this behavior within the church (215).

Another obstacle in the Asian church is that female leadership is seen as a Western construct. As we have seen, however, the traditional role of women is both a Confucian and a Western construct, and there are varying responses. Among the first generation, many churches support women pastors, even though there is a significant power imbalance and, in some cases, abuse. Among the second generation, there is growing discontentment with the first generation, and their rejection of the first generation has also included some rejecting women in formal leadership. While it may be tempting to dismiss the second generation's response as reactionary, it is more helpful to see their response as simply another outcome of the same discipleship continuum that has been passed on from the time of the initial Protestant mission to Asia.

This outcome is indicative of a shift toward neo-Calvinism and complementarianism. Fenggang Yang notes that when there were missions for Chinese people in America, those churches tended to stay in those denominations (such as the Presbyterians, United Methodists, Episcopalians, and so on) (Yang 1999, 6–7). But those churches established *by* the Chinese tended to either be independent or to belong to denominations that allowed for autonomy and were known for their theological conservatism—such as the Southern Baptist Convention and Christian and Missionary Alliance (7).[22]

Yang makes several observations: within independent or autonomous *Chinese* churches, Chinese people could establish their North American identity on their own terms (as opposed to by their North American white counterparts) (127). Secondly, the Southern Baptist association is interesting (given their historically racist positions), but not when the influence of Southern Baptist missionaries in China and their emphasis on the homogenous unit principle are taken into consideration (130). In such a way, Chinese churches were able to establish respectability in the North American church as well as keep their theological

---

21 Hong's experience with the senior pastor who, regardless of paternal intent, gave her a hundred dollars and patted her on the rear, would fall under this category.

22 Given that Canada and the US were treated as one district in CCOWE, it is not a far stretch to imagine that what was influencing the States also made its way into the Chinese Canadian church.

conservatism, congregational autonomy, and preserve their language and culture (130). Particularly, as Hong Kong students emigrated en mass to study in North America in the 1980s, they converged upon a Southern Baptist movement that was beginning to craft a complementarian response in opposition to what John Piper and Wayne Grudem (1991) identified as "liberal" and "feminist" ideologies in evangelicalism (xiii). By 1989, the Danvers Statement had been published and the Council for Biblical Manhood and Womanhood (CMBW) established by esteemed figures like Grudem, Piper, and James Dobson, to name a few.[23] Is it any surprise, then, that while there has been a deep history of Chinese women being empowered and released for ministry, Chinese women began to be suppressed by the desire to defend Christianity at this time?

As the structures began to form, the openness exemplified in missions was verbally proclaimed, but the structures meant to facilitate that openness began to harden. It is therefore posited that one of the reasons why complementarianism was adopted by the Chinese (diaspora) church is because it presented a logical, consistent, seemingly biblical justification for the particular Confucian values that pertained to gender and the home. Nevertheless, although the practicality of Chinese (in particular, Hong Kong-diaspora) culture leads to a teaching of the conservative position on women in leadership, in application the churches are more open (Lau 1999, 260).[24] The second-generation adoption of neo-Calvinist values and norms should also not be a surprise. In fact, church leaders are only bearing the fruit of what they have been raised in.

With Reformed tradition and doctrine dominant in Korean churches, the leap to neo-Calvinism has been a more obvious pathway than in the Chinese churches. It remains rare today—even among the second generation—to see a female elder in a decision-making position or as a senior pastor. It remains true that a noble, biblically Christlike and culturally "becoming" woman serves her male counterparts. A woman who overreaches and disrupts the accepted norm, however, is thoroughly shamed by her peers and elders.

Still, the Chinese and Korean church remains a place of hope and belonging for many women. Korean American Aram Bae shares how meaningful the Korean church community was to her in her formative years (Lee 2017, 80–89).

---

23 One wonders if New Testament scholar Ronald Y. K. Fung's change of view from allowing the ordination of women to disallowing it is in part because of the growing influence of this view. Fung is not, however, the only scholarly voice. Khiok-khng Yeo and Wing-Sung Cheung both emphasize mutuality and the granting of leadership by virtue of gifting.

24 There is diversity in response too, dependent on the senior pastor's theological education. The first Chinese female pastor to be ordained in the Canadian Baptists of Ontario and Quebec was Rev. Dorothy Wong in the late 1990s. Shortly thereafter, the Association of Christian Evangelical Ministries (ACEM) ordained a number of women in the early 2000s. Anita Leung was the first Chinese woman to be ordained in the C&MA in Vancouver.

Later, though, when she returned to the Korean American church as a pastor, the "once-upon-a-happy-place" had become toxic.

> I want to run away from the overt sexism and stifling nature of patriarchy found in the church. I want to run away from the ageism that works against me. I want to run away from the sometimes subtle but always telling way certain older adults have when they speak to me, or rather, *at* me… . And I really want to stay away from adults who, having been spoiled by both their parents and culture, still expect women to remain ignorantly agreeable, alluringly quiet, and alarmingly thin. (Lee 2017, 82–83)

It would seem that the more things change, the more things stay the same (Bae 2015, 84–87).[25]

Like Christine Hong, and despite her inclination to run away from her diaspora home church, Bae (2015) returns with hope, seeing herself as an agent of change "of the place that has loved and nurtured" her (88–89). Both Hong and Bae are courageous women, confronting and challenging the Confucian gender norms that have defined traditional Korean culture for centuries. There is still a long way to go. But changes are being made, and more young women—and older women—are recognizing the significant role that women have played and must play in the Korean church, both on the peninsula and throughout the diaspora communities.

Despite the frustrations, it is encouraging to know that Asian women are finding their voice in order to share their experiences. Whether or not they are formally recognized, women have been overcoming obstacles and stepping into positions of leadership—some within the church, as lay ministers, and others in the parachurch world. In 1929, the ratio of female to male missionaries was two-to-one, both in and from China (Lau 1999, 176). In the last century, two-thirds of all missionaries in and from China have been women.

Women are not leading merely to fill a gap that men have been unable to fill. The reality is that the church needs both men and women, empowered by the Spirit and released in their giftings so that the world might come to know Jesus. No longer should Asian women be relegated to the private domestic sphere; but instead they should be confident in their calling to minister and serve in the communities that they call home. Their place is not hidden and silent. Their place is where God has called and placed them—for his kingdom, and for his glory.

---

25 As Bae unpacks her experience and the collective social narrative behind the Korean American church, she points to the work of Georgia State University professor, Jung Ha Kim. As a result of studying the relationship between gender and the sociology of religion, Ha notes some significant observations in the history of the Korean American church—namely, "patterns of feminization, the permanence of patriarchy, and an ethos of religion (one's actions) over faith (one's beliefs)." The Korean diaspora churches in North America have imported and preserved the Confucian gender ideology of traditional Korea, perhaps as an unconscious way of preserving Korean culture as an immigrant population in North America.

The Proper Place for Women to Minister

The proper place for women to minister is not limited to the kitchen or to children's ministry. There is "no immovable sex line drawn on God's employment sheet" (Lau 1999, 141). Women are useful not only in the "inner place" and domestic sphere, but also in the public community: to lead, to teach, to preach, and to serve. With every passing generation of Korean and Chinese women and their daughters, the confidence and willingness to challenge established gender norms builds. As women distinctly feel God's calling and the Spirit's leading in their lives, they are discovering that their place in ministry leadership is not dictated by culture and tradition, but rather by God and where he places them.

But just acquiring a ministry leadership position is not the goal. The calling of Korean and Chinese women for the good of the body is at stake. Hence Unzu Lee, with the wisdom of experience, cautions women leaders about getting used to the established leadership, even if they eventually become insiders (Lee 2017, 122).

An intentional effort by women leaders to continue to push for change is needed, especially to open doors of opportunity that have never been available to emerging women leaders. Women should be given the opportunity to lead, not only because they "bring a woman's perspective," but because they bring many different perspectives, experiences, talents, gifts, and skills. Therefore, global leaders should aim to be mindful in making space for women to raise their voices and have opportunities to lead in order to optimize all the gifts God has given to the church for the *missio Dei*.

The relationship between Christian liberty and gender roles remains a tense tightrope for many women, not just for Chinese and Korean women. The call to leadership and ministry is also very personal, and God's prerogative—this "divine ministry placement"—belongs neither to man, nor woman, nor cultural tradition. What the Chinese and Korean churches have failed to do, in varying degrees, is to recognize, encourage, and empower women in their calling to lead and to minister. Perhaps now, in the twenty-first century, it is time to restore women to their proper place as full participants, ministers, and leaders in God's mission.

References Cited

Bae, Aram. 2015. "Home Sweet Diaspora Home." In *Here I Am: Faith Stories of Korean American Clergywomen,* edited by Grace Ji-Sun, 80–89. Valley Forge, PA: Judson Press.

Chan, Joyce Chung-yan. 2013. *Rediscover the Fading Memories: Early Chinese Canadian Christian History.* Burnaby, BC: Chinese Christian Missions.

Choi, Hyaeweol. 2009. *Gender and Mission Encounters in Korea: New Women, Old Ways.* Los Angeles: University of California Press.

Chow, Alexander. 2018. "The Remarkable Story of China's 'Bible Women.'" *Christianity Today,* https://www.christianitytoday.com/history/2018/march/christian-china-bible-women.html.

eL. 2017. "Women in China's Protestant Church and Missions." *China Source,* September 18, https://www.chinasource.org/resource-library/articles/women-in-chinas-protestant-church-and-missions.

Hong, Christine J. 2015. "Go Somewhere Else." In *Here I Am: Faith Stories of Korean American Clergywomen*, edited by Grace Ji-Sun, 58–62. Valley Forge, PA: Judson Press.

Kim, Ai Ra. 1996. *Women Struggling for a New Life: The Role of Religion in the Cultural Passage from Korea to America.* Albany, NY: State University of New York Press.

Kwok, Pui-lan. 1992. *Chinese Women and Christianity, 1860–1927.* Atlanta: Scholars Press.

Lau, Wai Lin. 1999. "Am I a Pastor? Woman in Ministry in a Chinese Church in Canada." DMin diss., Western Seminary.

Law, Gail. 1982. *Chinese Churches Handbook.* Hong Kong: CCOWE.

Lee, Unzu. 2017. "Foolishness of Wisdom." In *Leading Wisdom: Asian and Asian North American Women Leaders*, edited by Su Yon Park and Jung Ha Kim, 115–37. Louisville, KY: Westminster John Knox Press.

Leung, Ka-lun. 2001. "China." In *A Dictionary of Asian Christianity*, edited by Scott Sunquist, 139–46. Grand Rapids: Wm. B. Eerdmans.

Noll, Mark, and Carolyn Nystrom. 2011. *Clouds of Witnesses: Christian Voices from Africa and Asia.* Downers Grove, IL: InterVarsity.

Piper, John, and Wayne Grudem, eds. 1991. *Recovering Biblical Manhood and Womanhood.* Wheaton, IL: Crossway.

Spence, Jonathan D. 1990. *The Search for Modern China.* New York: W. W. Norton & Co.

Wang, Robin R. 2000. "The Classic of Changes." In *Images of Women in Chinese Thought and Culture: Writings from Pre-Qing to Song Dynasty*, edited by Robin R. Wang, 25–45. Indianapolis: Hackett.

———. 2006. "Virtue, Talent, and Beauty: Authoring a Full-Fledged Womanhood." In *Lienuzhuan (Biographies of Women) in Authority in the Confucian Culture*, edited by Peter Hershock and Roger Ames, 93–115. New York: State University of New York Press.

Wu, Silas. 2002. "Dora Yu (1873–1931): Foremost Female Evangelist in Twentieth-Century Chinese Revivalism." In *Gospel Bearers, Gender Barriers: Missionary Women in the Twentieth Century*, edited by Dana L. Robert, 85–98. Maryknoll, NY: Orbis Books.

Yang, Fenggang. 1999. *Chinese Christians in America: Conversion, Assimilation, and Adhesive Identities.* University Park, PA: Pennsylvania State University Press.

PART 2

Revisiting
Long-Held Models

CHAPTER 6

Five Decades,
Four Questions,
and One Which Remains:
Queries Concerning the Unreached People Group Movement

KEN BAKER

In his book *Team of Teams*, Stanley McChrystal succinctly demonstrates the watershed difference between that which is *complicated* and that which is *complex* (2015, 56–57). A car is a complicated machine: an extensive collection of parts and processes which function in precise patterns. Despite the intricacy, any issue can be resolved, because relationships between the parts are specifically known; the problem is merely complicated. On the other hand, international relations, warfare, economics, social dynamics, health care, etc. are intensely complex, because the interdependencies in these living systems involve a cascade of unpredictable variables. Using this contrast as an example, a major sector of global mission—the unreached people group (UPG) movement—has chronically operated on the assumption that this endeavor is complicated but manageable, when the reality of global mission is exceedingly complex.

Presuming to be the dominant narrative of global mission, the UPG movement has suffered from a chronic reductionism that has led to prolonged simplification. The pressures of mobilization and funding have tended to reduce global mission to completing a church-planting movement (CPM) agenda, asserting that a CPM for every *ethne* is the comprehensive goal of Christian mission. All this to say that global mission is beset with a reductionistic and simplistic model that resists nuanced thought and praxis for our complex world today. In this chapter, I will first examine the UPG church-planting movement over five decades through the lens of five questions: *Where? Who? What? How?* and *Why?* After evaluating typical responses to these questions, my intent is to introduce an understanding of global mission as a role for God's people, rather than merely a task, and demonstrate how this missional role embodies the character of our King as he establishes his reign over all things.

Five Decades, Five Questions

The chart below summarily depicts the predominant church-planting outlook over the last five decades, at least from a mostly North American perspective. The chart represents the recognition that the realm of CPMs has increasingly received the most attention. Four questions have dominated this period, and my thesis is that one additional question remains.

	1974	2000	2020
WHERE?	**WHO?**	**HOW?**	**WHY?**
geopolitical outlook	"hidden" people groups	10/40 Window paradigm	
"national" churches in every country	**WHAT?**	Adopt-a-People Group AD2000&Beyond People-Group Mapping	
	a viable, reproducing church for every UPG	Insider Movements Church-Planting Movements Finishing The Task Disciple-Making Movements Business as Mission T4T NoPlaceLeft etc.	

Where?

Until the early 1970s, the prevailing question was *Where?* Which countries needed a church? Since the predominant perspective was to see the world as a collection of geopolitical nations, the general approach to global evangelization was to plant and develop strong national churches. However, Ralph Winter's address at the 1974 International Congress on World Evangelization in Lausanne, as well as the first *Unreached Peoples Directory*, introduced thinking focused on "people groups"—i.e., thousands of distinct groups which had been "hidden" from a geopolitical vision (Datema 2016, 49–51).

Who?

As a result of acceptance of the people-group model, the key question was no longer *Where*, but *Who*? Who were these hidden, unreached peoples? During this time, there was a shift in emphasis, away from geography and toward ethnolinguistic identity. The quest to

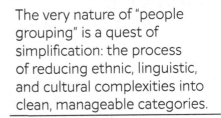

The very nature of "people grouping" is a quest of simplification: the process of reducing ethnic, linguistic, and cultural complexities into clean, manageable categories.

craft a consensus definition of "people group" (described in Datema 2016, 45–54) eventually evolved into this wording:

> For evangelization purposes, a people group is the largest group within which the Gospel can spread as a church planting movement without encountering barriers of understanding or acceptance. (Joshua Project n.d.)

Despite the fact that the category of "people group" is not specifically defined in Scripture, is not a recognized sociological category, and has endured wide critique (Appadurai 1988; Rynkiewich 2002, 2007; Lee and Park 2018), "people group" remains the principal category for identifying and promoting church-planting goals.

Interestingly, the migration/diaspora phenomenon exposes the inherent weakness of people-group categorizing. The very nature of "people grouping" is a quest of simplification: the process of reducing ethnic, linguistic, and cultural complexities into clean, manageable categories. Why the insistence that every person must fit into a people-group box, or that new boxes must be created? (We need look no further than the reification of race for an example of simplistic categorization.) Since people have their own notion of identity, why do we feel compelled to generate an identity or category for them? The UPG task appears to drive the need for clear people-group boundaries in order to focus the endeavor and quantify progress. One can understand the mobilization motivation to graphically present the status of world evangelization, and this has clearly brought many into global gospel ministry. Yet, what is lost in the process?

Defining *unreached* has been an equally thorny challenge. Beyond the unsatisfactory binary nature of the concept (reached/unreached) (Datema 2016, 52), there is the extended confusion over the percentage of Christians necessary within a people group to consider the group "reached." From the 1970s to the early 1990s, the general consensus was that the population of a reached people group was at least 20 percent "Christian" (Datema 2016, 47–60); but after the mid-1990s, the criteria changed to 2 percent "evangelical" (Hadaway 2014, 22; Datema 2016, 60). However, the principal missiologists of the day recognized that these percentages were arbitrary and intended only for purposes of clarification (Datema 2016, 55). Even though there is no sociological research evidence to justify their use (Datema

2016, 60), these percentages, especially the 2-percent threshold, have played a massive part in UPG mission promotion (Datema 2016, 50). Despite the imprecise and confusing definitions of "unreached" and "people group," an enduring project of creating and maintaining UPG lists began (Datema 2016, 60).

What?

The issue of populating these lists led to the next abiding query: *What?* What was needed within these UPGs? The standard answer is a church for every UPG—or more specifically, disciples who make disciples who form a church movement that will provide gospel access within a people group. But when is a church a church? A clear description of what constitutes a "church" within a CPM has also evolved. Currently, the general expectation for a CPM that arises within a UPG is that it would be indigenous (Datema 2016, 53), that its growth will develop as a homogeneous unit (McGavran 1990, 69–71), and that it would function as "rapidly reproducing" house churches (Garrison 2004, loc 294 and 2918) that will give the gospel a foothold within a people group. Given the movement's need for rapid multiplication, such a specific image of "church" is required for quantification purposes. Likewise, the terminology of "movement" has gained a life of its own. The concern with a movement is that it can become a narrative about itself and, as Lesslie Newbigin asserts, run "the risk of becoming chiefly interested in its own existence and development" (quoted in Stroope 2017, 351).

How?

As the *Who?* (UPGs) and *What?* (UPG church planting) gained extraordinary momentum in the 1980s and beyond, this began a continuing innovative period answering the question *How?* How should the UPGs be "reached"? Thus, from the 1980s onward, there has been a constant stream of "how-to" resources, programs, approaches, networks, and methodologies with regard to "reaching" UPGs. While the previous chart only lists several of these, we recognize the faith, time, commitment, and perseverance invested in these efforts. Many thousands of global workers have benefitted from these initiatives, as movements to Jesus proliferate.

Why?

Such are the four questions which have characterized the last five decades. The *Where? Who? What?* and *How?* over this time period have coalesced around the expansion of movements to Jesus within every people group (*ethne*). However, one question remains: *Why?* Why are we supposed to be engaged in launching CPMs within every *ethne*? In the remainder of this chapter, I will address the implications of this abiding question.

Exploring the Dynamics of Why?

The query *Why?* invokes one's vision of outcome. *Why?* anticipates a "so that …" response. For example, why are we involved in global witness? Typically, the response has been "so that" we can make disciples of all nations, or "so that" there will be movements to Jesus within every people group. The way we respond to *Why?* directly impacts our answers to *Where? Who? What?* and *How?* It is the "one ring that rules them all." Naturally, if our response to *Why?* is incomplete, then our responses to *Where? Who? What?* and *How?* will necessarily also be incomplete. An incomplete response to *Why?* has cascading ramifications. The popular response to the *Why?*—church expansion among every people—has become the dominant narrative, but it is incomplete, because it neglects the full purposes of the kingdom reign of God.

The Why? And the Where?

As the *Why?* (UPGs) gained prominence, the *Where?* was largely abandoned as a motivation. Clearly the emphasis upon geopolitical borders and national churches was an insufficient and inaccurate rendering of global reality. However, as I have proposed elsewhere (Baker 2017), relationship to *place* still matters, because context matters. People do not live in "people groups"; they live in specific places in space and time. People live in *communities*. It is in communities that people live, move, and have their being, where there is a distinctive rhythm and narrative. In such contexts, life "happens." Likewise, it is in communities—in real places— that global gospel workers live, learn, and engage with people in all their uniqueness and diversity. Place and context matter, not just "people group" identity.

The Why? And the Who?

If the *Why?* is incomplete, then that impacts the *Who?* Much has been written about the *panta ta ethne* in the New Testament, and it is not my purpose in this chapter to rehash the arguments regarding this Greek phrase. I will say, though, that the popular usage of this expression has emphasized the "each and every" aspect. The whole point of the focus on "hidden, unreached people groups" is that each and every *ethne* must have access to the gospel. However, this emphasis seems to overlook the "all" part of the phrase. All people, *humanity* as a whole, are in view as well; it is the "whosoever believes" of John 3. There is an "all of humanity" aspect to disciple-making: our "collective identity ... which shapes our sense of mission" (Wu 2019, 30). Thus, just as the geopolitical country focus of the *Where?* period was incomplete, the "people group" focus of the *Who?* period is also incomplete if it does not keep the this-is-for-all-humanity vision alive.

The Why? And the What?

Reexamining the *Why?* not only encourages us to nuance our understanding of the *Who?* but also to have another look at the *What?*—popularly expressed as "disciples who make disciples who form a church movement that will provide gospel access within a people group." This, though, raises the question, What sort of disciples are we making? There is substance behind the Great Commission. It functions as a skeleton, giving the basic elements of the role Jesus was entrusting to his followers; but the rest of the New Testament fleshes out the character and life Christ expects these followers to live and display. We have traditionally received the Great Commission mandate as a call to make disciples (going, baptizing, teaching) among every *ethne*. Yet we seem to overlook the orbit of implications unleashed through the realization that movements to Jesus among each people are *one comprehensive movement of the reign of God*—a kingdom movement.

Global mission envisions the reign of God reclaiming and transforming humanity as he calls his people to holistic kingdom living. Increasingly, we recognize the need to embody biblical themes such as justice, peacemaking, creation care, reconciliation, risk, suffering, and persecution as we encounter and engage with complex global realities such as globalization, urbanization, migration, climate change, world economics, human conflict, and pandemics. Are these global realities distractions from the goal or an integral part of God's kingdom scope? Lalsangkima Pachuau observes, "What [God] calls humanity to be is also what he expects culture to be.... By his redemptive and reconciling work in Christ, God is calling the entirety of humanity, together with their structures of existence (society) and ways of living (culture), back to his image" (2019, loc 4564).

These domains challenge us to conclude that an orientation toward the reign of God involves more than the task of viable church movements among each people group. The focus must be on the whole picture: the vertical work of the cross, the horizontal work of the cross, and the cosmic work of the cross. Space does not permit me to address each of these themes, so below I will concentrate on the implications of one of them—reconciliation. Renewed global consciousness is especially pointing to a collective recognition of reconciliation and healing as an abiding paradigm of kingdom endeavor (Schreiter 2005, 75).

The Why? And the How?

Lastly, an incomplete picture of the *Why?* leads us to examine the *How?* I propose that the main concern lies in casting the Great Commission as a *task*. We have shaped it as something for us to *do* and *finish*. A task is necessarily linear, procedural, and agenda-driven, which means that "measuring" and "completing" naturally take a central focus. The mere conceptualization of the Great Commission as a task molds involvement toward measurable goals, seemingly discounting the limitations of such empiricism (Datema 2016, 66). The term *mission* itself accentuates accomplishment. Michael Stroope makes this point in claiming that "mission" terminology has significantly skewed our understanding of God's kingdom purpose (2017, 15). The focus on quantification is an unfortunate example of the axiom that *if we can't measure what is truly important* (that is, transformative kingdom values), *then we make important what we can measure.*

Furthermore, if "mission" undertaking is a task, then the urgency narrative is its taskmaster. In the UPG/CPM perspective (and its progeny—

> Furthermore, if "mission" undertaking is a task, then the urgency narrative is its taskmaster.

DMM, T4T, etc.), urgency is *presumed* without robust reflection upon its implications. As a foundational motivation, urgency fuels the task-needs-efficient-methodology mentality. It is not my intent in this chapter to address this issue, but does this foundational commitment to urgency rest on interpretive deficiencies (Terry 2017; Bennett 2018)? Nevertheless, the UPG movement is popularly presented as Urgent Task + Mobilization + Every People Engaged + Rapid Church Multiplication = All People Groups Reached = Finished Task. Some go so far as to add "in our generation" to their purpose statement ("NoPlaceLeft.net n.d."). Others push back against the criticism (see Bennett 2018 and Moore 2019) of this stance, while insisting that it is possible to hasten the Lord's coming (Coles 2020). Given the tone of "hastening the day," it is no surprise that rapidity and efficiency characterize church-planting methodologies, rendering simplification and reductionism inevitable.

Task Versus Role

The task perspective clearly sets a tone of doing and measuring how we are doing. We cannot avoid it, since the task mindset resonates well with Western cultural values of goal-setting, linear productivity, efficiency, etc. Thus, it serves us well to acknowledge that such traits can subtly dominate Western involvement. Likewise, while task-oriented approaches and methods unfold in global contexts, they are largely conceived and promoted by those who are guests in the Majority World (Tan 2019, loc 6062).

Of course, there *is* a task aspect of global kingdom engagement; there *is* much *to do.* The problem, though, is seeing our involvement as *only* a task. I propose that we are better prepared for global engagement when we see our involvement as a *role* to live, instead of (only) a *task* to do. Role focuses on *who we are* as much as on *what we do.* As the people of God, it is our role to live and proclaim the reign of God. It is an incarnational role: the people of God as the presence of God, giving of ourselves into the life of our social and physical context. "Our concern is primarily to live authentically as Christians in the midst of the non-Christian world" (Tan 2019, loc 6072).

Our role is *being* and *making* disciples who will *be* and *make* disciples in the fullness of all that God intends for the flourishing of his kingdom. As Michael Goheen says, "The story of God's mission is the path he follows to make this good news known to the ends of the earth. The mission of God's people is to take their role in this drama" (2014, 39). Who we are reveals what we are to do.

As much of Scripture attests, the people of God have always had this role—i.e., a people among whom God dwells and through whom God intends to display an authentic witness of himself before the world. At any given time, the presence of God in his people declares to the world that he reigns. Jesus Christ manifested God in the midst of humanity; he is the second Adam, the perfect human. As God's people "in Christ" (Eph 2:10) and "clothed with Christ" (Gal 3:27), our role is to live and display perfect human community, as those "conformed to the image of his son" (Rom 8:29). Our role, as the collective people of God in Christ, is to display and proclaim Jesus Christ before the watching world. As we live and proclaim the life of Christ, we announce to the world the reign of God over all things.

The foundation and power of this role as the people of God before the watching world is that we *belong* to each other, and *with* each other, as brothers and sisters in Christ. *If we belong to Jesus, then we belong to those who belong to Jesus.* To be "in Christ" means that we belong (relationally joined) with all those "in Christ" through the indwelling of his Holy Spirit; we are one body in Christ. Fittingly, *belonging* carries ethical obligation, for "obligation is an inherent aspect of relationships" (Wu 2019, 185). Relationship characterizes both God and human beings, and it is not optional; likewise, distortions in human relationships are distortions of humanity (Deddo 2007, 31).

Relational alienation and distortion characterize life in a Genesis 3–11 world. At the cross, Christ's death reconciled all things, making way for a new creation. However, popular church-planting and disciple-making approaches appear to concentrate on the call for people(s) to be reconciled to God, which addresses the Genesis 3 problem. Unfortunately, though, these approaches may neglect the call for people to be reconciled to each other, which addresses the Genesis 11 problem. It reveals that the commonness of "people group" usage inevitably shapes thinking, and the use of "multiplication" language—the multiplying of disciples and "reached peoples"—emphasizes this "silo" perspective of self-contained people-group movements. "When we are used to thinking along one track (the gospel within a people group), we think only about the role of intra-ethnic relationships, not inter-ethnic relationships" (Baker 2017, 10). Our missional vision is not merely a Jesus movement within a people group manifesting reconciliation with God, but a Jesus movement which envisions comprehensive reconciliation, expressing the fullness of Christ's reign over all human relationships. Both Leviticus 19 and Luke 10 command that God's people are to "love God" and "love neighbor." Likewise, in John 13:35, Jesus said to his disciples, "All people will know that you are my disciples, if you love one another" (ESV). These Scriptures demonstrate that the vertical and horizontal obligations are never separate. Love and reconciliation typify our role as God's kingdom-ambassadors.

David Garrison claims that oneness in Christ is the "devil's candy"—sweet and enticing, but a trait that can prevent a church-planting movement (2004, loc 4009–68). Given the prominent place that God gives to love and oneness in Scripture, how can we so easily cast these aside as stumbling blocks to urgent gospel work? John 17:20–23 is crystal clear that Jesus' primary prayer for "those who will believe in me" is "that they may become perfectly one, so that the world may know that you sent me and loved them even as you loved me" (ESV). Why aren't love and oneness an intrinsic part of gospel planting strategy? They are a sign of the presence of God in his people, not an impediment to kingdom growth.

The Character of the King

When we view movements to Jesus as a task to do rather than as a role to live, we miss the opportunity and obligation to display the fullness of God's kingdom in humanity. It is as though we are so caught up in the management of the global mission enterprise that we are forgetting the character of the kingdom. When we shape the goal as "finishing the task," we focus more on the expansion of the kingdom than on its character. But *the character of the King must accompany the expansion of his kingdom.*

One of the primary themes of King Jesus' character is reconciliation, which emerges from redemption and anticipates restoration. "Reconciliation is increasingly being understood as an 'integrating' metaphor, helping us to understand both the essence of mission and the way in which we are called to engage with the world" (Langmead 2008, 6). However, when we lose focus on the reconciling reign of God, "the reconciling deeds of the kingdom are diminished or lost" (Stroope 2017, 361). God's intent through his kingdom people is "the reordering and renewing of relationships so that humanity may live fully in relationship to God, each other and creation" (Langmead 2008, 10).

Role and Reconciliation

Since reconciliation is concurrently vertical and horizontal, how can anyone be reconciled to Jesus and not to his *whole* church? Individual reconciliation ushers one into a gathered community, with "love of one another" as its principal character trait.

> Reconciliation to God is inseparable from reconciliation to one another. Christ, who *is* our peace, *made* peace through the cross, and *preached* peace to the divided world of Jew and Gentile. The unity of the people of God is both a fact ("he made the two one") and a mandate ("make every effort to preserve the

unity of the Spirit in the bond of peace"). God's plan for the integration of the whole creation in Christ is modelled in the ethnic reconciliation of God's new humanity. (The Cape Town Commitment 2011, 33–34; italics in original)

The promise of blessing to Abram "is an answer to the sin and the scattering of Genesis 3–11" and signals the eventual provision of reconciliation for every nation, tribe, people, and language (Hays 2003, 61). "The separation of Abraham and Israel was always overshadowed by the promise that the one God would one day bless humanity as *one* humanity" (Leithart 2016a, loc 230; italics in original).

Reconciliation with God is the "foundation of all Christian discourse on reconciliation: what God has done for humanity through Jesus Christ. What is new is the deeper exploration of the 'horizontal' dimension of reconciliation; that is, reconciliation between humans, as individuals and as groups" (Schreiter and Jørgensen 2013, 13). Salim Munayer concurs: "It is clear that the Christian vision of reconciliation is expansive. It cannot be limited to our personal salvation, as it must also encompass a believer's personal relationships, and ultimately the reconciliation of all things under God's rule" (2019, loc 6738). And Robert Schreiter adds, "Reconciliation encompasses the message of a call to conversion to Christ and situates it in a larger cosmic drama of all things being brought together in Christ" (2005, 23).

Reconciliation seems otherworldly because human discord is endemic to society. But reconciliation is not ethereal and detached; it is personal. As Jesus attests in Matthew 5:24, there is no acceptable worship (or obedience) without reconciliation. To be "in Christ" means to be in right (reconciled) relationship with God and all those in Christ (Duvall and Hays 2019, 231). The vision of reconciliation through the cross is humanity restored to divine intimacy and presence: "oneness" in God and his people. God's longing for reconciliation with humanity is so that those who are reconciled would "be one" in him and each other. Jesus' prayer in John 17 emphasizes this constant theme: "I am not praying for the world but for those whom you have given me ... that they may be one" (John 17:9, 11 ESV). God's heart for the nations is that they would be reconciled to him *and to each other* to the praise of his glory (cf. Psalm 87). Even though reconciliation may not be fully felt, we pursue it nonetheless, because reconciliation is not a destination but a daily process of relational obligation. Likewise, reconciliation is not merely a theological reality; it is an *actual ministry*. As the reconciled people of God, we have been given the ministry of reconciliation (2 Cor 5:17–19).

Any conception of global engagement which leaves out the ministry of reconciliation is not fully Christ-centered or cross-centered. Why haven't we seized on this ministry of reconciliation—the Great Calling—in the same way that we have embraced Matthew 28:19–20? The Great Calling is a companion to the Great Commission and the Great Commandment. Unfortunately, the popular image of reconciliation—"Let's all just get along"—is an impediment to the biblical presentation of reconciliation (Nordstokke 2013, 117). Reconciliation is not diversity training; it is *proclaiming* and *appropriating* what the cross made possible. Reconciliation returns humanity to the relational design which God intended from the outset. Reconciliation envisions and renders transformed relationships in all dimensions; it restores "with*ness*" and renews "belonging."

Reconciliation recognizes belonging as an integral part of human existence; "humanity was created one but was divided by sin" (Leithart 2016a, loc 206). Humanity still belongs to each other. This is intrinsic to human identity; and even though we are "in Christ," we remain a *companion* community with all of God's image-bearers. The people of God in Christ also represent human community as God intended—a "*contrast* community" (Goheen 2011, 194; italics mine) destined to display a preview of Christ's kingdom before the watching world. As a contrast community, we are also a *covenant* community, which embraces all that we are as diverse people, and "the very identity of each is formed through relation to others; the alterity of the other enters into the very identity of each" (Volf 1996, 154).

Thus, when we consider those mentioned in Revelation 5:9—every "tribe, language, people and nation" (additionally in 7:9 and 14:6)—we recognize that all these designations fall under the biblical theology of "neighbor," for "no matter what the *ethnos,* we remain, first of all neighbor" (Deddo 2007, 31–32). As such, we experience human existence as neighbors together in relationship, with all its accompanying ethical obligations. We equally recognize that we (the church) are sent to represent all that God intended for human community to be. "For Paul, the gospel announces the fulfillment of God's one plan for the one human race: the plan to unify all tribes, tongues, nations, and peoples in Christ … the reunion of humanity in Christ *is* the gospel … it is a *future* reality that gives present actions their orientation and meaning" (Leithart 2016a, loc 252, 266, 335; italics in original). This means that *ethne* and other designators have relative value in the face of "one new humanity" as the body of Christ.

Belonging means personal and collective obligation, because the Spirit wants to make present the future kingdom of God. What, then, are the implications? As those committed to gospel ministry in Christ, do we see "belonging"—with all its kingdom obligations—to our diverse, global brothers and sisters in Christ, as an asset or liability? Do we see such a connection propelling us forward or slowing us down? More specifically, what is our attitude and action toward fellow Christians/Christ-followers in our local ministry context? Are we befriending, trusting, and collaborating? Or avoiding, neglecting, and bypassing? To resist the latter and embrace the former may not be linear or efficient, but it calls for "faith to walk in a way of being church" (Leithart 2016a, loc 436) that is forming and evolving through redemption and reconciliation. This is where the balance between the Great Commandment, Great Calling, and Great Commission displays the reign of God among his people. The church of Christ is humanity reborn, reconstituted as the body of Christ. Therefore, by what rationale can we justify ignoring, dismissing, or bypassing fellow Christians in our ministry context, or in our ministry strategies?

Contextual Implications

If kingdom witness is best understood as a role rather than a task, one of the key implications is to be wholly present in one's context. How can we think of kingdom witness as transformation unless we are fully engaging in the context, to walk with people in their life experiences? The Incarnation demonstrated that "God's rule and reign have arrived precisely in the person and ministry of Jesus of Nazareth … [fulfilling] the long-standing promise of Yahweh to dwell among his people" (Duvall and Hays 2019, 179). Thus we are reminded that there is always an incarnational component in the ministry of God's people as Christ's reign is lived and proclaimed. People cannot be understood apart from the narrative of their cultural and social context. This vision calls us to an authentic role, living as Christians in a non-Christian world (Tan 2019, loc 6068). It means self-contextualization—an obligation to identify with the context where the gospel is lived and proclaimed.

> All proclamation of the gospel has to have the Incarnate mode of articulation. That means it has to have the commitment and orientation of identifying with the context where the Word of God is to be preached, being responsive to the life issues in a life situation, not for the expediency of generating quick response and wide acceptance of the gospel. (Yu 2019, loc 62640)

Thus, it requires hyper self-awareness of what we bring to a context, whether ourselves and/or our methods.

Likewise, embracing kingdom witness as a role has significant implications for mobilization, funding, and strategy. If each of these domains leads with ticking off people-group boxes in order to "finish the task," then serious reckoning awaits. When speed toward a movement controls the mission narrative, efficiency and expediency inevitably dominate church-planting endeavors and methods (Massey 2012, 105). Consequently, the full intent of the Great Calling, Great Commandment, and Great Commission is lost.

Summary

In this chapter I have asserted that the UPG church-planting movement and the standardly accepted responses to *Where? Who? What? How?* and *Why?* appear to operate on the presumption that the entire endeavor is a complicated task reducible to a set of linear, manageable, and measurable approaches which will see the task finished. These responses reveal a reductionism which has neglected an entire dimension of kingdom witness, the character of the King in the life of his people, the incarnate role of Christ in and through his body, the church. A complete response to *Why?* involves the fullness of all that God's reign intends through the life and witness of his people.

Likewise, a revised response to *Why?* recasts as well the responses to *Where? Who? What?* and *How?*

WHERE: not fixated on political nations, but on real places; the myriads of human communities; the contexts where people live, relate, and have a story.

WHO: not just about UPGs, but the whole of humanity; God's image-bearers, who are alienated from him and each other, striving in sin and human discord.

WHAT: not merely viable churches within every people group, but the living manifestation of the reign of God through one new humanity in Christ.

HOW: not only launching movements to Jesus, but the presence of the people of God in Christ, living and proclaiming the reign of God and his kingdom; the embodiment of the Great Calling, Great Commandment, and Great Commission.

WHY: not just that there would be Jesus movements within every people, but the flourishing of the reign of God through the redeeming and reconciling work of the cross, reclaiming and transforming humanity for shared intimacy and presence with God and his people.

Since God's people belong to each other, in all their diversity—our collective testimony of the transformative reign of God—global witness for Christ is not merely a task to finish, but a role for Christ's body to live and proclaim before the watching world. The church, as the diverse representation of "transformed human society" (Leithart 2016b, 217), manifests all that God intends for humanity to experience this side of the consummation of all things. Through ministry in the world, "they will fulfill God's purpose of filling the earth with his glory through image-bearers who reflect his character and kingship in their exercise of God-like authority and responsibility over the new creation" (Berry 2016, 193).

References Cited

Appadurai, Arjun. 1988. "Putting Hierarchy in Its Place." *Cultural Anthropology* 3 (1): 36-49.

Baker, Ken. 2017. "Beyond People Groups: Why the Term 'Communities' May Be Preferable." *Evangelical Missions Quarterly* 53 (4): 8–13.

Bennett, Michael. 2018. "Finish the Task: When Mottos Hijack the Mission." International Mission Board website, https://www.imb.org/2018/12/27/finish-task/.

Berry, Donald. 2016. *Glory in Romans and the Unified Purpose of God in Redemptive History*. Eugene, OR: Pickwick. Kindle.

Bessenecker, Scott A. 2014. *Overturning Tables: Freeing Missions from the Christian-Industrial Complex*. Downers Grove, IL: InterVarsity.

Brewster, Tom, and Betty Sue Brewster. 1984. "Bonding and the Missionary Task." In *Perspectives on the World Christian Movement*, edited by Ralph Winter and Steven C. Hawthorne, 450–61. Pasadena, CA: William Carey Library.

Coles, Dave. 2020. "24:14 Goal: Movement Engagements in Every Unreached People and Place by 2025 (72 Months)." *Mission Frontiers*. January/February 2020. http://www.missionfrontiers.org/issue/article/2414-goal2.

Corwin, Gary. 2018. Personal communication.

Datema, Dave. 2016. "Defining 'Unreached': A Short History." *International Journal of Frontier Missiology* 33 (2): 45–71.

Deddo, Gary W. 2007. "Neighbors in Racial Reconciliation: The Contribution of a Trinitarian Theological Anthropology." *Cultural Encounters* 3 (2): 27–46.

Duvall, J. Scott, and J. Daniel Hays. 2019. *God's Relational Presence: The Cohesive Center of Biblical Theology*. Grand Rapids: Baker Academic. Kindle.

Garrison, David. 2004. *Church Planting Movements: How God Is Redeeming a Lost World*. Monument, CO: WIGTake Resources. Kindle.

Goheen, Michael W. 2011. *A Light to the Nations: The Missional Church and the Biblical Story*. Grand Rapids: Baker. Kindle.

———. 2014. *Introducing Christian Mission Today: Scripture, History and Issues*. Downers Grove, IL: InterVarsity. Kindle.

Hadaway, Robin Dale. 2014. "A Course Correction in Missions: Rethinking the Two-Percent Threshold." *Southwestern Journal of Theology* 57 (1): 17-28.

Hays, J. Daniel. 2003. *From Every People and Nation: A Biblical Theology of Race*, edited by D. A. Carsm juj7on. NSBT. 14. Downers Grove, IL: InterVarsity.

Joshua Project. n.d. "What is a People Group?" https://joshuaproject.net/resources/articles/what_is_a_people_group.

Keller, Timothy. 2012. *Center Church: Doing Balanced, Gospel-Centered Ministry in Your City*. Grand Rapids: Zondervan. Kindle.

Langmead, Ross. 2008. "Transformed Relationships: Reconciliation as the Central Model for Mission." *Mission Studies* 25: 5–20. https://repository.divinity.edu.au/371/.

Lee, Peter T., and James Sung-Hwan Park. 2018. "Beyond People Group Thinking: A Critical Reevaluation of Unreached People Groups." *Missiology: An International Review* 46 (3): 212–25.

Leithart, Peter J. 2016a. *The End of Protestantism: Pursuing Unity in a Fragmented Church.* Grand Rapids: Brazos Press. Kindle.

———. 2016b. *Delivered from the Elements of the World: Atonement, Justification, Mission.* Downers Grove, IL: InterVarsity. Kindle.

Massey, John D. 2012. "Wrinkling Time in the Missionary Task: A Theological Review of Church Planting Movements Methodology." *Southwestern Journal of Theology* 55 (1): 110–37.

McChrystal, Stanley. 2015. *Team of Teams: New Rules of Engagement for a Complex World.* New York: Penguin Publishing Group. Kindle.

McGavran, Donald A. 1990. *Understanding Church Growth,* 3rd ed., edited by C. Peter Wagner. Grand Rapids: Eerdmans.

Moore, C. J. 2019. "Can We Hasten the Parousia? An Examination of Matt 24:14 and Its Implications for Missional Practice." *Themelios* 44 (2): 291–11.

Munayer, Salim J. 2019. "Reconciliation and the Kingdom of God." In *Asian Christian Theology: Evangelical Perspectives,* edited by Timoteo Gener and Stephen T. Pardue, loc 6607–7021. Cumbria, UK: Langham Global Library. Kindle.

NoPlaceLeft.net. n.d. "Who We Are." https://noplaceleft.net/#toggle-id-3.

Nordstokke, Kjell. 2013. "Diakonia in Context: Transformation, Reconciliation and Empowerment." In *Mission as Ministry of Reconciliation*, edited by Robert Schreiter and Knud Jørgensen. Oxford, UK: Regnum. Kindle.

Pachuau, Lalsangkima. 2019. "Cultural Identity and Theology in Asia." In *Asian Christian Theology: Evangelical Perspectives,* edited by Timoteo Gener and Stephen T. Pardue, loc 4273–724. Cumbria, UK: Langham Global Library. Kindle.

Peñamora, Aldrin M. "God's Basilea in Asia's Res Publica: Situating the Sacred in Asia's Public Sphere." In *Asian Christian Theology: Evangelical Perspectives,* edited by Timoteo Gener and Stephen T. Pardue, loc 5214–5621. Cumbria, UK: Langham Global Library. Kindle.

Rynkiewich, Michael A. 2002. "The World in My Parish: Rethinking the Standard Missiological Model." *Missiology: An International Review* 30 (3): 301–22.

———. 2007. "Corporate Metaphors and Strategic Thinking: "The 10/40 Window" in the American Evangelical Worldview." *Missiology* 35 (2): 217–41.

Schreiter, Robert J. 2005. "Reconciliation and Healing as a Paradigm for Mission," *International Review of Mission* 94 (372): 73–84, https://onlinelibrary.wiley.com/doi/pdf/10.1111/j.1758-6631.2005.tb00487.x.

Schreiter, Robert, and Knud Jørgensen, eds. 2013. *Mission as Ministry of Reconciliation.* Oxford, UK: Regnum. Kindle.

Stroope, Michael W. 2017. *Transcending Mission.* Downers Grove, IL: InterVarsity. Kindle.

Tan, Kang-San. 2019. "Hans Frei's Typology of Theology for Religious Encounters in Asian Contexts." In *Asian Christian Theology: Evangelical Perspectives,* edited by Timoteo Gener and Stephen T. Pardue, loc 5901–6238. Cumbria, UK: Langham Global Library. Kindle.

Terry, George A. 2017. "A Missiology of Excluded Middles: An Analysis of the T4T Scheme for Evangelism and Discipleship." *Themelios* 42 (2): 335–52.

The Cape Town Commitment. 2011. *A Confession of Faith and a Call to Action* http://lausanne.org/content/ctcommitment#capetown.

Volf, Miroslav. 1996. *Exclusion and Embrace: A Theological Exploration of Identity, Otherness and Reconciliation.* Nashville: Abingdon. Kindle.

Wu, Jackson. 2014. "The Influence of Culture on the Evolution of Mission Methods: Using Church Planting Movements as a Case Study." *Global Missiology* 1 (12), http://ojs.globalmissiology.org/index.php/english/article/view/1712/

———. 2019. *Reading Romans with Eastern Eyes.* Downers Grove, IL: InterVarsity. Kindle.

Yu, Carver. T. 2019. "Theology in a Context of Radical Cultural Shift." In *Asian Christian Theology: Evangelical Perspectives,* edited by Timoteo Gener and Stephen T. Pardue, loc 6252–599. Cumbria, UK: Langham Global Library. Kindle.

CHAPTER 7

To the Ends of the Earth through Strategic Urban Centers:

Reexamining the Missions Mandate in Light of the New Testament's Use of the Old Testament

MICHAEL D. CRANE

When I was young, my family moved from Taiwan to a country with a large Muslim population. My parents were told to focus on the Chinese in that country and *not* to try to reach the Muslims. During that paradigm of missions, the goal was to establish the church in every geopolitical nation-state. The hope was that the church in that country would then reach the rest of the country. That approach represented a geopolitical missiology.

In the 1990s, the organization my parents served with shifted paradigms to a focus on unreached people groups. In the nation I grew up in, this meant that missionaries dropped engagement with the existing churches, which were primarily Chinese, and began to engage a Muslim unreached people group (UPG). The goal, then, was to establish the church among every ethnolinguistic people group. Each people group would have an "indigenous" church. During this time, missionaries went from a geopolitical missiology to a people-group missiology. It was built on the assumption that people remain very ethnically siloed. When I moved overseas as an adult, I discovered a complicated landscape of ethnic and cultural identity, particularly in urban contexts.

In this chapter, I will examine people-group missiology both from a practical and a biblical perspective. The goal, however, is not merely to deconstruct past perspectives, but to suggest another way of understanding the church's biblical task—that of a geographical framework starting in strategic urban centers.

People-Group Thinking:
The Good, the Bad, and the Biblical Concerns

In 1974, evangelicals began to rethink the missionary task by questioning and redefining "nations" (*ethne*). More complete accounts of this shift are found elsewhere (Gill 2016; McGavran 2005; Payne and Terry 2013). In the following decades, missions agencies shifted their approach from a country focus (nation-state) to a focus on ethnolinguistic people groups (Baggett and Arnett 2016; Datema 2016). Agencies listed "every" UPG on missions websites, with a goal of "finishing the task" by 2000 ("AD2000 Joshua Project Overview" n.d.; Jenkins n.d.; Winter and Koch 2009). "People group thinking" (Robb 1989) became the battle cry of the emerging generation of missionaries (e.g., Frontiers, Pioneers, and Ethnos360). As Elliot Clark and Darren Carlson (2019) note, "The subsequent strategic primacy of reaching every ethnolinguistic people group now shapes evangelicalism's global missionary enterprise." The missions community came up with lists of these people groups and decided how to define which ones were "reached" and which ones were "unreached" ... then added "unengaged" ... and then added "undiscovered."

While the sketch above is an oversimplification, ethnically defined "people groups" became the grid (framework) through which many evangelicals understood the task. While this approach has some good aspects, it also raises some biblical concerns.

The Good

Some important and necessary adjustments came with this paradigm shift. Ralph Winter and others were right to point out the deficiencies in the way missions had been done. The previous paradigm had established churches and denominational structures in countries where huge swaths of people had no meaningful opportunity to hear the gospel. The people-group paradigm also helped missionaries see more clearly parts of the world devoid of gospel witness, which then allowed for a reallocation of resources to reach these areas. Central to the understanding of people groups is to think of populations where the gospel will flow freely. These were good developments.

The Bad

But things went too far with people-group missiology. Evangelical missiology was being driven more by people-group lists than by biblical concepts. Ethnic categories based on outdated anthropological models became more important than human beings in need of a Savior (Howell and Paris 2011, 77–78; Lee and Park 2018). In some circles, people-group missiology even took on eschatological undertones (Piper and Mathis 2012; Smith and Kai 2011; Trousdale and Sergeant 2019), believing that mission agencies could get all the people groups checked off as if they were items on a grocery list. At the very least, this was an ill-suited paradigm for cities and other heterogeneous communities. Cities are far too mixed and blended. There was a time when people thought of cities like a waffle, with neat and tidy ethnic enclaves (Holste 2012, 327). Troy Bush argues that the more appropriate image is an omelet, where there are some distinctive groupings but the proximity brings flavors together (2010, 320).

Again, much good came from people-group thinking. Our first assignment on the field was to an unreached people group that would have been ignored under the previous paradigm. It was and is right to engage unreached people groups. I am suggesting, however, that limiting the church's global missions mandate to a list of people groups is *not* the biblical mandate. Ultimately, the church needs to look to the Scriptures for guidance on this.

The Biblical Concerns

Contemporary evangelical missions literature nearly always assumes that *nations* is synonymous with *people groups* (Pratt, Sills, and Walters 2014, 19). The missions community has assumed that people groups are static ethnic sets. Missiologists have interpreted the concept of people groups this way until recently. A growing number of scholars, particularly biblical scholars, understand "nations" to represent the great mass of humankind which is in rebellion against God (Goldsworthy 1996, 6; Köstenberger and O'Brien 2001, 50). It might surprise many that even Israel was not homogeneous, but rather was an "ethnically diverse crowd" (cf. Ex 12:38, 48; Num 11:4; Neh 13:3) (Mathews and Park 2011, 98). Although space does not permit an exhaustive exegetical overview of "nations" in the Bible, I will simply direct readers' attention to a few key passages.

Genesis 12:3. Abram's call to go to a new land involved a promise of blessing to every *mishpahoth* on earth. The precise meaning of the Hebrew word *mishpahoth* has been debated: Does it refer to "families," "peoples," or "nations"? Again, missiologists and biblical scholars seem to be at odds here (Robb 1989, 13–14). Recent scholarship indicates the term is familial, referring to families or kinship groups (Brown, Driver, and Briggs 1977, 1046; Harris, Archer, and Waltke 1999, 947; Koehler and Baumgartner 2001; Wright 2006, 216). The Septuagint confirms a translation that involves a shared bloodline (Gr. *ai phylai*; cf. Matt 24:30; Rev 1:7) (Walter 2000, 1069). As a number of related Hebrew and Greek words have been translated with imprecise English words,

Quite simply, a missiology that does not include everyone everywhere, because some do not fit in the people-group boxes, is inadequate.

missiologists have tended to combine everything under "nations," attaching to it the notion of ethnolinguistic people groups. Missiologists have not gone far enough to consider how "tribes," "clans," and "nations" differ from one another (Crouch 2014; Crüsemann 1997; Mbuvi 2016). If missionaries build their missions paradigm on this passage in Genesis 12, they must exegete it with hermeneutical integrity.

Matthew 28:19 (and 24:14). In recent decades, the Great Commission has been the go-to passage for a missions mandate. The phrase "to all the nations" (*panta ta ethne*) has been the center of much of this discussion about the focus of the missionary task. John Piper's exegesis of this passage has been highly influential in evangelical missions (Bierig 2018). Famously, Piper argued that *ethne* refers to all the people groups of the world (1996, 22). I was among those influenced deeply by *Let the Nations Be Glad,* including Piper's argument on *ethne* as people groups, until I began to see the world in tones and hues rather than in a simple set of crayon colors.

When I served in Indonesia, I would go to the city of Medan and meet people in the city who were grouping themselves based on aspects of their identity other than ethnic origin (class, neighborhood, religious affiliation, subculture). Meanwhile, missionaries with a "people-group missiology" would go out of the city to find UPGs in a homogeneous setting, because urban dwellers were less ethnically defined.

This motivated me to look back at the biblical evidence. While it is true that missionaries cannot conceive of *ethne* as geopolitical nation-states, neither can they reduce the word to people groups (Williams and Moss 2019, 131–32). A growing number of scholars are addressing this (mis)interpretation (Williams and Moss 2019; Baggett and Arnett 2016; Lee and Park 2018; Bush 2013; Clark and Carlson 2019; Bennett 2018; Brawner 2014). It is noteworthy that biblical scholars, even those close to Piper, never reduced *ethne* to "people groups" (Carson, Wessel, and Strauss 2010, 9:597). Scholarly consensus is that the phrase intends to refer to "everyone everywhere" (Baggett and Arnett 2016, 71; Köstenberger and O'Brien 2001, 50; Nolland 2005, 1266).

Revelation 5:9 and 7:9. The case becomes even more clear when Christians consider passages that use several connected terms. For example, Revelation 5:9 (and 7:9) proclaims that God ransomed people from every tribe (*phyle*), language (*glossa*), people (*laos*), and nation (*ethnos*).[1] An echo can be found in the references

---

1 Bush describes *ethnos* as the "weakest" of these terms, meaning that it is the broadest category (2013, 8).

in Genesis 10 to lands, languages, clans, and nations (Gen 10:5, 20, 31) (Osborne 2002a, 261) and in Daniel using a threefold formula of "all peoples, nations, and languages" (Dan 3:4, 7; 4:1; 5:19; 6:25; 7:14) (Beale 1998, 360).

These different terms do not give the impression of ethnic specificity, but rather of all-encompassing mission. The way the people of God are described in the book of Revelation indicates diverse representation constituting a *tertium genus* ("a third race") (Aune 1997, 362; McNicol 2011, 18–19; Osborne 2002b, 260–61). In other words, globally diverse representation, rather than ethnic homogeneity, is highlighted. This important distinction should not be missed. It does not negate the value of identifying unreached population segments, including unreached people groups. But it does call into question a missiology built solely around the notion that *ethne* only refers to ethnolinguistic people groups. In a simplistic translation equivalence, *ethne* became "ethnic" (Jenkins 2006). Quite simply, a missiology that does not include everyone everywhere, because some do not fit in the people-group boxes, is inadequate.

To the Ends of the Earth through Urban Centers

I have presented a brief argument for the fact that the biblical mandate is to reach "everyone everywhere." However, missionaries cannot reach "everyone everywhere" all at once. Missionaries need to think through starting points and strategies. What does the Bible say about this?

Thinking Geographically: Beginning in Strategic Centers

The Bible does not give a concrete command regarding mission starting points and strategies. (If Acts 1:8 is an exception, it reinforces my point below.) However, when the Bible speaks of the nations, it often does so in geographical terms. Some key passages can help us recover the geographic language used in the Bible. Each of these passages has an emphasis on geographic universality, with the city of Jerusalem as the point of orientation (cf. Ezek 5:5; 38:12). The nations are drawn to the city and sent from the city as heralds of the gospel (Scott 1995, 11).

Genesis 10 (Table of Nations). The seventy nations listed in the "Table of Nations" found in Genesis 10 represent a worldwide geographic horizon, which has implications for God's people (Dempster 2003, 74; Filbeck 1994, 55; Von Rad 1961, 139). Surprisingly, this passage receives sparing attention from missiologists, yet it functions significantly throughout the biblical narrative. The list shows a wide-ranging geographical distribution based on "three geographical arcs reflected in the table, with the intersection of the three arcs appearing at the land of Canaan" (Mathews and Park 2011, 74–75). Richard Bauckham (2004) notes that this begins a pattern of "representative geography" that intends to capture a universal scope (59–60). James Scott (1995) records

The city attracts the nations to hear the gospel and disperses them to bear witness to the ends of the earth.

in great detail the many echoes of the Table of Nations found in the Bible (cf. 1 Chr 1; Ezek 38–39; Isa 66; Acts 2) (5–6, 9, 54). Hays (2003) observes this pattern in the fourfold formula in Revelation (195).

Isaiah 60 and 66. The final chapters of Isaiah demonstrate a geographical orientation of the nations. In Isaiah 60, a long poem describes the nations arriving in the New Jerusalem from Midian, Ephah, Sheba, Kedar, Nebaioth, and Tarshish. Alec Motyer (1998) explains these "names assembled impressionistically to create the sense of a world-wide surge to Zion" (495). What is implicit in Isaiah 60 becomes explicit in Psalm 107, where people are gathered from all four points on the compass (v. 2). Isaiah 66:18–24 demonstrates a vision with the ends of the earth in mind. A reference to "all nations and tongues" (v. 18) echoes the Table of Nations (cf. Gen 10:5, 20, 31). God sends survivors (the remnant) as apostles (sent ones) with a message of his salvation to the edges of the known world, as Christians see in the New Testament (Köstenberger and O'Brien 2001, 52; Oswalt 1998, 689). The notion of missions *to* the nations in every direction is clear here (Motyer 1998, 541). Although some scholars debate the precise locations of the places mentioned in Isaiah, they seem to represent the farthest reaches in each direction from Jerusalem (Watts 1987, 365).

Acts 2:9-11. In Acts 2, the reader again sees geography, rather than ethnic groups, emphasized. The passage highlights places represented by the people who had come to Jerusalem for Pentecost, giving the reader the impression of geographic expanse (G. L. Stevens 2019, 169). Theories abound regarding the origin or source of the list of nations in Acts 2 (Barrett 2004, 120–24; Gilbert 2002; Taylor 1999). Even so, a few important observations can be made here. First, the passage highlights geographic expanse, forming a circle around Jerusalem (Lenski 1961, 66). Second, Luke switches between names of places and the people from that place. If, as most presume, those in Jerusalem for a religious festival were Jews, then ethnicity seems to take a back seat to places and languages. Third, the account portrays people from afar coming to Jerusalem and becoming a new people (see Eph 2:15).

The city attracts the nations to hear the gospel and disperses them to bear witness to the ends of the earth. The mission mandate stated in Acts 1:8, echoing Isaiah 49:6, compels us "to the ends of the earth." Thinking geographically enables us to focus on the world comprehensively. Nobody is left out.

Paul's Mission: Geographic Representativeness Starting in Cities

All of the disciples of Jesus were commissioned to give witness to the ends of the earth. Of the disciples of Jesus in the New Testament, readers have the most information about Paul. The apostles sought to accomplish the mission of the church in a way that matches the missions mandate (Merkle and Guyer, 2014, 63). If missionaries accept this assertion, then Paul's missionary work can further elucidate the call to make disciples of all nations. Of note here are the geographical orientation of Paul's movement and the concentration of his work in cities.

The Geographical Orientation of Paul's Movement

Paul thought geographically, using Roman provinces as his grid. Richard Bauckham (2004) calls this "representative geography" (59–60). Paul's missions effort moved geographically through Roman provinces to the northeast, planting churches in strategic locations.

The clearest statement of Paul's self-understanding regarding his geographical movement is found in Romans 15:19. Some have suggested that Paul thought of his mission with Isaiah's geography in mind. Romans 15 gives an indication of Paul's mission in response to the geographical scope in Isaiah 66:19 (Hengel and Schwemer 1997, 86, 98; Rabens 2017, 106; Riesner 1998, 245–53; Scott 1995, 141). Scott (1995) asserts that Paul's mission strategy is best understood in terms of territory or geography informed by Genesis 10: "When Paul's mission is viewed in light of a territorial strategy based on the Table of Nations, many aspects of his relationship to the Jerusalem apostles and his opponents begin to fall into place" (150). Scott might be overstating his case, but Christians can see how reliant Paul is on the Old Testament, especially Isaiah. Although conclusive evidence of Paul's reliance on Genesis 10 or Isaiah 66 cannot be found, it is an entirely plausible theory, and the influence of the Old Testament on Paul's missiology is evident. Here we return to Bauckham's notion of "geographical representativeness," which then leads us to examine the New Testament (2004, 65).

The Concentration of Paul's Work in Cities

Early Christianity took hold in cities (Bosch 1991, 130; Kaiser 1989, 16; Allen 1962, 13; Meeks 1982, 118; Rabens 2017; Stark 2006; 1997). Many have noted that Paul's missions efforts were concentrated in cities. The question before us is whether Paul's focus on cities was an intentional strategy or simply his response to where the Spirit led him. Some argue that Paul did *not* have an intentional urban strategy, even though he did focus much of his ministry on cities. Roland Allen and Eckhard Schnabel are key proponents of this view. Allen (1962) concedes that Paul planted churches in the "centres of Roman administration, of Greek civilization, of Jewish influence, or of some commercial importance" (13). Nevertheless, he argues that it is impossible to say that Paul was intentional with his strategy (10). Herbert Kane (1976) brings clarity to this discussion by observing that people mean different things by "strategy." If missionaries understand Paul's strategy as a thought-through plan that remained flexible and sensitive to the leading of the Holy Spirit, "then Paul did have a strategy" (73).

Schnabel (2004), like Allen, agrees that Paul did much of his ministry in cities and that he had a geographically oriented strategy (1299). Schnabel (2007) further states that Paul was more focused on cities than the provinces of the empire (258). But he describes the urban nature of his strategy as almost incidental. He is skeptical that Paul thought to establish the church in these urban centers so that the gospel would radiate from these cities. Schnabel lists four reasons for his skepticism:

1. Hellenistic cities governed their own affairs, thus making it unlikely that the gospel would travel from one city to the next, despite proximity.
2. Cities were in competition with each other.
3. Personal identity was wrapped up in the city one was from, making cities insular.
4. Urban dwellers in the Roman Empire were obsessed with hierarchy and ambition. Schnabel suggests that because this was at odds with the Christian gospel, the message would not spread.

Schnabel (2007) concludes, "Planting churches in cities certainly had strategic value, but it was no guarantee that the gospel would spread from the cities into the countryside" (258–59). One of Schnabel's arguments against the idea that Paul had an urban strategy is that Paul did not prioritize cities the way Schnabel thinks he should have. At different points, Schnabel comments that if Paul truly had an urban strategy, he would have gone to a particular city or would not have gone to this or that place off the main highways (241, 247). Can a case be made for an intentional Pauline urban strategy?

The city was Paul's natural habitat. Wayne Meeks (1982) establishes Paul was thoroughly urban to the degree that "the city breathes through his language" (9). Paul, as an urban dweller, used rhetoric and verbal images and metaphors from the urban context (Rabens 2017, 113; Doohan 1989, 36). Paul knew how to communicate with urban dwellers and how to communities that thrived in busy, diverse cities. Paul knew how to establish churches with clear boundaries without disconnecting from the broader urban society (Campbell 2018, 118; Meeks 1982, 190).

Much of Paul's ministry was in cities, with the expectation that the gospel was spreading further. Bible readers are not privy, in most cases, to the reasons for Paul's missionary movements (Evans 2016, 145). Christians can, however, make observations about common features of the places he went. Paul went to large and influential cities. He visited eight of the more Hellenized cities (Rabens 2017, 100). It can also be noted that Paul went to a number of cities with Roman administration, like Philippi (Kaiser 1989, 15). The cities Paul went to were often major points of trade, located at crossroads or important ports (Rabens 2017, 100). He also went to diverse cities "with substantial Jewish diaspora communities" (Rabens 2017, 101, 122; Kaiser 1989, 15). This pattern of going to major cities does not prove intent, but it does show a pattern that is distinctly urban.

Paul planned to take the gospel to key cities. In contrast to Allen and Schnabel, other missiologists and biblical scholars do claim Paul was intent on an urban strategy (Peskett and Ramachandra 2003, 225). Bosch (1991) puts it simply: "Paul thinks regionally, not ethnically; he chooses cities that have a representative character" (130). The weight of opinion from scholars is that Paul had an intentional strategy that included going to key cities (Rabens 2017, 101; Gibbs 2013, 69). There is clear evidence of planning in Paul's letters (e.g., 1 Thess 2:18; 1 Cor 16:5–6).

God used Paul to establish and strengthen churches in cities from Jerusalem to Illyricum (Rom 15:19). Paul claims that he has fulfilled his gospel ministry in this geographical expanse. Although we don't know for certain what Paul had in mind in Romans 15:19, scholars make the case that he sought to establish a gospel presence in key cities with the expectation that the gospel would radiate out to the surrounding areas (Cranfield 1998, 762–66; Dunn 1988, 881; Scott 1995, 144–45). These churches became the anchor for missions to the rest of the empire (cf. Ephesus in Acts 19:9–10) (Witherington 1997, 226). Rabens (2017) summarizes: "Paul's mission strategy among the cities demonstrates a close interconnection between basic missiological principles and the praxis based upon them" (121).

Paul then established healthy churches in key urban centers in these provinces. Some scholars have pushed against this understanding of missions in the New Testament, but their arguments have failed to make their case.[2] Even if Paul didn't tackle an urban strategy the way some missiologists think he should have, going to urban centers first was his *modus operandi*.

Observations about Paul's Missiology

If Paul is compelled by the same mandate that compels the church today, then his missiology demands close examination. Sometimes missionaries take their marching orders from the Great Commission and look to Paul for his methods without examining his missiology.

---

2 Although Robinson argues against urban priority, he still defaults to say that rural populations "orbit the polis," thus emphasizing the outsized importance of urban centers. Schnabel does generally lean toward a geographic orientation for Paul, but he resists the notion that Paul had an urban strategy. These concerns are addressed in my (2019) paper "Urbanization and the Great Commission."

The Old Testament informed Paul's missiology. Paul was deeply entrenched in the Scriptures (the Old Testament). His writings are drenched with direct quotations, echoes, and symbolism drawn from the Old Testament. Even his biographical statements echo the Old Testament (cf. Gal 1:15; Rom 1:1) (Dickson 2003, 313). It stands to reason, then, that "Paul was rooting the Christian mission fully in Old Testament traditions, for 'while Israel is the people of God, the people of God is broader than Israel' (Fretheim 1977, 26)" (Okoye 2006, 158). For Paul, Jesus was indisputably the Messiah described in the Jewish Scriptures. Paul's reading of them provided a geographical framework to herald the gospel in places remaining without a church.

Paul's missiology was not a people-group missiology. Missionaries have viewed Paul as a model missionary (Allen 1962; Schnabel 2008; Plummer 2006; Brooks 2019; Campbell 2018). If the missionary task is to prioritize ethnolinguistic people groups, does Paul demonstrate a people-group strategy? Paul doesn't seem concerned with establishing the church in each ethnolinguistic people group, even though he and his team were intent on crossing cultural barriers (cf. Acts 14:8–23). Rather, Paul was concerned with planting churches in cities that were composed of all people in the city. Given the cultural chasm between Jews and Gentiles, it would have been logical and easier to plant homogeneous churches. However, everything in Paul's writings indicates that he established multicultural churches, because the breakdown of ethnic divisions was a demonstration of Christ's work (cf. Eph 2) (Campbell 2018, 32–35; D. E. Stevens 2012).

Given the present centrality of people-group thinking in missiology and missions practice, it is important to point out that the goal of reaching ethnolinguistic people groups was not the modus operandi of New Testament missions. The believers' vision seems broader—to make the gospel known to all people—and their way to do this seems more *geographically oriented* (cf. Romans 15) (Riesner 1998, 243). Regardless of ethnic background, new converts were incorporated into the one body of Christ (Hays 2011, 83–87). Thinking about the mission geographically does not mean missionaries default back to a simplistic geopolitical missiology. In a geographic area, a missionary must consider how to reach the many different population segments. But missionaries must do so with a framework that is concerned for everyone everywhere, as opposed to an ethnically fixated framework (LaGrand 1995, 44; Lee and Park 2018, 7). The goal is to faithfully give witness to Christ (Acts 1:8) and "present everyone mature in Christ" (Col 1:28). Again, the goal is everyone, but the path requires some fluidity.

Cities: The Heart of Missions to the Ends of the Earth

With more than half of the world's population living in cities, the church is presented with an opportunity to reexamine missions strategy. The Bible offers the church some handles on considering missions strategy with cities playing a central role.

The Pulse of Missions

How, then, does the church reach the billions who remain lost and are often cut off from hearing the gospel? I propose missionaries follow a biblical model of starting in the cities, and from the cities sending out missionaries. Just as the heart is the center of blood circulation, cities are the centers of human circulation. Recent research on cities has moved from the study of buildings and districts (static) to the movement of people in, through, and around cities (flow).

If the calling to bear witness is truly to everyone everywhere, then cities are an excellent place to start. In the Old Testament, God's people were called to be a light to the nations. Jerusalem was to be the one place where ethnicity, wealth, and status were unimportant and the heart's devotion to God was what mattered (Fujino and Cheong 2012, 36). Jerusalem defaulted to the ways of the world; oppression and injustice were the norm. The prophets began to speak of a new city—one that welcomed the nations, and where all joined in worship. There is a pulsing action in the city. The nations are drawn to the city (Isa 2:2–3; 60:1–9; 66:18) and sent back out again with a message of salvation (Isa 2:3; 66:19). The language of "all nations and tongues" is similar to the language of Daniel ("peoples, nations, and languages"; 3:4, 7, 29; 4:1; 5:19; 6:25; 7:14). These passages evoke the language of Genesis 10–11 (clans, languages, lands, and nations; vv. 5, 20, 31), listing nations in every direction of the compass.

Jesus entered the world as the true light of the nations. In Acts 2, representatives of the nations came to the city of Jerusalem. From Jerusalem, missionary witness went out in every direction. Paul only has one small part in this mission, which was to go in a northeastern direction with the goal of getting as far as Spain (Rom 15:24). He went about this by concentrating on important cities in the provinces he visited. Christians catch a glimpse of the way this strategy works in the important trade city of Ephesus, where Paul taught in the city and "all the residents of Asia heard the word of the Lord, both Jews and Greeks" (Acts 19:10 ESV). The church took root in the cities of the Mediterranean basin and gradually reached an empire that had been hostile to the gospel for 250 years.

Layered Identity in an Urbanizing World

Urban people often live with layered identities (Jansen 2017, 149). In Kuala Lumpur, Malaysia, a Malay man might only speak Malay or he might not speak any Malay. He might be very devoted to his faith or he might be more devoted to working out or to the arts. He might live in a predominantly Malay neighborhood or he might live in a high-rise apartment with many different kinds of people. *A rigid people-group approach expects people to be one thing.* Such rigidity can lead to stereotyping and to unhealthy churches (Cheong 2018, 27).

City people have layered identities, and that can increase with each generation. In the past, missionaries placed a lot of emphasis on the indigenous church and ethnic-based contextualization. Now a missionary needs to ask what "indigenous" means in a city and what urban-based contextualization might look like ("Indigenous" 2021; Ponraj 2002, 152). If missionaries are serious about reaching the world with the gospel, then they must operate with a missiological framework that includes the world.

Conclusion

The Great Commission calls the church to make disciples of "all nations." Biblical study has revealed that this mandate is best understood to mean everyone everywhere. People-group thinking helped the church see large segments of the world that were closed off from the gospel. But as a missiological framework, people-group missiology fails to engage everyone everywhere. And in cities, people-group missiology has not served the church well. In a world that is aggressively urbanizing, the missions community must reevaluate its missiological framework.

Although missions is always about people, Scripture recognizes that all people are placed geographically. A missiology that includes geography ensures that missionaries consider all to be included in this mission. The Bible shows a pattern of God drawing the nations to urban centers and then dispersing this witness to distant places. An emphasis on urban centers does not preclude missions to rural places. A geographical framework can aid in determining the priorities of missions. But the intersection of rural and urban should not be overlooked. Cities offer us a staging ground to get to all nations. Roger Greenway (1978) affirmed the importance of cities, writing, "As the cities go, so go the nations. If winning the nations to Christ is our assignment, to the cities we must go" (27).

References Cited

AD2000. Joshua Project Overview. n.d. http://www.ad2000.org/joshovr.htm.

Allen, Roland. 1962. *Missionary Methods: St. Paul's or Ours?* Grand Rapids: Eerdmans.

Aune, David. 1997. *Revelation 1–5, Volume 52A*. Dallas: Word Publishing.

Baggett, Kevin, and Randy Arnett. 2016. "Redefining Global Lostness." *The Southern Baptist Journal of Missions and Evangelism* 2: 65–88.

Barrett, C. K. 2004. *Acts: Volume 1:1–14*. London: T&T Clark International.

Bauckham, Richard. 2004. *Bible and Mission: Christian Witness in a Postmodern World.* Grand Rapids: Baker Academic.

Beale, G. K. 1998. *The Book of Revelation: A Commentary on the Greek Text*. New International Greek Testament Commentary. Grand Rapids: Eerdmans.

Bennett, Matthew. 2018. "Finishing the Task? A Cautionary Analysis of Missionary Language." *Southeastern Theological Review* 9 (2): 33–53.

Bierig, Samuel. 2018. "The Book That Mobilized a Generation of Missionaries Turns 25." International Mission Board (blog), https://www.imb.org/2018/12/31/book-mobilized-generation-missionaries/.

Bosch, David. 1991. *Transforming Mission: Paradigm Shifts in Theology of Mission.* Maryknoll, NY: Orbis Books.

Brawner, Jeff. 2014. "Proper Missiology Requires Sound Biblical Interpretation Or … Proof Texting—The Best Path to Bad Missiology." *The Journal: Mid-America Baptist Theological Seminary* 1 (Spring).

Brooks, Will. 2019. "Paul as Model for the Practice of World Mission." In *World Mission: Theology, Strategy, and Current Issues*, edited by Scott M. Callaham and Will Brooks, 291–317. Bellingham, WA: Lexham Press.

Brown, Francis, S. R. Driver, and Charles A. Briggs. 1977. *Enhanced Brown-Driver-Briggs Hebrew English Lexicon.* Oxford, UK: Clarendon Press.

Bush, Troy L. 2010. "The Great Commission and the Urban Context." In *Great Commission Resurgence: Fulfilling God's Mandate in Our Time*, edited by Chuck Lawless and Adam W. Greenway, 299–324. Nashville: B & H Academic.

———. 2013. "Urbanizing Panta Ta Ethnē." *Journal of Evangelism and Missions* 12: 3–16.

Campbell, Douglas A. 2018. *Paul: An Apostle's Journey.* Grand Rapids: Eerdmans.

Carson, D. A., Walter W. Wessel, and Mark L. Strauss. 2010. *Matthew and Mark.* Rev. ed. Vol. 9. The Expositor's Bible Commentary. Grand Rapids: Zondervan.

Cheong, John. 2018. "Polycentrism in Majority World Theologizing: An Engagement with Power and Essentialism." In *Majority World Theologies: Theologizing from Africa, Asia, Latin America, and the Ends of the Earth*, edited by Allen Yeh and Tite Tienou, 24–42. Evangelical Missiological Society Series 26. Pasadena, CA: William Carey Publishing.

Clark, Elliot, and Darren Carlson. 2019. "The 3 Words That Changed Missions Strategy—and Why We Might Be Wrong." The Gospel Coalition (blog), https://www.thegospelcoalition.org/article/misleading-words-missions-strategy-unreached-people-groups/.

Crane, Michael D. 2019. "Urbanization and the Great Commission: Hitting the Refresh Button on Missiology." Paper presented at the Urban Mission and Transformation Consultation, March 21, in Kuala Lumpur, Malaysia.

Cranfield, Charles E. B. 1998. *A Critical and Exegetical Commentary on the Epistle to the Romans: Introduction and Commentary on Romans IX-XVI, Vol. 2.* 5th ed. Edinburgh, UK: T&T Clark International.

Crouch, Carly L. 2014. *The Making of Israel: Cultural Diversity in the Southern Levant and the Formation of Ethnic Identity in Deuteronomy.* Supplements to Vetus Testamentum 162. Leiden, Netherlands: Brill.

Crüsemann, Frank. 1997. "Human Solidarity and Ethnic Identity: Israel's Self-Definition in the Genealogical System of Genesis." In *Ethnicity and the Bible*, edited by Mark G. Brett, translated by Rainer Schack and Mark G. Brett. Biblical Interpretation 19. Leiden, Netherlands: Brill.

Datema, Dave. 2016. "Defining 'Unreached': A Short History." *International Journal of Frontier Missiology* 33 (2): 45–71.

Dempster, Stephen G. 2003. *Dominion and Dynasty: A Theology of the Hebrew Bible*. Leicester, England; Downers Grove, IL: IVP Academic.

Dickson, John. 2003. *Mission-Commitment in Ancient Judaism and in the Pauline Communities: The Shape, Extent and Background of Early Christian Mission*. Tübingen, Germany: Mohr Siebeck.

Doohan, Helen. 1989. *Paul's Vision of Church*. Wilmington, DE: Michael Glazier.

Dunn, James D. G. 1988. *Word Biblical Commentary, Vol. 38B, Romans 9–16*. Nashville: Thomas Nelson.

Evans, David. 2016. "The City in Acts: The Relevance of Paul's Urban Mission for Luke's Purpose." *Reformed Theological Review* 75 (3): 145–69.

Filbeck, David. 1994. *Yes, God of the Gentiles, Too: The Missionary Message of the Old Testament*. Wheaton, IL: Billy Graham Center.

Fujino, Gary, and John Cheong. 2012. "Emerging Global Mega-Regions and Globalization: Missiological Implications." In *Reaching the City: Reflections on Urban Mission for the Twenty-First Century*, edited by Gary Fujino, Timothy R. Sisk, and Tereso C. Casino, 35–57. Pasadena, CA: William Carey Library.

Gibbs, Eddie. 2013. *Rebirth of the Church: Applying Paul's Vision for Ministry in Our Post-Christian World*. Grand Rapids: Baker.

Gilbert, Gary. 2002. "The List of Nations in Acts 2: Roman Propaganda and the Lukan Response." *Journal of Biblical Literature* 121 (3): 497–529.

Gill, Brad. 2016. "Editorial Reflections: The Unfortunate Unmarketability of 'Unincorporable.'" *International Journal of Frontier Missiology* 33 (2): 72–76.

Goldsworthy, Graeme L. 1996. "The Great Indicative: An Aspect of a Biblical Theology of Mission." *Reformed Theological Review* 55: 2–13.

Greenway, Roger. 1978. *Apostles to the City: Biblical Strategies for Urban Missions*. Grand Rapids: Baker.

Harris, R. Laird, Gleason L. Archer Jr., and Bruce K. Waltke. 1999. *Theological Wordbook of the Old Testament*, electronic ed. Chicago: Moody.

Hays, J. Daniel. 2003. *From Every People and Nation: A Biblical Theology of Race*. New Studies in Biblical Theology, Leicester, UK; Downers Grove, IL: IVP Academic.

———. 2011. "Paul and the Multi-Ethnic First-Century World: Ethnicity and Christian Identity." In *Paul as Missionary: Identity, Activity, Theology, and Practice*, edited by Trevor J. Burke and Brian S. Rosner, 76–87. Library of New Testament Studies 420. London: T&T Clark International.

Hengel, Martin, and Anna Maria Schwemer. 1997. *Paul Between Damascus and Antioch: The Unknown Years*. Louisville, KY: Westminster John Knox Press.

Holste, J. Scott. 2012. "Finishing the Task." In *Discovering the Mission of God: Best Missional Practices for the 21st Century*, edited by Mike Barnett, 323–39. Downers Grove, IL: IVP Academic.

Howell, Brian M., and Jenell Williams Paris. 2011. *Introducing Cultural Anthropology: A Christian Perspective*. Grand Rapids: Baker Academic.

"Indigenous." 2021. In *Cambridge English Dictionary*, Cambridge, UK: Cambridge University Press, https://dictionary.cambridge.org/us/dictionary/english/indigenous.

Jansen, Mechteld. 2017. "Christian Migrants and the Theology of Space and Place." In *Contested Spaces, Common Ground: Space and Power Structures in Contemporary Multireligious Societies*, edited by Ulrich Winkler, Lidia Rodriguez Fernandez, and Oddbjorn Leirvik, 147–61. Leiden, Netherlands: Brill/Rodopi.

Jenkins, Orville Boyd. 2006. "'Nation' and 'People' in Hebrew and Greek." Strategy Leader Resource Kit, http://strategyleader.org/peopledefinitions/nationpeopleshebgreek.html.

———. n.d. "What Is a People Group?" IMB Global Research, https://peoplegroups.org/.

Kaiser, Walter. 1989. "A Biblical Theology of the City." *Urban Mission* 7 (1): 6–17.

Kane, J. Herbert. 1976. *Christian Missions in Biblical Perspective*. Grand Rapids: Baker.

Koehler, Ludwig, and Walter Baumgartner. 2001. *The Hebrew and Aramaic Lexicon of the Old Testament*, rev. electronic ed., translated by M. E. J. Richardson. Leiden, Netherlands: Brill Academic Publishers.

Köstenberger, Andreas, and Peter T. O'Brien. 2001. *Salvation to the Ends of the Earth: A Biblical Theology of Mission*. Downers Grove, IL: InterVarsity.

LaGrand, James. 1995. *The Earliest Christian Mission to "All Nations" in the Light of Matthew's Gospel*. Grand Rapids: Eerdmans.

Lee, Peter T., and James Sung-Hwan Park. 2018. "Beyond People Group Thinking: A Critical Reevaluation of Unreached People Groups." *Missiology: An International Review* 46 (3): 212–25.

Lenski, Richard C. H. 1961. *Interpretation of the Acts of the Apostles 1–14*. Minneapolis: Augsburg Fortress Publishers.

Mathews, Kenneth, and M. Sydney Park. 2011. *The Post-Racial Church: A Biblical Framework for Multiethnic Reconciliation*. Grand Rapids: Kregel.

Mbuvi, Amanda Beckenstein. 2016. *Belonging in Genesis: Biblical Israel and the Politics of Identity Formation*. Waco, TX: Baylor University Press.

McGavran, Donald. 2005. *Bridges of God: A Study in the Strategy of Missions*. Eugene, OR: Wipf & Stock Publishers.

McNicol, Allan J. 2011. *The Conversion of the Nations in Revelation*. Library of New Testament Studies 438. London: T&T Clark.

Meeks, Wayne A. 1982. *The First Urban Christians: The Social World of the Apostle Paul*. New Haven, CT: Yale University Press.

Merkle, Benjamin, and Michael Guyer. 2014. "The Great Commission According to Paul." *The Journal: Mid-America Baptist Theological Seminary* 1: 51–66.

Motyer, J. Alec. 1998. *The Prophecy of Isaiah: An Introduction and Commentary*. Downers Grove, IL: IVP Academic.

Nolland, John. 2005. *The Gospel of Matthew: A Commentary on the Greek Text*, New International Greek Testament Commentary. Grand Rapids: Eerdmans.

Okoye, James Chukwuma. 2006. *Israel and the Nations: A Mission Theology of the Old Testament*. Maryknoll, NY: Orbis.

Osborne, Grant R. 2002a. *Revelation*. Baker Exegetical Commentary on the New Testament. Grand Rapids: Baker Academic.

———. 2002b. *Revelation*. Baker Exegetical Commentary on the New Testament. Grand Rapids: Baker Academic.

Oswalt, John N. 1998. *The Book of Isaiah: Chapters 40–66*. The New International Commentary on the Old Testament. Grand Rapids: Eerdmans.

Payne, J. D., and John Mark Terry. 2013. *Developing a Strategy for Missions: A Biblical, Historical, and Cultural Introduction*. Grand Rapids: Baker Academic.

Peskett, Howard, and Vinoth Ramachandra. 2003. *The Message of Mission: The Glory of Christ in All Time and Space*. Downers Grove, IL: InterVarsity.

Piper, John. 1996. "The Supremacy of God Among 'All the Nations.'" *International Journal of Frontier Missions* 13 (1): 15–26.

Piper, John, and David Mathis, eds. 2012. *Finish the Mission: Bringing the Gospel to the Unreached and Unengaged*. Wheaton, IL: Crossway.

Plummer, Robert L. 2006. *Paul's Understanding of the Church's Mission: Did the Apostle Paul Expect the Early Christian Communities to Evangelize?* Paternoster Biblical Monographs. Milton Keynes, UK: Paternoster.

Ponraj, S. Devasagayam. 2002. *Biblical Models for Strategic Mission*. Chennai, India: Mission Educational Books.

Pratt, Zane, M. David Sills, and Jeff K. Walters. 2014. *Introduction to Global Missions*. Nashville: B&H Academic.

Rabens, Volker. 2017. "Paul's Mission Strategy in the Urban Landscape of the First-Century Roman Empire." In *The Urban World and the First Christians*, edited by Steve Walton, Paul R. Trebilco, and David W. J. Gill, 99–122. Grand Rapids: Eerdmans.

Riesner, Rainer. 1998. *Paul's Early Period: Chronology, Mission Strategy, Theology*. Grand Rapids: Eerdmans.

Robb, John D. 1989. *Focus: The Power of People Group Thinking*. Monrovia, CA: MARC.

Robinson, Thomas A. 2009. *Ignatius of Antioch and the Parting of the Ways: Early Jewish-Christian Relations*. Peabody, MA: Hendrickson.

———. 2017. *Who Were the First Christians? Dismantling the Urban Thesis*. Oxford: Oxford University Press.

Schnabel, Eckhard J. 2004. *Early Christian Mission, Volume 2: Paul and the Early Church*. Downers Grove, IL: InterVarsity.

———. 2007. "Paul's Urban Strategies: Jerusalem to Crete." *Stone-Campbell Journal* 10 (2): 231–60.

———. 2008. *Paul the Missionary: Realities, Strategies and Methods*. Downers Grove, IL: IVP Academic.

Scott, James M. 1995. *Paul and the Nations: The Old Testament and Jewish Background of Paul's Mission to the Nations with Special Reference to the Destination of Galatians*. WUNT 84. Tübingen, Germany: Mohr Siebeck.

Smith, Steve, and Ying Kai. 2011. *T4T: A Discipleship Re-Revolution*. Monument, CO: WIGTake Resources.

Stark, Rodney. 1997. *The Rise of Christianity: How the Obscure, Marginal Jesus Movement Became the Dominant Religious Force*. New York: HarperOne.

———. 2006. *Cities of God: The Real Story of How Christianity Became an Urban Movement and Conquered Rome*. San Francisco: HarperSanFrancisco.

Stevens, David E. 2012. *God's New Humanity: A Biblical Theology of Multiethnicity for the Church*. Eugene, OR: Wipf & Stock.

Stevens, Gerald L. 2019. *Acts: A New Vision of the People of God*. 2nd ed. Eugene, OR: Pickwick Publications.

Taylor, Justin. 1999. "The List of Nations in Acts 2:9–11." *Revue Biblique* 106 (3): 408–20.

Trousdale, Jerry, and Curtis Sergeant. 2019. "Completing the Task: 24:14–Partnering with King Jesus: The One Thing We Can Do to Hasten His Return." *Mission Frontiers* 41 (4): 22–23.

Von Rad, Gerhard. 1961. *Genesis: A Commentary*. Translated by John H. Marks, Old Testament Library. Philadelphia: Westminster Press.

Walter, Bauer. 2000. *A Greek-English Lexicon of the New Testament and Other Early Christian Literature*. Translated by Felix Wilbur Gingrich and William F. Arndt, 3rd ed. Chicago: University of Chicago Press.

Watts, John D. W. 1987. *Isaiah 34–66*. Vol. 25. Word Biblical Commentary. Waco, TX: Thomas Nelson.

Williams, Jarvis J., and Trey Moss. 2019. "Focus on 'All Nations' as Integral Component of World Mission Strategy." In *World Mission: Theology, Strategy, and Current Issues*, edited by Will Brooks and Scott M. Callaham, 131–48. Bellingham, WA: Lexham Press.

Winter, Ralph D., and Bruce Koch. 2009. "Finishing the Task: The Unreached Peoples Challenge." In *Perspectives on the World Christian Movement*, edited by Ralph D. Winter and Steven C. Hawthorne, 4th ed., 531–46. Pasadena, CA: William Carey Library.

Witherington, Ben, III. 1997. *The Acts of the Apostles: A Socio-Rhetorical Commentary*. Grand Rapids: Eerdmans.

Wright, Christopher. 2006. *The Mission of God: Unlocking the Bible's Grand Narrative*. Downers Grove, IL: IVP Academic.

CHAPTER 8

Missiology through the Lens of Disability:
Assessing the Unreached People Group Idea

ROCHELLE SCHEUERMANN

The Lausanne Movement has been a defining feature of evangelical missions. From the inaugural meeting in Lausanne in 1974, to its more recent congress in Cape Town in 2010, the declarations and statements produced from these gatherings, as well as the continuing conversations through occasional papers, consultations, and working groups, have helped to define, organize, critique, and catalyze evangelical mission activity around the world. The Lausanne Covenant remains central to the shared commitments of evangelicals. Each subsequent statement (i.e., the Manilla Manifesto and the Cape Town Commitment), represents continued elaboration of the core tenets of the Lausanne Covenant in light of changing global realities and the valuation of voices from around the globe. Central to all of these remains the need for the whole church to take the whole gospel to the whole world.

Every Christian—male and female, young and old, trained minister and layperson—is specifically called to personal evangelism and social responsibility (The Lausanne Covenant 1974, sec. 4, 5, and 6; Manilla Manifesto 1989, sec. A.6; Cape Town Commitment 2010, sec. II-F.3). But it is the Cape Town Commitment that, for the first time, includes people with disabilities within the scope of mission: both as those in need of being reached and as those with a ministry to give (2010, sec. II-B.4).

The Cape Town Commitment recognizes that people with disabilities are disabled as much by "social attitudes, injustice and lack of access to resources"

> The Cape Town Commitment recognizes that people with disabilities are disabled as much by "social attitudes, injustice and lack of access to resources" as they are by a physical or mental impairment.

as they are by a physical or mental impairment. The call to serve those with disabilities extends beyond physical, social, or medical provision to "fighting … for inclusion and equality," "resisting prejudice," and "advocating for their needs" both "in society and in the Church" (2010, sec. II-B.4). Church and mission leaders are encouraged to "think not only of mission *among* those with a disability, but to recognize, affirm, and facilitate the missional calling of believers with disabilities as part of the Body of Christ" (2010, sec. II-B.4; emphasis theirs). In the closing statement of this section, the commitment is made to "make our churches places of inclusion and equality for people with disability and to stand alongside them in resisting prejudice and in advocating for their needs in wider society" (2010, sec. II-B.4). This is no easy task. One way to live out our commitment is to do the hard work of evaluating our current missiological models to see if our philosophies, tactics, and practices of mission lend themselves toward the open welcome and inclusion of this minority group, which is estimated to exceed one billion people—15 percent of the world's population (World Health Organization 2020).

The preamble of the Cape Town Commitment gives us a good starting place. The preamble affirms the work of the previous two congresses and notes, particularly, that "among [the First Lausanne Congress's] major gifts to the world Church" was "a new awareness of the number of unreached people groups." During that 1974 congress, Ralph Winter argued that the task of reaching the world was far from over. He suggested that unreached peoples are less defined by geography and more defined by other social, ethnic, and linguistic barriers; and he introduced the E-Scale as one means for efficiently and systematically reaching the unreached. His formative address reshaped the ways that missionaries and missiologists understood the peoples of the world and strategized to reach them.

While this trajectory has not been without critique (both then and now), the unreached people group (UPG) idea has become a mainstay of evangelical missiology. But does this way of thinking about people and mission remain valid when seen through the lens of disability? In this chapter, I will argue that if we are to fulfill Cape Town's commitment to people with disabilities, we must critique some of the underlying assumptions of the UPG model and find new ways for the whole dis/abled church to engage the whole world with the whole gospel.

What Do We Mean by "Disability"?

Disability is tricky to define because it is both biological and social and it can be permanent or temporal. In general, Lausanne has followed the World Health Organization (WHO) in defining disability "quite broadly to cover impairments, activity limitations and participation restrictions from various physical and non-physical causes" (John 2019, 6). Amos Yong (2011, 9) follows this path of trying "to be as inclusive as possible regarding the spectrum of disabilities," but also recognizes that medical and social models of disability make it challenging to neatly identify what things "disable" a person: Mental impairment? Physical impairment? Social processes and norms that exclude wider ranges of abilities?

Benjamin Conner is more explicit in suggesting that definitions by the WHO and the American with Disabilities Act struggle to separate out medical and social forms of disability (2018, 18–19). Conner elevates the social construction of disability and says that while definitions "can be helpful for identifying and considering the impact of disabilities, whether sensory, intellectual, or physical," it is when people "think they need no help in identifying a disability" that they have forgotten "how socially embedded notions of normalcy, ability, and disability can be" (2018, 22).

It is here that Thomas Reynolds provides a helpful and holistic definition that balances the physical and social aspects. Disability, he says,

> is a term naming that interstice where (1) restrictions due to an involuntary bodily impairment, (2) social role expectations, and (3) external/social obstructions come together in a way that (4) preempts an intended participation in communal life. This stress is indeed on the social, but not in a way that neglects the body. (2008, 27)

In this chapter, I will think of disability in this way and with the goal of being as inclusive as possible. Even so, I must also acknowledge that I come with some measure of bias because of my personal story. Though I seek to include people with all manner of disabilities in this conversation, because I have a son with Down syndrome, I am most interested in finding ways to engage, include, and empower people with intellectual and developmental disabilities with and through the gospel.

And following Yong (2011), Conner (2018), and Reynolds (2008), I will use *people with disabilities*, rather than *the disabled* or *disabled people*, "in order to remind us that we are all people first, and with or without disabilities second" (Yong 2011, 9). As Yong says, this is not to ignore disabilities that are central to people's lived experiences, but to avoid reductionism. The language "of 'people with disabilities' reminds us of the richness of life, especially if such life includes disability" (Yong 2011, 9).

E-Scale and UPGs

Winter's 1974 Lausanne address challenged the idea that the world had been reached. Though churches were found on every continent, it was not geography that defined a group as reached. Within every geography, people were marked off by cultural, social, and linguistic barriers that prevented access to the gospel and participation in a viable indigenous church. Until each tribe and tongue had its own church and engaged in near-neighbor evangelism, the work of the Great Commission remained.

The crux of Winter's argument rested on his E-scale model of evangelism, which identified the cultural distance between the evangelist and the unreached. E-1 represented "near-neighbor" evangelism, in which there was negligible difference between evangelists and hearers. Both shared the same language and culture such that they could "witness without learning any foreign language or taking into account any special cultural differences" (Winter 1975a, 218). The only barrier to cross was the one between the church and the world. An E-2 scenario required the crossing of two barriers: (1) the barrier between the church and the world, and (2) an additional barrier marked by "significant but not monumental differences of language and culture" (Winter 1975a, 218). E-3 necessarily meant crossing such significant barriers that everything between the evangelist and the hearer was deemed significantly different.

Winter suggested that people sitting in E-2 and E-3 spaces were still waiting for gospel engagement, since the majority of missionaries were concentrated in E-1 work. This was not the most expedient strategy for finishing the Great Commission task. Local, indigenous churches are more capable of (and more responsible for) reaching those within their own culture. E-1 evangelism, then, should not be done by cross-cultural workers. Instead, cross-cultural workers should be strategically deployed to work in E-2 and E-3 spaces until there was a viable indigenous church. Once this church took over E-1 evangelism, the cross-cultural worker, no longer needed, moved on to the next E-2 or E-3 place. Following this model, the peoples of the world could be systematically cataloged, strategized, and reached. This fueled hope that making disciples of *pante ta ethne* (Matthew 28:19) was not only possible, but within reach.

Winter's presentation at Lausanne marked a significant shift in how missiologists viewed the mission task, and subsequent conversations over several decades worked to define and redefine the people-group idea.[1] While some fluidity

---

1 Tracing this history is outside the scope of this chapter. For detailed accounts of this history, see "Defining 'Unreached'" (Datema 2016); "Essential Frontier Missiology" (Hawthorne 2016); "Part I: Frontier Mission Movement's Understanding of the Modern Mission Era" (Johnson 2001a); "Part II: Major Concepts of the Frontier Mission Movement" (Johnson 2001b); "People Groups: How Many Unreached?" (Johnstone 1990); "Beyond People Group Thinking" (Lee and Park 2018); "Will the Earth Hear His Voice? Is Ralph D. Winter's Idea Still Valid?" (Parsons 2015); "Finishing the Task" (Winter and Koch 2002).

in the definitions remain, most have settled on the idea that a people group is "the largest group through which the gospel can flow without encountering significant barriers of acceptance or understanding" (LCWE 2004a, 4). An unreached people group, therefore, is "typically defined as those people groups which lack a movement strong enough to do the task of evangelizing the group without any cross-cultural assistance" (LCWE 2004a, 5).

Both the E-scale and the UPG idea have provided positive focus and strategy to the evangelical missionary endeavor. They have raised the visibility of peoples and cultures that have been historically overlooked in evangelism, refocused missionary efforts toward spaces and places where concentrated work was needed, provided motivation for continued cross-cultural missionary effort in a world some thought was reached, and provided assessment points by which to evaluate mission trends (e.g., the short-term missions movement; see Priest 2010, 99). The wide-scale acceptance of the UPG model birthed mission organizations, directed monetary flows and personnel, and galvanized evangelicals—both missionaries and laypersons—toward the attainable goal of seeing the evangelistic task completed.

E-Scale and UPGs through the Lens of Disability

Though the concepts of the E-scale and UPGs have become deeply entrenched in evangelical missiology, these ideas have garnered criticism. Some of the critiques are long-standing; however, my goal is not to simply reiterate critiques that have already been made, but instead to evaluate Winter's ideas—and the ways in which evangelicals have appropriated, modified, and engaged with these ideas through the lens of disability.

E-Scale

The E-Scale, Alan Johnson notes, "is the single most important concept that underlies [Winter's] thesis" (2001a, 87). The cultural distance between the reached and the unreached determines who should be involved in the work of evangelism and where those who are being saved will find church community. Winter reasons that the distance between people in E-2 and E-3 evangelism is significant enough that those reached with the gospel will not feel comfortable within established churches. While not "enforce[ing] segregation" (1975b, 241), Winter encourages separate churches for the expedience of church growth and comfort. Since people "tend to sort themselves out according to their own way of life pretty consistently" (1975b, 241), through the formation of "their own worshipping congregations" these congregations can "best ... win others of their own kind" (1975a, 223).

Respondents to Winter's Lausanne presentation immediately raised concerns with the notion that E-2 and E-3 evangelism necessarily required new, separate, indigenous churches. Philip Hogan (1975) and Pablo Pérez (1975) acknowledged the pragmatism of this approach, but critiqued the segregation it imposed and its perpetuation of "adverse existing conditions and prejudices simply because they can be labeled as culturally determined" (Pérez 1975, 256). Winter acknowledged these concerns in his response and maintained that if we forced people into existing churches, it would necessitate "uniformity." To avoid Western hegemony, Winter argued that we maintain the rich diversity of the body of Christ by fostering "unity and fellowship between *congregations* just as we now do between *families*" (Winter 1975b, 241).[2]

At a time when "mounting pressure from secularization and postcolonial reactions increasingly questioned the validity of international missions" (Lee and Park 2018, 213), we can appreciate that Winter sought to promote local autonomy and indigeneity. His response to his first critics, however, is not fully persuasive, and the underlying ideas that were accepted as givens and developed through the years are problematic in several ways.

First, the E-scale upholds the idea that boundaries are both distinct and given. The lives of people in our present, globalized world are complex. Interconnectedness leads to simultaneous actions of cultural rejection, cultural appropriation, and cultural embrace. To say people are "organic and indivisible wholes that are unchanging and clearly distinguished from others" is to follow outdated anthropology that essentializes cultures, elevating between-group differences and under-valuing interconnection (Lee and Park 2018, 215–16). To say that boundaries are a given overlooks "the production of difference within common, shared, and connected spaces" (Gupta and Ferguson 1997b, 45). Gupta and Ferguson (1997a) note that

> Identity and alterity are … produced simultaneously in the formation of 'locality' and 'community.' 'Community' is never simply the recognition of cultural similarity or social continuity but a categorical identity that is premised on various forms of exclusion and constructions of otherness. This fact is absolutely central to the question of who or what it is that 'has' such identities (a group? an individual?), for it is precisely through processes of exclusion and othering that both collective and individual subjects are formed. (Gupta and Ferguson 1997, 13; emphasis mine)

Not all boundaries are inherent. Social construction determines which markers rise to the top as desired and acceptable. As people organize around these shared markers, they encourage similarity in an "us" by excluding those construed to be deviant or "other."

---

2 It is ironic that Winter exalts families as places of homogeneity. Families exist only by inclusion. Marriages join separate families with diverse social, linguistic, and ethnic backgrounds together through the husband and wife, and children are welcomed into families both through natural birth and adoption. If anything, most families show that different people can come together in ways that create unity without erasing diversity.

Second, by not considering how boundaries are made or maintained, the underlying premise of the E-scale fails to consider whether perceived boundaries should be upheld or demolished. In leaving the boundaries within the realm of "Christian liberty" (Winter 1975b, 241), prejudice is neither confronted nor seen as troublesome. Rather, "boundaries of hatred and prejudice [are] treated as equivalent to boundaries of language and culture" (Priest 2009, 186).[3] This is a significant point.

Third, by upholding comfort for the sake of expedience, the E-scale does not motivate congregations toward inclusion, integration, or mutual submission. Inevitably, this works against the idea that congregations will take up E-1 evangelism among the disabled who are both like and unlike them. The language of comfort and reaching one's "own kind" leaves little space for persons with disabilities who challenge a group's comfort and sense of normalcy.

Disabilities often make people uncomfortable.[4] Though Winter suggests the comfort *of those being reached* is what allows for people to choose their own church spaces, the closed space of the local church is another mark of exclusion for people with disabilities, who struggle to feel welcome in many spaces. Such exclusion creates disability for people. Because Winter does not express hope or means for congregations to become welcome spaces of true inclusion,[5] the natural result is a distorted view of inclusion that assimilates by "imposing conformity on differences" and "at best [is] a paternalistic gesture of charity, helping 'those others' get along 'like us'" (Reynolds 2008, 46–47).

Fourth, by maintaining boundaries, the E-scale contributes to an incomplete gospel. This gospel is deficient in part because reconciliation between peoples and cultures is seen as a by-product of the gospel (Lee and Park 2018, 219) rather than "an intrinsic part of the gospel" (Bosch 1982, 27). But the gospel is also deficient because its theology is deficient. John Swinton argues that "we become who and what we are according to the types of relationships that we experience within our lives. In a very real sense we are responsible for the construction of the personhood of those whom we choose to relate with" (2003, 74).

---

3 Robert Priest levels this critique specifically against the homogenous unit principle; however, this, by association, also includes the E-scale. Tennent argues that E-1 evangelism is "an important evangelistic principle, which has given rise to what is known as the homogeneous unit (HU) principle" (2010, 363). Lee and Park argue that the UPG model makes the homogenous unit principle its "normative strategy" (2018, 218).

4 For a discussion on this, see Thomas E. Reynolds' (2008) *Vulnerable Communion: A Theology of Disability and Hospitality*, especially chapter 3 (pages 73–101), and pages 111–17.

5 In his address at Lausanne, Winter said "these few converts" of E-2 evangelism would "merely be considered somewhat odd additions to existing congregations" (1975a, 223). His purpose was to promote the freedom of people to worship through their own cultural expressions and languages; however, in suggesting that being "odd additions to existing congregations" is a valid principle, he implicitly promoted separateness rather than true welcoming, inclusionary hospitality.

Consequently, because of our freedom to choose our community relationships (Winter 1975b, 241), our "process of becoming persons-in-relation occurs through interaction with a very limited range of people ... pretty similar to ourselves" (Swinton 2003, 74). This lack of diversity limits our development. Swinton concludes that if everything about us, from our self-understanding to our interpretive grids, comes from people like ourselves, "we then assume that the theology and practices which emerge from such interactions are both real and universal" (2003, 74). Missiology argues that we need global voices for proper theological and missiological understanding. We also need the voices of people with disabilities. The World Council of Churches explicitly agrees. Section 98 of *Together Towards Life* says,

> The connection of evangelism with colonial powers in the history of mission has led to the presupposition that Western [and I would add *abled*] forms of Christianity are the standards by which others' adherence to the gospel should be judged. Evangelism by those who enjoy economic power or cultural hegemony risks distorting the gospel. Therefore, they must seek the partnership of the poor, the dispossessed, and minorities and be shaped by their theological resources and visions. (CWME 2012, 35–36).

The E-scale is a helpful tool insofar as it helps us to consider the cultural distance between evangelists and the people being reached. However, although the E-scale attempts to promote indigeneity and local cultural expressions of Christianity, it simultaneously promotes exclusion and separateness, thus creating disability by maintaining a "cult of normalcy" (see Reynolds 2008)

UPG in Definition
In the decades following Lausanne, missiologists tweaked, modified, and expanded the definition of unreached people. In 2002, Winter and Koch suggested four ways for considering people groups: blocs, ethnolinguistic people, sociopeoples, and unimax groups.[6] While sociopeoples are the initial points for evangelizing blocs and ethnolinguistic groups (2002, 17), because unimax people lack significant barriers in the spread of the gospel, we will get "missiological closure" when all unimax peoples are reached and have their own church-planting movement (2002, 21). But where do people with disabilities fit? Are they a sociopeople or a unimax people? There is little agreement among missiologists. This is most evident in the 2004 Lausanne Occasional Papers 35A (LCWE 2004a) and 35B (LCWE 2004b) and the events surrounding their creation.

---

6 Winter and Koch define sociopeoples as "a relatively small association of peers who have an affinity for one another based upon a shared interest, activity, or occupation" (2002, 17). A unimax people is a "**max**imum sized group sufficiently **uni**fied to be the target of a single people movement to Christ, where 'unified' refers to the fact that there are no significant barriers of either understanding or acceptance to stop the spread of the gospel" (2002, 18; emphasis theirs).

At the 2004 Forum for World Evangelism (Pattaya, Thailand), the only space for UPG conversation was to be held within the issue group "Hidden and Forgotten People," which was focused on people with disabilities. Steven Hawthorne notes that "consultations planners insisted that any discussion about unreached people groups would have to be a piece of a broad conversation about ministry to disabled persons," but that this did not satisfy attendees. "Several leaders," he says, "not wanting to diminish the importance of ministry to disabled people, and at the same time, adamantly passionate about completing the task among all peoples, organized a way for those focused on unreached people groups to meet separately" (2002, 27). The impromptu issue group garnered dozens of participants (who abandoned other issue groups) and called itself "Ministry among Least Reached People Groups." Forum organizers, "with some consternation," allowed this new group to present a report to the general assembly, but required group members to "share time with Group 6, which had come to call itself 'Ministry among People with Disabilities'" (Hawthorne 2016, 27).

Without firsthand knowledge of how these events played out, it is striking that while everyone acknowledged the need to discuss people with disabilities and evidenced concern to not overrun the agenda for a group focusing on disabilities, it was the disabilities group that was forced to surrender presentation time to accommodate others. Hawthorne says, "Disabled people are of course often overlooked and well deserving of a full discussion" (2016, 27). However, the group was not privileged to have their full discussion presented to the general assembly. Additionally, as Hawthorne describes in his footnotes, the original group focusing on disabilities became "Group 6B" and the "unreached peoples mini-consultation became 'Group 6A'" (2016, 32). While this doesn't necessarily mean that "A" is better, the relegating of the original disabilities group to the "B" designation does hint at an order preference. Disability was displaced.

Aside from this, however, is the apparent confusion as to whether or not disabilities fit into UPGs. The "Ministry among People with Disabilities" group notes that "the 2004 Forum was the first time that 'people with disabilities' was acknowledged as a sociologic 'people group'" (LCWE 2004b, 5) and a "definable people group" (LCWE 2004b, 5–6). And their paper identified the disability community as "one of the largest unreached—some say under-reached—or hidden people groups in the world" (LCWE 2004b, 7).

This is in considerable contrast to the impromptu UPG group. Though the new group published under the title "Hidden and Forgotten People, Including Those Who Are Disabled" (2004a), they only mentioned the disabled three times. Their opening definition dismisses the disabled as a "people group" (LCWE 2004a, 4), although the disabled—like the young, old, poor, and refugees—are among the "parts of society" that show up within the 25 percent who have "little access to the Good News" (LCWE 2004a, 66). The only other place disability is mentioned in the paper is within a list explaining that "ministry to social needs can include ministry to the disabled, street children, drug addicts and the building of strong community relationships" (LCWE 2004a, 37–38). In opposition to the paper's title, people with disabilities remained hidden and forgotten.

This example reveals the ways in which people with disabilities fall through the cracks because they don't easily fit within UPG definitions but need to be acknowledged as unreached. Though Lausanne has adopted the additional term of *unengaged* (often read together as "unreached and unengaged people groups," or UUPGs), this doesn't seem to solve the confusion. The Cape Town Commitment identifies *unreached* groups as having "no known believers and no churches among them," and *unengaged* groups as having no currently known "churches or agencies that are even trying to share the gospel with them" (sec. II–D.1). Where does this leave people with disabilities?[8]

Winter argues that E-1 evangelism is the responsibility of local churches. Church members are to reach their own near-neighbors. Are people with disabilities "near-neighbors"? If so, why is it that (in the United States) "having a disability label regrettably remains a reliable predictor of whether people with [Intellectual and Developmental Disabilities] and their families are present" within a church (Carter, Biggs, and Boehm 2016, 128–29)? Why is it that, of those who attend church, 89 percent of families thought their children were accepted by congregational leaders, but only 69 percent agreed that church leadership was "committed to including people with intellectual disability or [Autism Spectrum Disorder]" (Carter, Boehm, Annandale, and Taylor 2016, 386)? This says nothing of other types of disabilities or ages.

If comfort is a legitimate basis on which to establish separate churches, and people with disabilities (and the people reaching them) are not comfortable with being included in the local church, how might people with disabilities go about establishing their own churches? We do see the advent of Deaf churches. *Deaf* is on the Joshua Project's UPG list as an affinity block, people group, and people cluster (Joshua Project n.d.). But apart from the Deaf, people with disabilities are

---

7 In footnote 12 of the article "Developing Young Leaders with Disabilities," it is said that "Although people with disabilities do not fit the pattern of unreached people groups, Lausanne has proposed the more inclusive term 'unengaged peoples'" (Deuel 2016, 13). The usage suggested in this article is not supported after looking through Lausanne documents. The term was not introduced for the sake of including people with disabilities, and the definition itself seems equally problematic as "unreached."

8 There are examples of others using UPG with people with disabilities, but these lack in-depth engagement with how disabilities fits within standard UPG definitions (cf. Jennings 2017, 30; Martin 2019).

not establishing their own churches (indeed, depending on the type of disability, self-sufficiency might not even be possible). But why should they? If people with disabilities are supposed to be part of mainstream society, why not the local church?

If, as the definition of *unengaged* states, people with disabilities are not being reached by local churches or agencies, who should be reaching out to them? And once reached, what church do they join? The cycle seems endless; and while we loop around and around these questions, people with disabilities remain both unreached and unengaged.

UPG in Practice

Perhaps one of the more concerning aspects of the UPG practice is found within the managerial missiology critique raised by Samuel Escobar. Winter's UPG missiology was founded on the desire to make the missionary task quantifiable and manageable, all toward the goal of completion. In a very Western, pragmatic fashion, Winter was concerned with speed and efficiency, and thus his model sought to evangelize with minimal barriers. Escobar says that because this kind of missiology "reduce[s] reality to an understandable picture and then … project[s] missionary action as a response to a problem that has been described in quantitative form," missionary action "is reduced to a linear task that is translated into logical steps to be followed in a process of management by objectives, in the same way in which the evangelistic task is reduced to a process that can be carried on following marketing principles" (2000, 109).

Though Escobar points out several problems that arise from managerial missiology, this statement is most alarming:

> If the missionary effort is reduced to numerical growth, anything that would hinder it has to be eliminated. If the struggle for obedience to God in holistic mission involves costly participation in the processes of social transformation, it is simply eliminated. (Escobar 2000, 111)

Is it possible that people with disabilities are eliminated from evangelism if they hinder numerical growth and add to the cost of social transformation? It doesn't seem unreasonable to ask this question, because Winter and Koch, when establishing guidelines for approaching sociopeoples, note that

> Some types of groups may prove to be especially helpful when establishing churches, while others may hinder the process. Natural leaders and Bible teachers for churches might be discovered by first reaching businessmen or teachers… . On the other hand, you could choose the wrong group, such as focusing on children's ministry for initial evangelism within a people, which may be interpreted as a threat to their natural families. (2002, 18)

Winter and Koch essentially argue that if you reach people who can assist in the creation and oversight of the church, you can perhaps better sustain growth for the church plant. But does expedience make the methodology sound?

So many issues are involved in a conversation like this, but at some point we are forced to consider: Who decides which people are helpful and which people will hinder the process? If people with disabilities, as our definition suggests, includes a large segment of people who have a variety of physical and mental ailments and often are poor, are they to be seen as hindrances or assets to church growth? Reynolds (2008) argues strongly that the maintenance of a "cult of normalcy" follows capitalist principles with the body being a significant commodity that must sell itself as being useful in providing good for others and purchasing good (autonomy, freedom, and equality) for self.

Swinton says that "societies such as our own thrive on meritocracy and processes of valuing that are contingent on the exchange of particular social, psychological or material goods" (2003, 69). When people with disabilities do not have body capital (Reynolds 2008, 58) or are unable to participate in meritocracy in ways others expect, they are excluded as aberrant and unuseful. And "within a society that uses the criteria of independence, productivity, intellectual prowess and social position to judge the value of human beings," Swinton says, "there will always be questions relating to the value of people with [profound types of developmental] disability" (2003, 67).

Winter and Koch's strategy to reach "helpful people" can be seen as a call to reach the abled and privileged first. Again, while this does require many nuanced discussions, it begs the question of when those whom society calls lowly, weak, or disabled should be included in evangelistic strategy. And how does all of this fit with Jesus' call in Luke 14 to bring people with disabilities into the banquet as first priority (Luke 14:7–24; see LCWE 2004b; Eareckson Tada 2018)?

Concluding Thoughts

The church, like society, struggles with an ablest perspective. As the Cape Town Commitment itself acknowledges, disability is identified as much, if not more so, in the exclusion and lack of access that people face because of their perceived disabilities as it is in the actual impairments. Many people are uncomfortable when encountering a person with disabilities, and churches themselves often function—both physically and socially—in a way that, at best, accepts people with disabilities without necessarily including them to the point of true welcome and belonging (see Carter, Biggs, and Boehm 2016; Conner 2015, 17).

While the E-scale and the UPG idea have made many important contributions to how we view the world that has yet to hear the gospel, there are some concerning aspects of these ideas that must be addressed as we work to develop mission among and with people with disabilities. Winter and Koch argue that the "value of the unimax approach

The church, like society, struggles with an ablest perspective.

lies in the way it identifies the boundaries hindering the flow of the gospel" (2002, 19)—not so that the boundaries can be eliminated, but so that people can work within them. Implicitly this reinforces boundaries between people and elevates comfort. If people cannot be comfortable with "you," they should be with their "own kind." This is dangerous missiology. Conner notes that

> while cultures are always evolving and interacting, indigenization favors continuity with the past, and "the more the Gospel is made a place to feel at home, the greater danger that no one else will be able to live there" (Eiesland 1994, 84). When this happens, the "city on a hill" that is supposedly welcoming people and drawing them in becomes inaccessible on many levels. As Nancy Eiesland has interpreted it, "For many disabled persons the church has been a 'city on a hill'—physically inaccessible and socially inhospitable." (Conner 2015, 20–21)

There are ways forward. The idea of *missio Dei* reminds us that mission is never ours. We participate only through the enabling of the Holy Spirit. Christ is no respecter of persons, and neither is the Holy Spirit. Anyone who calls on the name of Christ is knit into Christ's body and indwelled by the Spirit. And only through this indwelling do any of us, in all of our varying levels of ableness, participate in God's good work in the world (Konz 2018, 340). Expedience, efficiency, and cultural ideas of valuable personhood tempt us to follow methodologies that favor the powerful and the abled. But God's kingdom is an upside-down kingdom, where the last become first. Connor powerfully challenges us,

> Since it is the Holy Spirit who enables witness, the only way that people with disabilities who are part of the body of Christ can fail to offer their contribution to the ministry and witness of the church is if they are not afforded a place within our congregations. The absence of their concerns and presence from theological schools and congregations diminishes the church's capacity for ministry and the fitness of her witness. No one is impaired such that they can't bear the witness of the Spirit, and no single person should be disabled from participating in the church's witness. (2015, 26)

The church, too, is called to hospitality, welcome, and inclusion. However, as opposed to Winter's thesis, unity does not necessitate uniformity. Newbigin says that "as the mission goes its way to the ends of the earth new treasures are brought into the life of the Church and Christianity itself grows and changes until it becomes more credible as a foretaste of the unity of all mankind" (1989, 123–24).

Missiology has been more cognizant of its need to embrace cultural diversity and listen to global voices, but it has been much slower to embrace diversity and listen to the voices of people with disabilities. While there are many reasons for this (see Conner 2018; Eiesland 1995; Reynolds 2008), these reasons do not need to remain rooted. We must revisit and revise missiological principles and methodologies like E-scale and UPGs in light of disability. "For it is only when the witness of the handicapped is an integral part of the witness of the whole Church, that this witness is true to the Gospel of the Crucified who is risen, the risen Lord who is Crucified" (Newbigin 1979, 24).

If exclusion of people with disabilities diminishes our theology, it also inherently diminishes our witness. It is through the welcome of people with disabilities—a welcome that helps them not only find their place but also "creatively contribute to the life of the community" that "the church becomes itself—that is, a place of redemption for all" (Reynolds 2008, 245). Perhaps as we witness among—and with—people with disabilities, we will find that other walls of exclusion will fall, and that prejudice and comfort will be eliminated as legitimate reasons for separate churches. Why? Because disability, as Reynolds argues,

> is redemptively fundamental: by welcoming people with disabilities into our church communities, our churches become communions bearing witness to God's creative-redemptive ability to give life. And when our church communities traffic in such power, they cannot help but spill outward to transform the world in a God-ward direction. (2008, 249)

References Cited

Bosch, David. 1982. "Church Unity amidst Cultural Diversity: A Protestant Problem." *Missionalia* 10 (1): 16–28.

Carter, Erik W., Elizabeth E. Biggs, and Thomas L. Boehm. 2016. "Being Present Versus Having a Presence: Dimensions of Belonging for Young People with Disabilities and Their Families." *Christian Education Journal* Series 3, 13, no. 1: 127–46.

Carter, Erik W., Thomas L. Boehm, Naomi H. Annandale, and Courtney E. Taylor. 2016. "Supporting Congregational Inclusion for Children and Youth With Disabilities and Their Families." *Exceptional Children* 82, no. 3: 372–89.

Conner, Benjamin. 2015. "Enabling Witness: Disability in Missiological Perspective." *Journal of Disability & Religion* 19, no. 1: 15–29.

———. 2018. *Disabling Mission, Enabling Witness: Exploring Missiology through the Lens of Disability Studies*. Downers Grove, IL: InterVarsity.

CWME, Commission on World Mission and Evangelism. 2012. *Together towards Life: Mission and Evangelism in Changing Landscapes*. https://www.oikoumene.org/resources/documents/together-towards-life-mission-and-evangelism-in-changing-landscapes

Datema, Dave. 2016. "Defining 'Unreached': A Short History." *International Journal of Frontier Missiology* 33 (2): 45–71.

Deuel, Dave. 2016. "Developing Young Leaders with Disabilities." *Lausanne Global Analysis* 5 (1). https://www.lausanne.org/content/lga/2016-01/developing-young-leaders-disabilities?_sf_s=disabled.

Eareckson Tada, Joni. 2018. "What Does the Gospel Have to Say to Disabled Persons?" *Lausanne Content Library*. https://www.lausanne.org/content/what-does-the-gospel-have-to-say-to-disabled-persons?_sf_s=disabled.

Eiesland, Nancy L. 1994. *The Disabled God: Toward a Liberatory Theology of Disability*. Nashville: Abingdon.

Escobar, Samuel. 2000. "Evangelical Missiology: Peering into the Future at the Turn of the Century." In *Global Missiology for the 21st Century: The Iguassu Dialogue*, edited by William D. Taylor, 101–122. Grand Rapids: Baker Academic.

Gupta, Akhil, and James Ferguson. 1997a. "Culture, Power, Place: Ethnography at the End of an Era." In *Culture, Power, Place: Explorations in Critical Anthropology*, edited by Akhil Gupta and James Ferguson, 1–29. Durham, NC: Duke University Press.

———. 1997b. "Beyond 'Culture': Space, Identity, and the Politics of Difference." In *Culture, Power, Place: Explorations in Critical Anthropology*, edited by Akhil Gupta and James Ferguson, 33–51. Durham, NC: Duke University Press.

Hawthorne, Steven C. 2016. "Essential Frontier Missiology: Its Emergence and Flourishing Future." *International Journal of Frontier Missiology* 33 (1): 23–33.

Hogan, J. Phillip. 1975. "Response to Dr. Ralph Winter's Paper." In *Let the Earth Hear His Voice: Selected Addresses from the International Congress on World Evangelization, Lausanne, Switzerland, 1974*, edited by J. D. Douglas, 242–45. Minneapolis: World Wide Publishers.

Jennings, Donna. 2017. "Those Who Seem to Be Weak: The Role of Disability within a Missional Framework." *Mission Round Table* 12 (3): 29–34.

John, Nathan G. 2019. "The Church's Treasure: People with Disability on Mission." In *Disability in Mission: The Church's Hidden Treasure*, edited by David C. Duel and Nathan G. John, 1–7. Peabody: MA: Hendrickson's Publishers.

Johnson, Alan. 2001a. "Part I: The Frontier Mission Movement's Understanding of the Modern Mission Era." *International Journal of Frontier Missions* 18 (2): 81–88.

———. 2001b. "Part II: Major Concepts of the Frontier Mission Movement." *International Journal of Frontier Missions* 18 (2): 89–97.

Johnstone, Patrick. 1990. "People Groups: How Many Unreached?" *International Journal of Frontier Missions* 7 (2): 35–40.

Joshua Project. n.d. https://joshuaproject.net/search.

Konz, D. J. 2018. "The Even Greater Commission: Relating the Great Commission to the *Missio* Dei, and Human Agency to Divine Activity, in Mission. *Missiology: An International Review* 46 (4): 333–49.

The Lausanne Movement, The Lausanne Covenant. 1974. https://www.lausanne.org/content/covenant/lausanne-covenant#cov.

The Lausanne Movement, The Manilla Manifesto. 1989. https://www.lausanne.org/content/manifesto/the-manila-manifesto.

The Lausanne Movement, The Cape Town Commitment. 2011. "A Confession of Faith and a Call to Action." https://www.lausanne.org/content/ctcommitment#capetown.

LCWE, Lausanne Committee for World Evangelization. 2004a. "Hidden and Forgotten People, Including Those Who are Disabled" (LOP 35A). September 29 to October 4, Pattaya, Thailand.

———. 2004b. "Ministry among People with Disabilities" (LOP 35B). September 29 to October 4, Pattaya, Thailand.

Lee, Peter T., and James Sung-Hwan Park. 2018. "Beyond People Group Thinking: A Critical Reevaluation of Unreached People Groups." *Missiology: An International Review* 46 (3): 212–25.

Martin, Stephanie. 2019. "The Unreached People Group That We Overlook." *ChurchLeaders.com*, September 12, https://churchleaders.com/children/childrens-ministry-articles/333339-special-needs-the-unreached-people-group-that-we-overlook.html.

Newbigin, Lesslie. 1979. "Not Whole without the Handicapped." In *Partners in Life: The Handicapped and the Church*, edited by Geiko Müller-Fahrenholz, 17–25. Geneva, Switzerland: WCC Publications.

———. 1989. *The Gospel in a Pluralist Society*. Grand Rapids: Eerdmans.

Parsons, Greg H. 2015. "Will the Earth Hear His Voice? Is Ralph D Winter's Idea Still Valid?" *International Journal of Frontier Missiology* 32 (1): 5–18.

Pérez, Pablo M. 1975. "Response to Dr. Ralph D. Winter's Paper." In *Let the Earth Hear His Voice: Selected Addresses from the International Congress on World Evangelization, Lausanne, Switzerland, 1974,* edited by J. D. Douglas, 25–258. Minneapolis: World Wide Publishers.

Priest, Robert J. 2009. "Afterword: Concluding Missiological Reflection." In *Power and Identity in the Global Church: Six Contemporary Cases,* edited by Brian M. Howell and Edwin Zehner, 185–91. Pasadena, CA: William Carey Library.

———. 2010. "Short-Term Missions as a New Paradigm." In *Mission after Christendom: Emergent Themes in Contemporary Mission,* edited by Obgu U. Kalu, Peter Vethunayagamony, and Edmund Kee-Fook Chia. Louisville, KY: Westminster John Knox Press.

Reynolds, Thomas E. 2008. *Vulnerable Communion: A Theology of Disability and Hospitality*. Grand Rapids: Brazos Press.

Tennent, Timothy C. 2009. *Invitation to World Missions: A Trinitarian Missiology for the Twenty-first Century*. Grand Rapids: Kregel.

Swinton, John. 2003. "The Body of Christ Has Down Syndrome: Theological Reflections on Vulnerability, Disability, and Graceful Communities." *The Journal of Pastoral Theology* 13 (2): 66–78.

World Health Organization. 2020. "Disability and Health." World Health Organization website, December 1, https://www.who.int/news-room/fact-sheets/detail/disability-and-health.

Winter, Ralph D. 1975a. "The Highest Priority: Cross-Cultural Evangelism." In *Let the Earth Hear His Voice: Selected Addresses from the International Congress on World Evangelization, Lausanne, Switzerland, 1974,* edited by J. D. Douglas, 213–25. Minneapolis: World Wide Publishers.

———. 1975b. "The Highest Priority: Cross-Cultural Evangelism." In *Let the Earth Hear His Voice: Selected Addresses from the International Congress on World Evangelization, Lausanne, Switzerland, 1974,* edited by J. D. Douglas, 226–41. Minneapolis: World Wide Publishers.

Winter, Ralph D., and Bruce A. Koch. 2002. "Finishing the Task: The Unreached Peoples Challenge." *International Journal of Frontier Missions* 19, no. 4: 15–24.

Yong, Amos. 2011. *The Bible, Disability, and the Church: A New Vision of the People of God.* Grand Rapids: Eerdmans.

CHAPTER 9

Hybridity, Borderlands, and Paul Hiebert:
A Latinx Missiologist Reexamines Critical Contextualization

MARTIN RODRIGUEZ

Contextualization and its analogues—inculturation, indigenization, contextual theology, local theology—have arguably been *the* central missiological issue for the last fifty years. Influential missiologists, including Eugene Nida, Charles Kraft, David Bosch, Andrew Walls, Robert Schreiter, and Stephen Bevans, have each lent their voice to this ongoing conversation, exploring ways to develop biblically faithful expressions of Christianity while preserving as much of the traditional culture as possible. In this ongoing missiological task, the church seeks methods of contextualization that remain faithful to the gospel without being irrelevant and that are relevant to the culture without being syncretistic. We seek methods that remain faithful to the gospel without falling into ethnocentrism and that are hospitable to a host of cultural expressions without falling into relativism.

Few, if any, contextualization methods have been more influential or more widely accepted than Paul Hiebert's critical contextualization (1984; 1987). Hiebert left an enduring legacy, for he challenged Western missionaries and missiologists to attain a deeper awareness of our own hidden worldviews and to embrace a critical consciousness of the ways our worldviews shape our interpretations. In many respects, my proposals here seek to advance Hiebert's aim to promote a more critical consciousness among the people of God.

The proposals that follow build on an original qualitative study of the experiences of multiculturality and leadership of twelve Latinx[1] pastors working in multicultural congregations in Southern California.[2] The argument I will put forward is straightforward: to insist that if we are to engage in genuinely relational mission in contexts of diversity, then Hiebert's model must be abandoned, not only because it is increasingly ill-equipped to address the challenges and opportunities presented by cultural diversification and hybridization, but more importantly because it fosters what Willie James Jennings calls a "distorted relational imagination" (2010, 4).

To explain the need to reconsider Hiebert's model in light of the increasingly complex commerce between cultures, I will begin by exploring Latinx experiences of hybridity. I will build on the aforementioned qualitative study, using the work of Mikhail Bakhtin and Gloria Anzaldúa as a hermeneutical lens in order to offer a situated and embodied conception of hybridity that honors our neighbor's agency, protects difference, and remains attentive to power asymmetries. Then I will show how a messier approach to culture—emerging from the qualitative research— exposes significant reductionisms at the heart of Hiebert's critical contextualization model. Finally, I will show how a critical conception of hybridity draws our attention to the ambiguous inner logic of Hiebert's contextualization project.

Hybridity in Latinx Experience

In 2018, the Latinx population in the United States reached 59.9 million. By 2050, demographers estimate that one in three Americans will identify as Hispanic/ Latino/a. Globalization and global migration patterns continue diversifying our neighborhoods and our churches (Martínez 2011; Rodriguez 2011; Mulder, Ramos, and Martí 2017). I am a Latinx minister of a multicultural congregation in Los Angeles, a city in which Latinx peoples account for more than half of the total population. Culturally speaking, Latinx peoples are a profoundly diverse group, and among us there are many whose cultural identities resist monocultural categorization—people whose (so-called) assimilation to the United States actually involves a hybridization of cultural narratives rather than the erasure of one and the wholesale adoption of another.

---

1 In North America, the contested terms "Hispanic," "Latino," "Latin," "Latino/a," "Latin@," and "Latinx" all refer to persons of Latin American and Caribbean origin or descent, each with distinct historical backgrounds, ethnic and racial backgrounds, immigration patterns, and levels of integration into United States social and economic life. For this chapter, I have chosen to use the pan-ethnic label "Latinx," mainly because this term is closely associated with the work of Gloria Anzaldúa, whose ideas ground my own approach to culture studies and Latinx identity.

2 This qualitative study lies at the heart of my dissertation submitted in partial fulfillment of my PhD in Intercultural Studies from Fuller Theological Seminary.

My own identity is typical: I am Mexican-American, although I am not quite Mexican and not quite American. I live in the hyphen. As missiologist Juan Martínez explains,

New generations of Latinos born in the United States are creating *hybrid cultures* that combine various cultural realities that they are experiencing. Since our identities are in constant flux, it is difficult to imagine a scenario in which these tensions are ever "resolved." Part of our US-Latino identity and culture is to live in the hyphen "-" between the multiple influences that affect our identity. (2008, 28)

I am Mexican-American, although I am not quite Mexican and not quite American. I live in the hyphen.

Urban centers of North America are increasingly populated with hybrid peoples like me, and yet the dynamics and significance of Latinx hybridity remain a relatively unexplored field of inquiry among missiologists. My own research on hybridity theories has been by way of discourses on *mestizaje*, a Latinx analogue for hybridity. For nearly forty years, Hispanic theologians like Virgilio Elizondo (1983; 1988), Allan Figueroa Deck (1992), Asa María Isasi Díaz (1996), and Justo L. González (1996; 1990) have been writing about *mestizaje* and its implications for theology. A survey of this mature conversation lies beyond the scope of this chapter; suffice it to say that we are increasingly aware of the need for hybridity frameworks that are attentive to the dynamics of agency, power, and plurality.

Today, a growing number of evangelical missiologists are engaging hybridity frameworks in their scholarship (cf. Uytanlet and Rynkiewich 2016; Shaw 2018; Ott 2015; Shaw and Burrows 2018). Many missiologists have been introduced to hybridity discourse by way of conversations on globalization, and in particular by Jan Nederveen Pieterse's immensely popular *Globalization and Culture: Global Mélange* (2019 [2003], now in its fourth edition; cf. Shaw 2018; Ott 2015; Lee and Harold 2019; Resane 2019), which defines hybridization as a process of adapting, adopting, and rejecting aspects of other cultures. Though Pieterse's arguments are nuanced, appropriations of hybridity within missiological conversations have been inconsistent, tending to fixate on the dynamic of fusion while neglecting the dialectic of twoness (which I describe below). In this respect, appropriations of hybridity among Western evangelical missiologists today are reminiscent of uncritical appropriations of mestizaje among Latinx theologians nearly forty years ago—appropriations that scholars like Néstor Medina (2009) and Michelle A. Gonzalez (2006) rightly criticize for their reifying and essentializing tendencies and their subtle erasure of oppressions. When used to promote inclusion and multiplicity, Medina and Gonzalez argue, mestizaje (usually under the guises of fusion and synthesis) too often becomes a rigid absolutizing and homogenizing mechanism.

In *Rethinking Mission in the Postcolony*, postcolonial missiologist Marion Grau (2011) explores the conflicted religiocultural identity (or polydoxy) formation that occurs in liminal spaces around empire and Christian mission. Though the thrust of Grau's argument addresses the harm caused by "civilizing" missions warped by imperialism, she perceptively notes a more subtle danger that Western evangelicals face today: "the too-enthusiastic affirmation of celebratory hybridity" (2011, 24). Grau argues that dominant representations of pluralism and inclusivism wrapped in labels like mestizaje and hybridity can unwittingly hide their own supersessionisms that slowly consume difference. Grau's warnings are timely, for our well-intentioned encounters with religious and cultural others, more often than we realize, are sites where "hybridizations" involve power struggles and result in the silencing of more vulnerable voices.

The model of Latinx hybridity I propose below suggests a more nuanced relationship between hybridization and power. I will delineate a dialectical model for cultural interaction: a tendency toward coalescence in conflict with a tendency toward contestation, both tendencies in continuous dialogical tension with the individual's/community's social context. My conception of hybridity is grounded both in my qualitative study of Latinx leaders in Los Angeles and in the scholarship of Mikhail Bakhtin and Gloria Anzaldúa, whose theories make room for agency, plurality, change, and situatedness as integral aspects of cultural identity.

Mikhail Bakhtin: Linguistic Hybridity

The writings of Russian literary theorist Mikhail Bakhtin (1895–1975) date to the tumultuous period immediately after the Russian Revolution until Stalin's clampdown in the 1920s. Ever since Bakhtin's works became accessible to anglophone scholars in the early 1980s, his frameworks have been at the center of critical discussions of hybridity in Western postcolonial discourse. His theories continue to garner interest because they propose a vision of intercultural life that does not lose sight of the agency of cultural-others, of the suffering generated by displacements and diasporas, or of the complex socio-historical contexts (marked by power imbalances) that give rise to and permeate these intercultural experiences. Sadly, there are as yet very few missiological works that extend discussion of Bakhtin's proposals beyond a few citations (cf. Moon 2009; Zene 2015).

Bakhtin's hybridity theory is grounded in his philosophy of dialogue. Dialogue, he explains, is a characteristic of life itself: "Life by its very nature is dialogic. To live means to participate in dialogue" (1984, 293). In Bakhtin, dialogue refers to all verbal and nonverbal acts ("utterances") used in communicating and relating with others, from body language to social behavior. Dialogue, Bakhtin insists, is always situated and always relational.

- It is *relational* because the generation of meaning only happens in dialogical relationship with others. No one "makes sense" on one's own.

- It is *situated* because the generation of meaning cannot be detached from the embodied experiences and activities of actual people in the context of their messy, everyday, on-the-ground interactions with others. No one "makes sense" apart from body and place.

Language, observes Bakhtin, "lives only in the dialogic interaction of those who make use of it" (1984, 183); which is to say, every society and every community has recognizable communication patterns that are socially structured and systematized into particular understandings. These structured communication patterns dictate, for instance, that I greet my Mexican friends and family differently than I greet my North American friends and family, and that we greet people at funerals differently than we greet people at a Dodgers game. Bakhtin reasons that, since all communication is shaped by contextual/dialogical interactions, any time we communicate we are drawing on a complex history of language use.

> There are no "neutral" words and forms—words and forms that belong to "no one;" language has been completely taken over, shot through with intentions and accents ... each word tastes of the context and contexts in which it has lived its socially charged life; all words and forms are populated by intentions. Contextual overtones ... are inevitable in the word. (Bakhtin 1981, 293)

There is no simple correlation between the motives of speakers and the meanings of their words in a conversation, insists Bakhtin. To participate in dialogue is to immerse ourselves in a plethora of alien words and discourses, which "inevitably leads to an awareness of the *disassociation* between language and intention, language and thought, language and expression" (Bakhtin 1981, 368–69, italics added; cf. Gardiner 2004, 36).

In Bakhtin's philosophy, dialogue is also the location of personal agency. Although our language is layered with rich histories and meanings shaped by our complex sociocultural situatedness and by our diverse experiences, Bakhtin nevertheless maintains that it is in the midst of each particular conversation between speakers/listeners that meaning emerges. In our dialogue, we give voice to words and constantly re-accent them with our own tone, our own pathos, our own particular grasp of the semantic content of the words, and our own sense of how our dialogue partners will understand and relate to our language. We are never simply bound to the ways in which language or words have been used before us. We can collaboratively "author" new meanings and fresh articulations of words to benefit our own purposes and contextual needs (Bakhtin 1984, 189). Though words resist being re-accented, there is always space (or loopholes) in our dialogue for what Bakhtin calls "creative understanding." This space for creative understandings emerges from the fact that every word draws on a host of prior dialogues, stories, and experiences and thus has a *plurality* of possible meanings. It is precisely this dynamic tension between the *situatedness* of meaning and the *plurality* of meaning that sets the stage for Bakhtin's hybridity theory.

Bakhtin uses the term *hybridization* to describe the way in which language, even within a single sentence or a single utterance, can be *double-voiced* and thus subvert authoritative speech ("monologue"). Foundational to Bakhtin's philosophy of dialogue is the dialectical assertion that hybridity involves not only the "mixing of two socio-linguistic consciousnesses" but also the simultaneous "collision between differing points of view on the world that are embedded in these forms" (1981, 360). Bakhtin labels these dialectical tendencies *intentional hybridization* and *organic hybridization*.

Intentional linguistic hybridity (or conscious hybridity) refers to "an utterance that belongs, by its grammatical [syntactic] and compositional markers, to a single speaker, but that actually contains mixed within it two utterances, two speech manners, two styles, two 'languages,' two semantic and axiological belief systems" (1981, 304). Organic hybridization (or unconscious hybridity), on the other hand, refers to the mixing of multiple languages within the boundaries of a single language. Organic hybridity is evident in the way our languages shift and change as they come into contact with new and distinct languages (1981, 358–59). Bakhtin cherished the storied layers of our dialogue. He insisted that this cacophony of meanings ("polyphony") enriched society, since, among other things, diversity and contradictions of meaning create space for people to deepen critical awareness of the stories that shape our language and to (re)accent creatively the language we use.

Bakhtin's philosophy places the dialogical construction of meaning at the fundamental level of every (specific and embodied) utterance. Because meaning, at its core, is dialogical and thus is marked at its most fundamental level by difference (between competing stories), difference is not to be overcome by consensus, but simply to be appreciated as such.

Gloria Anzaldúa: Borderlands

It is no overstatement to say that Gloria Anzaldúa's *Borderlands/La Frontera* (1987) was a watershed in Latinx identity conversations. A Chicana, queer, feminist, and postcolonial activist, Anzaldúa (1942–2004) was raised in the border country of south Texas. Her writings draw on her borderland experiences to paint vivid pictures of what it means to be a cultural hybrid, a *mestiza*, a person "alienated from her mother culture, 'alien' in the dominant culture, the woman of color caught between *los intersticios*, the spaces between different worlds she inhabits" (1987, 203). Anzaldúa called these spaces between worlds *borderlands* and the people who experience them *borderlanders*.

For Anzaldúa, the concept of borderlands is both a historical theme and a socio-psychological category—a "series of psychological, sexual, and spiritual sites, present whenever two or more cultures edge each other, where people of different races occupy the same territory, where under, lower, middle, and upper classes touch, where the space between two individuals shrinks to intimacy" (Delgado and Stefanic 1998, 641). Much of Anzaldúa's writing is preoccupied with the painful experiences of displacement, marginalization, and alienation of Chicana women of color. And yet, in a profound affirmation of agency, she consistently and resolutely moves beyond the realities of victimization and the experiences of exclusion by the dominant cultures to describe how we borderlanders can learn to incorporate our experiences to resist hatred, anger, and exploitation in order to become agents of healing in our communities (Anzaldúa 1987, 43; Anzaldúa and Keating 2009, 1).

Anzaldúa's most important contribution, however, was her theory of knowledge, which she described as *la conciencia de la mestiza* (the mestiza consciousness)—an imagination and intellectual posture characterized by a tolerance for ambiguity and contradiction, by a spirit of hospitality that includes rather than excludes difference, and by a resistance to attempts by those in power to control knowledge or define reality. Anzaldúa's most important application of her mestiza consciousness theory is in the field of cultural identity theory, where she challenges reductionistic and essentializing dichotomies of racial, cultural, ethnic, and sexual identity. She argues that our identities are never prepackaged nor fixed; they are fluid and in process. They are marked by plurality and riven by difference. The identities of borderlanders defy simple categories and refuse to stay within rigid borders.

Twoness, Fusion, and Displacement as Dimensions of Latinx Hybridity

Between June 2017 and June 2019, I conducted a series of semi-structured interviews as part of a narrative inquiry (Riessman 2008) of twelve Latinx pastors working in multicultural contexts in or near the city of Los Angeles. Research participants included eight male and four female pastors between the ages of thirty and seventy-eight who self-identified as Salvadoran-American, Mexican-American, Guatemalan-American, Peruvian-American, or Puerto Rican-American. Thematic analysis of these interviews in light of Bakhtin's linguistic hybridization and Anzaldúa's borderlands discourse suggests three interrelated psychosocial experiences for conceptualizing the dynamics of Latinx hybridity: *twoness, fusion,* and *displacement.* I propose that these interconnected experiences operate simultaneously and on a continuum, with each Latino and Latina identifying with each of these three experiences to differing degrees.

Twoness: Fronteras Por Dentro[3]
The experience of twoness takes as its theoretical point of departure Bakhtin's theory of intentional hybridity (a single utterance that contains within it two belief

---

3 "Borders within"

systems). The term twoness originates from W. E. B. Du Bois' (1903) concept of a divided consciousness—"an American, a black; two souls, two thoughts, two unreconciled strivings; two warring ideals in one dark body."[4] In Anzaldúa, twoness is the experience of borders within one's psyche (see fig. 1): "within us and within *la cultura chicana*, commonly held beliefs of the white culture attack commonly held beliefs of the Mexican culture, and both attack commonly held beliefs of the indigenous culture" (1987, 100, 195).

When I was a child I listened to my grandfather, a World War II veteran from the rich farmlands of Iowa, tell exciting stories of how a platoon of vastly outnumbered Marines under the command of General Winfield Scott fought their way from the Port of Veracruz to Mexico City, which they captured to help bring an end to the Mexican-American War. But I also grew up hearing and embracing a different telling of the same story—the tragic story of *la invasión norteamericana* and of how an unprovoked army invaded a peaceful country in an act of naked imperialistic aggression. I learned both stories, and they were both my story.

Twoness is the experience of living with the myths and worldviews of two (or more) cultures informing one's imagination. It feels like having a Mexican-American border running right through my heart and my imagination.

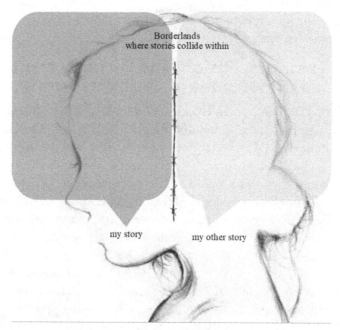

Borderlands
where stories collide within

my story   my other story

Figure I: Twoness as Borders Within

4 Twoness is something of a misnomer since the term implies dualistic or dichotomist conceptions of consciousness. Twoness, in light of Anzaldúa's rejection of binaries and Bakhtin's notion of polyphony, resonates more with Bernice Zamora's pithy dictum, "You insult me, when you say I'm Schizophrenic. My divisions are infinite" (Martínez 1998, 473).

Fusion: Café con leche

Theoretically, fusion is grounded in Bakhtin's notion of organic hybridity and in the creation of new stories through mixing multiple cultural narratives (see fig. 2). For Anzaldúa (1987), the experience of fusion in Latinx identity is like creating a unique tapestry using materials from the multiple worlds we inhabit.

When I was a child, I was often described as *café con leche* when I was introduced by friends and family. My father's dark, indigenous skin tones and my mother's light, Germanic skin tones blended in me, but the mixing was always much deeper than phenotype. I can remember how my mom encouraged me and my siblings to "choose your own culture," and by this she meant we should take the most life-giving aspects of each culture and merge them in our own ways of being in the world.

Where twoness is the experience of a divided or dual identity, the experience of fusion involves a continually mixing identity—that dynamic merger of cultures in one person's life experience.

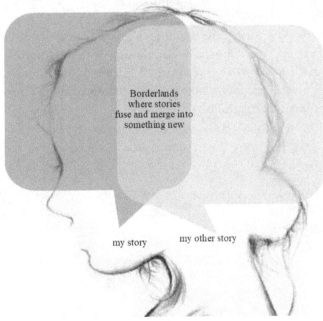

Figure 2: Fusion as Bridging and Creating Something New

Displacement: Ni de aquí, ni de allá[5]

Many individuals never feel fully at home or fully accepted in any single community. I refer to this experience of otherness and alterity as displacement (see fig. 3). For many Latinx scholars, our hyphenated cultural identity is tied up with the experience of being perpetual resident aliens, exiles, and "foreigners

---

5 "Neither from here nor from there"

in their native land" (Weber 2004). Anzaldúa describes an internal psychological experience of displacement using the indigenous Náhuatl concept of *nepantla*—a perpetual state of transition. *Nepantla* refers to "the liminal space between" that "uncertain terrain one crosses when moving from one place to another, when changing from one class, race, or sexual position to another, when traveling from the present identity into a new identity" (Anzaldúa and Keating 2009, 180). Sometimes the displacement is a distance we feel within—a sense of alterity and otherness—and other times the displacement is painfully forced on us when we find ourselves othered and reminded that we don't fully belong.

I was born in northern California, and my family moved to central Mexico when I was in elementary school. I remember the heartbreak I felt, as a fifth-grader, the day my teacher skipped me when my turn had finally come to carry *la bandera* (the flag) for our school's weekly flag salute. Even though I was indistinguishable from my classmates, my teacher explained that I was still an *extranjero* (foreigner, alien) and that the flag I loved was not *really* my flag. Years later, as a college student in the US, I experienced the other dimension of displacement. In the weeks after 9/11, as American flags appeared seemingly on every porch and back bumper, I began to associate the ubiquitous flag with the war fever and hunger for retaliation that swept through my community. I was reminded again that this (other) flag that I loved was not *really* my flag, at least not in the same way that it was for my friends and family whose patriotism and nationalism would always remain a sentiment foreign to me.

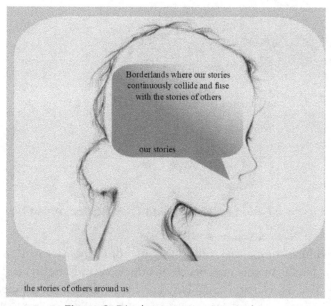

Figure 3: Displacement as *Nepantla*

The twelve Latinx leaders who participated in this study live with the dynamic tension of narratives of two (or more) cultures, and these cultural narratives continuously clash (twoness), coalesce into new shapes (fusion), and change as they are contested and revised in their encounters with the cultural narratives of neighbors (displacement; see fig. 4). By holding in tension the dialectics of twoness, fusion, and displacement, my framework suggests a complex vision of unity in which difference persists and the people of God are invited to lean into the tensions of real diversity without the monological compulsion to melt differences away. This dialectical vision of unity contrasts with the uncritical and assimilative versions of hybridity that perpetuate passive racisms and conceal lingering ethnocentrisms, even as they quietly stifle less powerful voices.

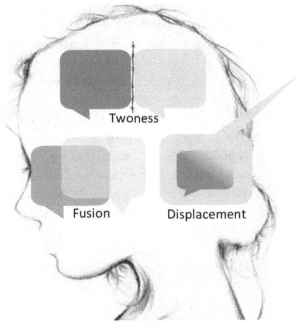

Figure 4: *Experiencias Mestizas*

A Relational Account of Culture

The narratives of these Latinx leaders suggest that missiologists need relational accounts of culture that create conceptual space for the experiences of borderlanders. We need agency-affirming accounts of culture that avoid essentializing, dichotomist, exclusion-oriented, victim-oriented, and boundary-marking configurations of cultural identity. Building on my qualitative research, I propose that a reimagining of culture that's attentive to Latinx experiences of hybridity entails (at least) the four following interrelated dynamics—dynamics that (not inconsequentially) resonate with key themes in Bakhtin's philosophy of dialogue.

1. *Cultural identities are situated.* Identities are tied to relationships, places, and bodies. The shape of one's cultural narratives is inseparable from dynamic constellations of one's relationships, places, and activities. These dynamic constellations are embodied experiences inexorably tied to social, political, and historical contexts.

2. *Cultural identities are shifting.* Our places are continuously shifting due to migrations and relocations. If contextual realities shape the structure and patterns of cultural identities, then it should come as little surprise that one's cultural narratives are only provisionally stable, as they remain linked to shifting contexts. This shifting is also linked to people's creative agency.

3. *Cultural identities are plural.* Communities and individuals experiencing hybridity describe how they navigate multiple (often incommensurate) cultural narratives, indicating that their cultural identities are not monolithic.

4. *Cultural identities are chosen.* Our contexts and relationships shape us, but they do not determine us. Experiences of hybridity can, to a certain extent, be chosen and embraced or muted and suppressed. For instance, survey participants sometimes experienced displacement, twoness, and fusion due to factors beyond their control (e.g., a participant's parents chose to move to a new country), but at other times participants experienced displacement, twoness, and fusion due to their own choices (e.g., a participant chose to fellowship with a congregation of an unfamiliar culture).

Paul Hiebert defines culture as "the *more or less integrated system* of beliefs, feelings, and values created and shared by a group of people that enables them to live together socially" (2009 150; italics added). Hiebert notes that cultures change and experience internal contradictions, but the clear tendency in his system-based conception of culture is toward commensurability—culture as a coherent system ("map") for interpreting reality. Dynamics of contestation and flux represent irregularities and contagions. Hiebert argues that people with belief systems that "contradict one another too much" are torn apart by "cognitive dissonance and the fear of meaninglessness" (2009 151). Nonetheless, the narratives of the Latinx pastors in my study suggest that at least some—and a growing number—of our neighbors' cultural identities are messier than Hiebert's tidy frameworks allow.

Western missiologists need conceptions of culture that address situatedness, flux, polyphony, and agency as *integral* dimensions of cultural identity—conceptions that integrate experiences of borderlands. To this end, I propose that missiologists might reimagine culture(s) as *webs of dialogue (collections of meanings) that are continuously constructed, renewed, and revised through dialogical relationships.*

Critical Contextualization in Light of Hybridity

In his scholarship, Paul Hiebert proposes a missiological bridge between biblical revelation and human contexts. At the heart of this undertaking we discover a simple and accessible method for appreciating cultures while critically evaluating them in light of Scripture: *critical contextualization*. Prominent missiologists from Bosch to Bevans have summarized and drawn on this method for their own work. Chang et al. (2009) maintain that Hiebert's model has been so influential because "it allowed Scripture to function normatively and correct the culture of recent converts" (204). To evangelicals concerned that contextualization might promote cultural relativism and lead to heresy, Hiebert offers a procedure explicitly designed to safeguard against any contextualization that might warp the true gospel.

A simple thought experiment, however, exposes two serious reductionisms embedded in the logic of critical contextualization. The first is related to issues of plurality, and the second is related to dynamics of power. For this thought experiment, I imagine trying to implement the four steps of Hiebert's method in my own context. I am the minister of an urban church in Los Angeles. My congregation reflects the diversity of our neighborhood. In step one of Hiebert's method, the missionary and local church leaders are instructed to engage in a phenomenological effort to understand relevant cultural customs.

Immediately, the first complication presents itself. Whose cultural customs are we evaluating: the customs of the elder from Nigeria or of the deacon from Oaxaca? the customs of the Mexican-American minister or of the Thai-American worship leader? It only grows "messier" when we consider the complexity *within experience*: Should we evaluate the worship leader's Thai customs or her North American customs? If the former, should we focus on the customs she acquired in rural Texas, where she grew up, or on the customs she adopted in California, where she has lived for the last ten years? Globalization and transnationalism trends indicate that the cultural diversification and hybridization of neighborhoods in Los Angeles portend demographic shifts throughout the urban centers of the West and the majority world (Hiebert recognizes these trends; cf. 2009, 118–21); so regardless of whether we live in Los Angeles, Lagos, Lima, or London, our methods should anticipate dynamics of plurality and flux. Unfortunately, Hiebert's method does not.

My faith community embodies a host of diverse practices—practices that we invest with a wide variety of meanings. Here, I note a second major reductionism. In Hiebert's model, the missionary and the church leaders are given the task to determine which Scriptures are relevant (step two), to critically evaluate their own past customs in light of Scripture (step three), and to bring old practices in line with Scripture (step four). In contexts of diversity, the questions that immediately present themselves are Who gets to define what is *relevant, critical,* and *in line with Scripture?* Which is to say, whose interpretive frameworks do we use?

Western theologians have often insisted that disagreements over whose reading is more "biblical" can be solved by recovering the "original meaning" through historical-critical methods. But this ignores not only that we have no direct access to original meaning, since discerning history is never an objective process, but also that historical-critical methods are tools to which wealthier, more educated, English-speaking Westerners have more access (cf. Dyrness 2016, 16–27; Jennings 2010, 136). In the end, it comes as little surprise that dominant conceptions of what is *relevant, critical,* and *in line with Scripture* reflect (pre-)determined and fixed standards that tend to align with the imaginations of those in power.

Our interpretive frameworks are never culturally neutral, yet Hiebert's models consistently overlook power asymmetries. (Hiebert admits this; cf. 2009, 14.) The issue is not only that critical contextualization is ill-equipped to help God's missionary people engage the growing diversity of our neighborhoods. The deeper issue is that Hiebert's model unwittingly perpetuates abuses of power that presume a convergence of opinion or unquestionable authority; such attempts to formalize meaning lead to monologue (Bakhtin) and repression (Anzaldúa). On the surface, then, critical contextualization appears to respect context (situatedness) and make space for differences in ways of thinking and being (plurality). But, in fact, the method hides deeper strategies of paternalistic manipulation and systems of control. It ultimately fails to challenge the hegemonic overlay that plagues Western evangelical missiology.

Contextualization's Distorted Relational Imagination

Latinx experiences of hybridity draw our attention to three critical reductionisms that underlie Hiebert's critical contextualization method: (1) an assimilative theory of culture that fails to incorporate situatedness, flux, polyphony, and agency as integral dimensions of cultural identity; (2) a method of intercultural discernment that fails to create space for real and persistent difference; and (3) an underdeveloped theory of power that fails to address hegemonic asymmetries. Yet these reductionisms represent only a superficial analysis of the real problem. There is a deeply contorted logic at the heart of the contextualization project. This contorted logic is evidenced by the way in which even non-essentializing conceptions of culture, inclusive models of discernment, and liberating uses of power continuously slip back into the same old reductionisms. The problem, I suggest, is that the very questions we ask in this work of contextualization serve to reintroduce those same tired reductionisms. Perhaps the enduring value of hybridity theory lies not so much in its answers to questions of cultural identity as in the way it helps deconstruct the questions and expose those *non-situated* and *unrelational* habits of mind and heart that lie behind the missionary questions that critical contextualization seeks to answer—questions like What does faithful communication of the gospel look like in this culture?

I begin by exploring our situatedness. Building on the theories of Mikhail Bakhtin and Gloria Anzaldúa, I have proposed a vision of culture in which our contexts and relationships shape us but do not determine us. In this vision, our relationships with our sociocultural contexts are dynamic, for "while society helps define a person, a person also helps to (re)define society" (Ochs 1993, 416). This constructionist conception of culture insists that a profound affirmation of our agency can *and must* be held in dialectical tension with a profound affirmation of our situatedness.

The importance of human situatedness falls into stark relief when we begin to unpack certain foundational assumptions of Hiebert's critical contextualization model. Hiebert anchors his method in a critical realist epistemology. Critical realism contends that reality exists and operates independent of our awareness or knowledge of it, but also that, with the right methods, people can make assertions about "what kind of entities actually exist in the social world and what [they are] like" (Archer et al. 2016). Hiebert claims that critical realism is a *post*-postmodern epistemology in that it "moves beyond postmodernism" by developing "metatheoretical models" and "metacultural models" that enable people to compare and translate meaning from one model or culture to another (2009, 28).

Critical realists argue that all human knowledge is a combination of objective and subjective elements. Knowledge is in human minds, so there is a subjective dimension. But Hiebert insists that our knowledge corresponds to the realities of the external world, so there is also an objective, "truthful" dimension to it (1987, 111). Thus, for Hiebert, cultures are mental maps that reflect in fundamental ways the order of reality itself (2009, 28). This theory of knowledge was foundational for Hiebert's proposals, since he believed that without (at least some) direct access to "truth" and "universal reality" there would be no way to judge whether our expressions of the gospel were faithful (biblical) or unfaithful (syncretistic).

At the heart of Hiebert's proposals, however, we discover a deep "forgetfulness of being" (Groome 1998, 75) in the presumption that humans can, through study and critical deliberation, approach a presuppositionless view of reality and set aside our situatedness in order to achieve a metatheoretical position to see truth/reality a little more clearly than (an)other person. From the perspective of the Bakhtinian-Anzaldúan hybridity theory I have proposed above, Hiebert's search for metatheories that can authoritatively translate meaning from one culture to another and judge between cultures is problematic for two interrelated reasons:

1. *Situatedness*: Hiebert's project is anchored in the belief that at some level our search for metatheory can happen independent of the cultural means (e.g., language) used to make sense of those things. There is no metacultural language: We are inextricably situated, embodied, and relational beings.

2. *Polyphony*: Hiebert's project is anchored in a fundamental rejection of polyphony. Hybridity theory insists that even when we agree, and it appears that our voices have converged (as critical realists claim of metatheoretical frameworks), here too we discover a dialogic encounter—we discover twoness. The multiplicity of meanings given for a single word resists efforts at developing metatheory, for the hybridity of our language relativizes the very words used to support our "metatheoretical model and thus deprives it of its naive absence of conflict" (Bakhtin 1981, 368).

The concept of people's situatedness ("place-centered identity") is a key theme in Willie James Jennings' *The Christian Imagination*: "The assumption at the heart of the contextualization project is that the faith of Jesus, the true spirit of the gospel, remains trapped in, first, Jewish culture, and then every other culture since then" (2010, 140). At their core, explains Jennings, Western contextualization projects build on three tragic fallacies: (1) that people are capable of some degree of non-situatedness (or cultural alienation), and consequently (2) that people are capable of prying apart the essence of the gospel from its cultural presuppositions (Jennings calls this a "docetic" mode of thought), and finally (3) that people are capable of then transplanting the gospel to a new culture ("adoptionist thinking").

This profound rejection of situatedness, at the heart of Hiebert's contextualization project, results in two relational tragedies: First, an unrelational habit of mind cultivates and sustains a conception of self that resists the relational risk and vulnerability involved in joining, belonging, connection, and intimacy with our neighbors. Second, an unrelational habit of mind cultivates an intellectual posture that engages neighbors as objects to control and reshape rather than as subjects to whom to listen and from whom to learn. Western missiologists need relational conceptions of mission rooted in a deep awareness that we do not have control over the semantic resonance of the words we use, for our neighbors are neither blank slates (*tabula rasa*) nor empty cups (Freire): they are culture-creators who draw on complex webs of dialogue that are at once situated, plural, shifting, and chosen. We need relational conceptions of missional engagement that willingly lean into the borderlands, refusing to turn away from the messiness and struggles of real, on-the-ground, embodied friendships with neighbors.

I have argued that hybrid cultures and contexts are shifting and moving; but so is the Holy Spirit. Western evangelical missiologies (shaped in the deeply contorted logic contextualization models) have tended to think of the growing pluralism of our neighborhoods as a challenge to overcome, but Latinx experiences of hybridity suggest a very different story. They invite us to reimagine the *borderlands* (those messy spaces marked by twoness, displacement, and fusions) and the *borderlanders* (those complex neighbors with identities marked by plurality and flux) of our neighborhoods as potentialities rather than problems. Why? Ultimately, because the *borderlander Spirit* is present and active in the messy spaces of contestation, collaboration, and critique.

Toward a Misiología Mestiza

Experiences of twoness, fusion, and displacement invite us to a misiología mestiza that shifts our missionary questions from *How can the Christian message be translated into this culture?* to *Where is the Spirit working in the borderlands of our neighborhoods? And how is the Spirit inviting us to participate in this work?* Thankfully, Paul Hiebert was mistaken. Plurality, fluidity, flux, and difference, far from being threats to God's mission, represent relational spaces where God's people can grow in awareness of our situatedness, in epistemic hospitality of conflicting narratives of others, in relational responsiveness to the agency of God and neighbor, and in willingness to step into discomfort for the sake of participating in the Spirit's redemptive initiatives. I end by noting that our experiences of hybridity, in many ways, reflect the activity and presence of the Spirit in the world, who also continuously spills out of our tidy categories and breaks free from our cherished (missiological) frameworks.

References Cited

Anzaldúa, Gloria. 1987. *Borderlands/La Frontera: The New Mestiza*. San Francisco: Aunt Lute Books.

———. 2009. *The Gloria Anzaldúa Reader*. Edited by AnaLouise Keating. Durham, NC: Duke University Press.

Archer, Margaret et al. 2016. "What Is Critical Realism?" *Perspectives: A Newsletter of the ASA Theory Section*. http://www.asatheory.org/current-newsletter-online/what-is-critical-realism.

Bakhtin, Mikhail Mikhailovich. 1981. *The Dialogic Imagination*. Edited by Michael Holquist. Translated by Caryl Emerson and Michael Holquist. Austin, TX: University of Texas Press.

———. 1984. *Problems of Dostoevsky's Poetics*. Edited by Caryl Emerson. Manchester: Manchester University Press.

Bevans, Stephen B. 1992. *Models of Contextual Theology*. Faith and Cultures Series. Maryknoll, NY: Orbis Books.

Chang, Eunhye, Rupert Morgan, Timothy Nyasulu, and Robert J. Priest. 2009. "Paul G. Hiebert and Critical Contextualization." *Trinity Journal* 30 (2): 199–207.

Deck, Allan Figueroa. 1992. *Frontiers of Hispanic Theology in the United States.* Maryknoll, NY: Orbis.

Delgado, Richard, and Jean Stefancic. 1998. *The Latino/a Condition: A Critical Reader.* New York: New York University Press.

Du Bois, W. E. B., and Brent Hayes Edwards. 2007. *The Souls of Black Folk.* Oxford: Oxford University Press.

Dyrness, William. 2016. *Insider Jesus: Theological Reflections on New Christian Movements.* Downers Grove, IL: IVP Academic.

Elizondo, Virgilio. 1983. *Galilean Journey: The Mexican-American Promise.* Maryknoll, NY: Orbis.

———. 1988. *The Future Is Mestizo: Life Where Cultures Meet.* Bloomington, IN: Meyer-Stone.

Gardiner, Michael E. 2004. "Wild Publics and Grotesque Symposiums: Habermas and Bakhtin on Dialogue, Everyday Life and the Public Sphere." *The Sociological Review* 52 (1): 28–48.

González, Justo L. 1990. *Mañana: Christian Theology from a Hispanic Perspective.* Nashville: Abingdon.

———. 1996. *Santa Biblia: The Bible through Hispanic Eyes.* Nashville: Abingdon.

Gonzalez, Michelle A. 2006. *Afro-Cuban Theology: Religion, Race, Culture, and Identity.* Gainesville, FL: University Press of Florida.

Grau, Marion. 2011. *Rethinking Mission in the Postcolony: Salvation, Society, and Subversion.* London: Continuum International Pub. Group.

Groome, Thomas H. 1998. *Sharing Faith: A Comprehensive Approach to Religious Education and Pastoral Ministry: The Way of Shared Praxis.* Eugene, OR: Wipf and Stock.

Hiebert, Paul G. 1984. "Critical Contextualization." *Missiology: An International Review* 12 (3): 287–96.

———. 1987. "Critical Contextualization." *International Bulletin of Missionary Research* 11 (3): 104–12.

———. 2009. *The Gospel in Human Contexts: Anthropological Explorations for Contemporary Missions.* Grand Rapids: Baker Academic.

Isasi-Díaz, Ada María. 1996. *Mujerista Theology: A Theology for the Twenty-First Century.* Maryknoll, NY: Orbis.

Jennings, Willie James. 2010. *The Christian Imagination: Theology and the Origins of Race.* New Haven, CT: Yale University Press.

Lee, Peter, and Harold Godfrey. 2019. "Potential or Threat? Adopting Cultural Hybridity as a Concept for Diaspora Missiology." *The South African Baptist Journal of Theology* 28: 2–14.

Martínez, Elizabeth. 1998. "Beyond Black/White: The Racisms of Our Time." In *The Latino Condition: A Critical Reader*, edited by Richard Delgado and Jean Stefanic, 466–77. New York: New York University Press.

Martínez, Juan Francisco. 2008. *Walk with the People: Latino Ministry in the United States*. Nashville: Abingdon.

———. 2011. *Los Protestantes: An Introduction to Latino Protestantism in the United States*. Santa Barbara, CA: Praeger.

Medina, Néstor. 2009. *Mestizaje: (Re)Mapping Race, Culture, and Faith in Latino/a Catholicism*. Maryknoll, NY: Orbis.

Moon, W. Jay. 2009. *African Proverbs Reveal Christianity in Culture: A Narrative Portrayal of Builsa Proverbs Contextualizing Christianity in Ghana*. American Society of Missiology Monograph Series, book 5. Eugene, OR: Pickwick Publications.

Mulder, Mark T., Aida Ramos, and Gerardo Marti. 2017. *Latino Protestants in America: Growing and Diverse*. Lanham, MD: Rowman & Littlefield.

Ochs, Elinor. 1993. "Linguistic Resources for Socializing Humanity." In *Rethinking Linguistic Relativity*. Edited by John Joseph Gumperz and Stephen C Levinson. Studies in the Social and Cultural Foundations of Language, No. 17. Cambridge: Cambridge University Press. 407-437.Ott, Craig. 2015. "Globalization and Contextualization: Reframing the Task of Contextualization in the Twenty-First Century." *Missiology: An International Review* 43 (1): 43–58.

Pieterse, Jan Nederveen. 2019. *Globalization and Culture: Global Mélange*. Oxford: Rowman & Littlefield.

Resane, Kelebogile Thomas. 2019. "Hybridity, Diaspora, and *Missio Dei*." *The South African Baptist Journal of Theology* 28.

Riessman, Catherine Kohler. 2008. *Narrative Methods for the Human Sciences*. Los Angeles: Sage Publications.

Rodriguez, Daniel A. 2011. *A Future for the Latino Church: Models for Multilingual, Multigenerational Hispanic Congregations*. Downers Grove, IL: IVP Academic.

Shaw, Daniel. 2018. "Beyond Syncretism: A Dynamic Approach to Hybridity." *International Bulletin of Mission Research* 42 (1): 6–19.

Shaw, R. Daniel, and William R. Burrows, eds. 2018. *Traditional Ritual as Christian Worship: Dangerous Syncretism or Necessary Hybridity?* American Society of Missiology Series, Number 56. Maryknoll, NY: Orbis.

Uytanlet, Juliet Lee, and Michael A. Rynkiewich. 2016. *The Hybrid Tsinoys: Challenges of Hybridity and Homogeneity as Sociocultural Constructs among the Chinese in the Philippines*. American Society of Missiology Monograph Series, book 28. Eugene, OR: Wipf and Stock.

Weber, David J. 2004. *Foreigners in Their Native Land: Historical Roots of the Mexican Americans*. Albuquerque, NM: University of New Mexico Press.

Zene, Cosino, 2015. *The Rishi of Bangladesh: A History of Christian Dialogue*. London: Routledge.

CHAPTER 10

Social Action as Christian Social Apologetics:
Through the lives of Pandita Ramabai and Amy Carmichael

ALLAN VARGHESE

Christian apologetics has traditionally been understood as an intellectual endeavor for theologians to provide a rational defense (*apologia*) for Christianity. However, the history of Christian missions demonstrates another kind of apologetics that is often ignored by popular Christian apologists: apologetics through social action. Intentionally or unintentionally, missionaries and pioneering local Christians have used social action and grassroots reform efforts as a reasonable defense for their Christian beliefs. Hence, in this chapter I will put forth a case for social action as apologetics, which I term as *social apologetics*.

To propose the case effectively, first I will evaluate contemporary approaches to apologetics and offer social action as an alternative apologetic method through a concise exegetical analysis of 1 Peter 3:13–16. Second, I will provide a brief account of the lives of Pandita Ramabai and Amy Carmichael, giving attention to their social efforts and ethical living in India that stands as a testament of lived Christianity, where evangelism[1] and social action[2] were held in a holistic nature to provide a social defense (apologetic) for the gospel against social injustices.

1 In this chapter I use the term *evangelism* to denote "an entirely, or mostly, verbal activity" where the gospel of Jesus Christ is proclaimed verbally to "facilitate conversions to Jesus Christ and to Christianity" (Ireland 2015, 14–15).

2 In this chapter I use the term *social action* in reference to "compassionate ministry, Christian ethics, and/or social justice" (Ireland 2015, 15). Although I am aware that scholars have made distinctions between "social action" (compassionate ministry or development work) and "social justice" (a direct effort that influences the political structures), I am not making such distinctions. The phrase "social action" is used in the broader sense to encompass both these nuanced meanings.

Third, based on my discussion of 1 Peter 1:13–16 and the lives of Ramabai and Carmichael, I will provide three tenets of social apologetics, taking into consideration the ambivalent American evangelical relationship between social action and evangelism.

Defining Apologetics as Social Apologetics

The concept of apologetics derives from the Greek word ἀπολογία (*apologia*). It is said to have originated from the judicial system of ancient Greece, where the plaintiff brought an accusation before the court and then the accused had the right to make a reply (*apologia*) to the accusation (Beilby 2011, 11). The response often sought to show the falsity of the accusation (Rosas 1989, 113). This gave rise to the verb *apologesthai*, meaning "to give an answer, legally to defend one's self" (Rosas 1989, 114). In the New Testament, whenever the Greek term *apologia* is used,[3] this concept of *giving an answer* is assumed by readers today.

However, in Christian apologetics, the New Testament idea of *giving an answer* has gone through a process of evolving over history, contributing to its nuanced meaning today.[4] As James Beilby states, modern apologetics involves "an action (defending), a focus of the action (the Christian faith itself), a goal (upholding Christianity as true) and a context (the circumstances in which apologetics occurs)" (Beilby 2011, 13). Subsequently, it has become popular among apologists to assume the primary *action* of defending the faith as solely a philosophical, intellectual affair. However, such a presupposition that neglects any nonverbal, nonphilosophical approaches toward defending or understanding the truth has not only led some to adopt an unfavorable attitude toward the contemporary apologetics enterprise, but it also caused the view that an apologist is "an aggressive, opportunistic person who tries, by fair means or foul, to argue people into joining the Church" (Dulles 2005, xix).

As a response, before abandoning the apologetics enterprise altogether from the missiological landscape, it is important to explore other ways of understanding apologetics. Proposals by Mikel Neumann and Paul Louis Metzger offer such alternative approaches. Neumann proposed an "incarnational approach," where cultural interactions, relational encounters, personal involvement, and long-term commitments take a central role, as opposed to confrontational, propositional, argumentative apologetics approaches (Neumann 2004). Along a

---

3 *Apologia* is used eight times in the Greek manuscripts: Acts 22:1, Acts 25:16, 1 Corinthians 9:3, 2 Corinthians 7:11, Philippians 1:7; Philippians 1:16, 2 Timothy 4:16, and 1 Peter 3:15 (Beilby 2011, 12–13).

4 See Dulles (2005) for a comprehensive introductory reading on the history of apologetics—encompassing Catholic and Protestant views. See Campbell-Jack and McGrath (2006, 1–51) for introductory discussions on Christian apologetics, including its historical progress and current relevance.

similar line, Metzger called for a "relational-incarnational apologetics" (2012, 5), where Christians imitate the incarnational living of Christ by sharing life with the religious other. Apologetics within the context of friendship is one way of engaging in relational apologetics, as James L. Fredericks notes (1998, 169). Such apologetics not only "include rational discussion of God's great ideas and pays careful attention to the context, so the truth is communicated meaningfully to others of different faiths" (Metzger 2012, 12), but also "accompanied, undergirded and energized by lives lived with the people with whom we are sharing" (Metzger 2012, 59). These suggestions from Neumann and Metzger are examples of engaging in apologetics through actions and relations, along with using verbal intellectual persuasion. I am presupposing such an eclectic apologetics approach, where social action is presented as a relational and incarnational way of providing a reason for the gospel.

Canadian scholar John Stackhouse briefly explores the relationship between social action and apologetics in his pursuit to put forth *Humble Apologetics*. Stackhouse says that if the church is to meet "our neighbors" to whom the church is called to witness the gospel, then we are to meet the neighbors "in a manner appropriate to each person's authentic need" (Stackhouse 2002, 206). Consequently, Stackhouse discusses "justice and charity" as other modes of apologetics to consider as "God furnishes the church with the resources necessary to accomplish [the] mission"[5] (206). However, Stackhouse did not explore in detail how such an alternative mode of apologetics is biblically warranted. Therefore, I will turn my attention to explore this question: Does the Bible warrant such a kind of apologetics where social action or "justice and charity" take the lead? I will attempt to answer the question by offering a brief exegetical reading of 1 Peter 3:13–16.

Does the Bible Warrant Social Apologetics?

"Always be ready *to make your defense* to anyone who demands from you an accounting for the hope that is in you" (1 Peter 3:15b NRSV) is often used as the core biblical text for Christian apologetics. Although the verse is taken by apologists to indicate the intellectually driven, verbal act of defending the Christian faith, a contextual reading of the text conveys that there is a social and ethical prelude within the act of apologetics before one gets to the point of providing the verbal *apologia* mentioned in 1 Peter 3:15b.

Verse 13—"Now who will harm you if you are eager to do what is good?"—provides a framework for Peter's apologetic mandate, where it is implied that moral integrity from social engagement is necessary for Christian witness and it

---

5 For Stackhouse, this means to appropriate the gospel based on a person's authentic need.

cannot be easily disputed by unbelievers (see Longman and Garland 2006, 334). The Greek text in verse 13, τοῦ ἀγαθοῦ ζηλωταὶ, which is often translated as "eager to do what is good" (NRSV), can also be translated as "zealots for what is good," conveying the full meaning of the word ζηλωταὶ (*zelotai*), which implies a deeper sense of zealous devotion to doing good frequently rather than just having a desire to do good. In Peter's time, engaging in such good works could be equal to engaging in social action today.

In verse 14a, Peter places the act of social action and justice in the context of suffering. The verse says, "Even if you should have to suffer in the cause of justice, you are blessed" (see Michaels 1988, 185). Peter is not referring to suffering as a hypothetical situation; rather, it is a likely reality that led to Peter's exhortation. However, Peter's appeal here is that Christians should not respond to such suffering by inflicting violence or other ways of retaliation; instead, they should return good works from their "blessed" status.[6] Therefore Peter instructs, "Do not fear their threats; do not be frightened" (verse 14b NIV).[7]

In verse 15a, the readers are reminded to "revere *only* Christ as Lord"—i.e., they should accept Christ as the one determining their lifestyle and attitude toward life (Van Rensburg and Moyise 2002, 280), even in the midst of suffering. It is implied that non-Christians may ask questions about what fuels Christians to engage in morally good social action in the midst of suffering. It is within this context that Peter exhorts believers to "Always be ready to make your defense to anyone who demands from you an accounting for the hope that is in you" (verse 15b). In other words, as Timothy E. Miller observes, the "apologetics opportunities may arise because of one's hope-filled response to suffering for doing good" (Miller 2017, 209). Peter's appeal to the early Christians was to lead an ethical Christian life in such a way that it invites curiosity among non-Christians. It is out of that social and ethical life that Christians are to be prepared to make their case for the hope they have in Christ.

In verse 16, Peter adds the attitudinal qualification of "gentleness and respect" as essential while doing *apologia*. The moral reference to the Christian's mannerism is consistent with the moral basis that guides one's zealousness to do good, implying that maybe "a quiet dignity is far more effective than argument and belligerence" (Longman and Garland 2006, 335). The reference to "keeping a clear conscience" (verse 16) is an indication of yet another reminder to make sure that the charges that are presented against Christians are from their good works and not for their participation in anything unethical.

---

6 For Peter, the Christians who are suffering for doing good are "blessed," which means they are already the "privileged recipients of divine favor" (Michaels 1988, 186), even in suffering.

7 Peter is quoting Isaiah 8:12, which resulted in the word formation in this verse. For more, see Van Rensburg and Moyise (2002).

The contextual exegetical analysis makes it clear that Peter's apologetics mandate has "Christian moral existence" (Hovey 2012, 109) as a precursor for the verbal witness, and it provides a rationale for apologetics driven more by

Social action and ethical living are the first act on the stage for providing the apologia for the gospel.

social action than by proving arguments. The nature of Christian moral existence that 1 Peter 3:13–16 demands is to live a life of love and good works in a manner that presents lives as full gifts for others, especially in suffering, which becomes a testimony of the "hope within" (1 Peter 3:15).

As Craig Hovey puts it, in this kind of living there will not be anything more one could say using words "than the claims our living make" (Hovey 2012, 110). As a result, the apologetic task (verbal defense) becomes "a subset of witness" (Hovey 2012, 111), which is only put to use when asked to provide a reason for the hope and rationale of this social and ethical living. The Christian moral existence becomes the first task of Christian witness, as "witnesses do not dare to point to the truth of something without themselves displaying the life that issues from the conviction" (Hovey 2012, 111). When asked to provide a reason, it is crucial to not fall in the trap of argumentative apologetics; instead, Christians should provide the answer in a manner that is consistent with moral existence—with respect and gentleness.

In summation, a contextual reading of 1 Peter 3:15b demands a Christian moral existence, making it clear that social action and ethical living are the first act on the stage for providing the *apologia* for the gospel. The second act of providing a verbal reason assumes or follows the persuasive nature of the first act. Therefore, when the opportunity emerges for the second act, the only required element is to communicate the reason for the ethical living—i.e., to verbally present the life-giving revelation of Jesus Christ. Argumentative-based apologetics do not find a rationale in the reading of 1 Peter 3:13–16. Just the contrary, as Miller makes clear:

> Peter warns them [the ones who love argumentative-based apologetics] that proper apologetic speech is filled with meekness and respect for the listener. Those who lose sight of pointing to Christ through gracious words and good works may win an intellectual battle ... but lose the war for the unbeliever's soul. (2017, 209)

Such is the biblical premise for what I call social apologetics. However, to solidify my case for social apologetics, it is also important to demonstrate how such action-oriented apologetics might be lived out. Therefore, I will turn our attention to the lives of Pandita Ramabai and Amy Carmichael to illustrate how their lives embody social apologetics as an alternative to traditional apologetics methods.

Social Apologetics through the Lives of Pandita Ramabai and Amy Carmichael

Pandita Ramabai and Amy Carmichael were Christian mission pioneers to India in the late nineteenth and early twentieth centuries who, through their lives, advocated for a holistic approach—social action *and* verbal evangelism. Although they were not intentionally trained or engaged in Christian apologetics, I will make the case that their lives resonate an apologetic witness. Specifically, their social actions carried an apologetics dimension that stood out in their acts of kindness and justice, in contrast to the Hindu-influenced oppressive practices against girls and women at the time.

The Life of Pandita Ramabai

Pandita Ramabai's life of social reform did not begin with her Christian conviction.[8] Instead, it developed out of her "disillusionment with the orthodox Hindu faith" (Kosambi 1992, 63) that she found oppressive toward women. Ramabai, who became the first Indian woman to be named "Pandita" (learned one) at the University of Calcutta (Blumhofer 2003, 154), also founded the reform organization Arya Mahila Samaj in June of 1882, "to correct the androcentric bias inherent in the male leadership" of other liberal Hindu reform organizations at the time (Kosambi 2004, 21).[9]

However, in 1883 during her visit to England—namely, the visit to the Sisters of Wantage—Ramabai's life took an unexpected turn, as she encountered the radical and apologetic nature of applied Christianity. For Ramabai, her visit to the Homes run by Sisters of Wantage did not just provide a social institutional vision, but it provided an ideological imagination, a Christian ontological foundation to build up her reform, in contrast to her existing reformative Hinduism. She saw her Hindu foundations crumbling, as it lacked the restorative principle that she witnessed at the Homes.[10] This experience led her to Christianity and influenced

---

8 Even though Pandita Ramabai spent most of her childhood in the South Indian state of Karnataka, her adult life, and her social reform efforts, were mainly centered in the central and western parts of India. For an introduction to Ramabai from a broad Christian perspective, see Blumhofer (2003, 152–70) and White (2005). From a Pentecostal perspective, see Anderson (2006) and Suarsana (2014). From a feminist perspective, see Shetty (2012) and Kosambi (1992; 2004).

9 During this time, Ramabai published her first book, *Stri Dharma Niti* (1882), articulating her reformative ideas along the line of emphasizing the need for education to empower women. Meera Kosambi translated this work from Marathi to English and published it in 2000. See Ramabai 2000, 35–101.

10 Ramabai writes, "I had never heard or seen anything of this kind done for this class of women in Hindus in my own country. I had not heard anyone speaking kindly of them.... The Hindus Shastras do not deal kindly with these women. The law of the Hindus commands that the king shall cause the fallen women to be eaten by dogs in the outskirts of the town. They are considered the greatest sinners, and not worthy of compassion.... [But] after my visit to the Homes of Fulham ... I began to think that there was a real difference between Hinduism and Christianity" (Ramabai 2000, 307).

her reform pursuits thereafter. For Ramabai, Christianity provided an egalitarian understanding where all are treated equal in the sight of God and salvation is offered freely, in contrast to Hinduism, which "stressed conformance to duty and linked the fruits of one's karma to future rebirths and possible salvation" (Kosambi 1992, 66).

In 1889, Ramabai started a school, Sharada Sadan (Home of Learning), in Bombay, which "was the first ever residential school for high caste Hindu widows and unmarried girls in Maharashtra" (Kosambi 1992, 63). The Sadan's goal was to provide education to women by upholding their equality and dignity and maintaining religious neutrality.[11] However, Ramabai's lifestyle at the Sadan reflected her Christian belief, where she did not keep her daily devotion and prayers a private affair. As Parinitha Shetty notes, "Ramabai's habit of reading the Bible and praying within sight of her institute's residents were seen as a blatant display of her Christianity" (Shetty 2012, 38). Ramabai believed that her lifestyle and social engagement served as evidence of the love of Jesus Christ for her students to see, similar to what the Rescue Home (in England) did for her. Ramabai, in her lifestyle and social engagement, became an embodiment of Christian apologetics.

However, in 1891 Sharada Sadan came under severe scrutiny, as some of the residents converted to Christianity, following Ramabai's path. The accusation of direct proselytization intensified, resulting in the alienation of Ramabai from the mainstream Hindu reform society. In the following months, Ramabai had a fresh experiential encounter with Jesus Christ that made her missionary activity, as Kosambi noted, "obsessive" (Kosambi 1992, 65), actively reaching out to rescue temple prostitutes and engaging in more verbal evangelism. Subsequently, Ramabai established the *Mukti Mission* (Home of Salvation) and a rescue home named *Kripa Sadan* (Home of Mercy), which carried a more evangelistic expression.

After 1891, Ramabai's mission works became more conjoined, with evangelism (as proclamation) and social action complementing each other as she recognized Christ as her "inexhaustible treasure,"[12] which needed to be communicated. Even though the institutions remained as educational and vocational centers for women, her conviction and purpose for these shifted from bringing hope through education (as implied in the name *Sharada Sadan*: "home of learning") to allowing social action to be a preview for others to meet the "inexhaustible treasure," which leads them to salvation (which was typified in the name *Mukti Sadan*, meaning "Home of Salvation"). In other words, Mukti Mission had become a public display of the kingdom of heaven preached by Jesus Christ—a new social order

---

11 Ramabai was careful not to make enemies and thus attempted to maintain religious neutrality. One of the visible marks of this neutrality was seen in "making Hindu and Christian texts freely available side by side" (White 2005, 16) in the institute.

12 In 1907, Ramabai wrote her testimony bearing witness for Christ being the reason for her work so far. She titled this essay "a testimony of our inexhaustible treasure."

where justice was practiced in stark contrast to the injustice around them and a testament for the social effectiveness of the gospel.

Toward the latter part of her life, Ramabai had transformed into a Christian evangelist[13] and a social reformer who embodied effective witness and defense for Christianity. Although Ramabai was able to hold verbal witness and social action together without conflict, her social setting demanded more social engagement, which became the primary means of witnessing to the gospel in the face of lived Hinduism.

While Ramabai engaged in social apologetics in the central and western parts of India, Amy Carmichael led a similar mission in the South Indian state of Tamil Nadu. Even though both Ramabai and Carmichael adopted a holistic mission— evangelism and social action together in their Christian witness—Carmichael's journey toward that realization was different than Ramabai's.

The Life of Amy Carmichael

Amy Carmichael arrived in India in 1882, becoming the first Keswick missionary to be fully sponsored by the Keswick mission committee (Houghton 1955, 51).[14] Carmichael's first book, *Things as They Are* (1905), illustrates her life as an itinerant evangelist missionary in late nineteenth-century Tamil Nadu, traveling from one village to another. Soon Carmichael came to realize that the caste system not only influenced the religious understanding of the Tamils, but it had shaped their "very psyche, thought pattern, and behavior" (Jeyaraj 2005, 224). Carmichael equated this pervading nature of the caste system to electricity, as "it is not merely birth, class, a code of rules, though it includes all these. It is a force, an energy; … hidden as the invisible essence which we call electricity" (Carmichael 1905, 80).

The invisible essence of the caste system was brought even closer to her when she encountered a young girl named Preena on March 7, 1901. Preena had escaped from the "clutches of temple women, (and) came to Carmichael requesting her protection" (Jeyaraj 2005, 222). It was the moment that changed Carmichael's life mission for good. Carmichael had to reconsider her missiological approach, moving from a purely evangelism-based ministry to a social action-oriented Christian witness.

---

13 This is more evident in her address at the Keswick Convention in July 1898. While at the convention, she said, "the Lord led me to ask those present to pray for an outpouring of the Holy Spirit on all Indian Christians… I requested God's people to pray that 100,000 men and 100,000 women from among the Indian Christians may be led to preach the Gospel to their country people" (quoted in Adhav 1979, 216).

14 Amy Carmichael spent her entire missionary life in the South Indian state of Tamil Nadu, which is the neighboring state of Karnataka, where Pandita Ramabai grew up. Although their lives and works were not dependent on each other, Ramabai came across Carmichael's book *Things as They Are* and wrote an endorsement for it. For more analysis of her life and work, see Jeyaraj 2005; Tucker 1999; Sharpe 1996; Daughrity 2008; Elliot 1970. For a more critical and feminist analysis, see McCarthy 2014.

Through Preena, Carmichael entered into the atrocious reality of temple children or temple women, which was perpetuated by the practice of the Hindu caste system.

She writes:

> When first, upon March 7, 1901, we heard from the lips of a little child the story of her life in a Temple house, we were startled and distressed and penetrated with the conviction... . The subject was new to us; we know nothing of the magnitude of what may be called "The Secret Traffic of India"—a traffic in little children, mere infants often times, for wrong purposes. (1912, 247)

The realization of the "secret traffic" reality, which was the *devadasis* ("slaves of gods") system, moved Carmichael to see the importance of social action. Subsequently, as Elizabeth Elliot put it, "The overwhelming desire to save the children became a fire in her bones" (Elliot 1987, 171). Even though Carmichael continued to engage in evangelism as an itinerant, her missional focus shifted to an action-oriented approach of rescuing and taking care of the *devadasis*, girl children who were considered as the "slaves of the gods" (Carmichael 1905, 147).

The devadasi system, which Carmichael encountered through Preena, was a long-standing tradition in Tamil Nadu that could be traced back to the eleventh century.[15] However, as Anandhi points out, "In later years, they had been referred to in day-to-day vocabulary as *thevadial*, a pejorative term representing devadasis as prostitutes" (Anandhi 1991, 739). From the time the young devadasi (before attaining puberty) was married away to a god by the temple priest in the *tali*-tying ceremony,[16] she becomes temple property. Then onwards, the devadasi becomes subjected to the will of her patron—often the temple priest or the ones who took care of the temple income (Brahmins and the high-caste non-Brahmin landlords). The patron "would also act as her sexual partner without having to marry her" (Anandhi 1991, 739).

> The sexual contract between the devadasi and her patron neither ensured her the status of wife nor any say in the household matters of the patron. The offspring of such unions became the children of the devadasis only, without any inheritance claim over the property of their father. (Anandhi 1991, 739)

---

15 Carmichael writes, "Inscriptions show that in A.D. 1004 the great Temple of the Chola king at Tanjore had attached to it four hundred women of the Temple, who lived in free quarters in the four streets round it, and were allowed tax-free land out of its endowments" (Carmichael 1912, 255). For a more socio-historical analysis, see Anandhi (1991).

16 *Tali* is a thread that is tied around the neck of men and women during the Hindu marriage ceremony. The use of *tali* in the devadasi system resembles this marriage system and provides the symbolic meaning of marriage, even though the woman is not being married to a physical person but to a divine one.

Carmichael's mission became to rescue and take care of these young devadasis and the children who were born in the temple, "who are innocent of wrong" (Carmichael quoted in Jeyaraj 2005, 228), but would end up being devadasis if not rescued. Often Carmichael lamented that she "could not legally prove what she knows as truth, because repeatedly she had heard not only 'a cry of tears, but also a cry of blood'" (Jayaraj 2005, 226). Therefore, through whatever means, Carmichael decided to take on the devadasi system and be known as the child-rescuing *amma* (mother), as part of her missionary work, which led to the establishment of the Dohnavur Fellowship.[17]

Carmichael's life and work demonstrate an important missional expression in which social action and evangelism are tied together. Her understanding of mission moved from a purely verbal evangelism framework to a more holistic approach, where her social action ended up being the face of her mission. Carmichael's social setting necessitated that social action would be an expression of applied Christianity and a defense for the uniqueness of Christianity in light of the unjust practices of the time.

Analysis of Ramabai's and Carmichael's Biographical Accounts

Both Ramabai's and Carmichael's lives were examples of lived Christianity, as they held both evangelism and social action inseparably. They verbally proclaimed the good news of Jesus Christ, and at the same time, their life—ethical and social living—spoke loudly.

On one end, Ramabai began her life as a social reformer whose actions prioritized initially, but later, after her spiritual experiences that brought her closer to Jesus Christ, she sought opportunities to engage in evangelism—verbal witness. Nevertheless, in the remaining years, her Christian-influenced social engagement stood as a defense against Hinduism, which perpetuated injustice against women and children. On the other end, Carmichael began as an itinerant missionary who brought the good news of Jesus Christ only through verbal evangelism, but had to incorporate the social-action approach of witnessing as she encountered Preena. Even though Carmichael remained convinced of the conjoined nature (evangelism and social action) of the mission, social action remained as the public face and, at the same time, provided an undeniable defense for the effectiveness of Christianity to bring justice in unjust situations.

However, in speaking of social action as an *apologia*, it should also be made clear that Ramabai's and Carmichael's social actions for justice and love stood as

---

17 In 1901, "Carmichael had moved her mission to a compound covering an area of about 107 acres in Dohnavur, a village about fifteen miles south of Tirunelveli. This became the permanent residence of her mission" (Cho 2009, 358). However, Carmichael remained as a missionary of the Church of England Zenana Missionary Society (C. E. Z.) till 1925. However, in 1925 Carmichael officially parted ways with the C. E. Z., and the compound came to be known as the Dohnavur Fellowship and was officially registered in 1927.

an *apologia* for the good news of Jesus Christ, which strengthened their witness and verbal proclamation. Their lives were an apologetic for Christianity mainly because their actions demonstrated a critical response to the Hindu cultural framework, which let injustice flourish. Simultaneously, their social actions provided an alternative belief system that could bring justice by replacing the social system which was influenced by the Hindu caste system.

Pandita Ramabai's and Amy Carmichael's lives demonstrate that social action inspired by Christianity could be an *apologia,* acting as persuasion without having to provide a verbal, rational argument for the Christian faith. Even though it is essential to use words to clarify the historical truth of Jesus Christ, the argumentative element of providing the historical evidence of the person of Jesus Christ, or the scientific rationality for the existence of God, does not have to come into play as a defense for the Christian faith if social action is present. Ramabai's and Carmichael's ethical living and social action were persuasive to the women and others to consider the good news of Jesus Christ, which leads us to see social action as apologetics.

Christian Social Action as Social Apologetics

To make social apologetics contextual and relevant to the present and future evangelical church, I will present three tenets that encompass the above discussion, while also briefly engaging with the evangelical tendency to divorce social action from evangelism.

Social Apologetics Acknowledges Our Neighbors' Unjust Realities

In an attempt to construct an *Urban Apologetics*, Christopher W. Brooks makes it clear that "Our willingness to embrace the realities of our neighbor's difficulty is what empowers our witness and makes our testimony of Christ effective and hearable" (Brooks 2014, 34). It is vital for Christians to listen actively, engage, and embrace our neighbors' unjust realities in order for them to see the truthfulness of the gospel. Today's unjust realities of our neighbors could vary from racial injustices, gun violence, immigration issues, poverty, human trafficking, sex industry, and so on. Christians should not ignore our neighbors, but listen and acknowledge these social realities to present the gospel through words and actions so that they may know that the gospel can be transformational. Ramabai's and Carmichael's lives are examples of such willingness to embrace the realities of the "neighbor" and demonstrate love and justice in action.

Social Apologetics Demands Action

For both Ramabai and Carmichael, similar to Brooks, "True followers of Christ are duty-bound" to join the cause for the rights of the oppressed and neglected as "the truest and highest expression of Christian ethics" (Brooks 2014, 132). Ramabai and Carmichael lived out their duty in pursuit of social action.

> It is vital for Christians to listen actively, engage, and embrace our neighbors' unjust realities in order for them to see the truthfulness of the gospel.

In doing so, Christ was presented in the application, which provided in itself a social defense for the gospel. Hence Ramabai's and Carmichael's missional model challenges evangelicals, whose primary goal has been to solely "uphold the doctrines of the faith" (Brooks 2014, 132) by negating any social engagements.

Carl Henry, through his 1947 book *The Uneasy Conscience of Modern Fundamentalism*, called for a need to rethink the American evangelical attitude toward social engagement. Nearly seventy-five years later there seems to be an imminent need for another reconsideration, since whenever the thought of social action or justice is brought forward for discussion among evangelicals, the underlying sentiments are "Just preach the gospel," "Only the gospel can change an individual's heart," and "The gospel is the answer to problems of injustice" (see Anyabwile 2019). There seems to be an assumption that the priority of evangelism (verbal proclamation of the gospel) somehow precludes any need for social action in practice. However, as a response to this prioritization, it is necessary to obtain a clear understanding of the holistic nature of evangelism and social action.[18] Social apologetics presupposes such an inseparable nature of evangelism and social action, even when it demands social action as a rightful response in the midst of social problems.

Social Apologetics Advocates for a Better Solution in Addressing Social Injustices
Ramabai's and Carmichael's social action efforts emerged out of their confidence that the Bible provides a better moral framework for pursuing justice. Their social actions— providing education for widows and shelter for orphans, and rescuing young girls from temple prostitution—challenged the systemic nature of injustice perpetrated by the Hindu cultural framework, which was an integral part of their witness and defense of the gospel. Ramabai and Carmichael were not the first people to see these abuses as injustices; liberal Hindu reform groups were also attempting to bring justice. As we see in Ramabai's life, however, those *samajs* (activistic reform organizations) lacked an ontological moral basis to challenge Hinduism. For both Ramabai and Carmichael, Christian faith, informed by the Scriptures, provided such a moral foundation, not only to challenge the injustices perpetuated by Hinduism but also to other political ideologies that sought to bring justice. Therefore, Ramabai and Carmichael served not only as an *apologia* for the Christian faith but also as a better moral solution to injustice. Hence, social apologetics provides a better and alternative ethical and moral solution for contemporary social injustices in which people are continually looking for answers in political and non-Christian ideologies.

---

18 For a brief historical account of the evangelical understanding of holistic mission, see Tizon (2010).

Conclusion

Through an exegetical reading of 1 Peter 3:13–16 and a brief analysis of the lives and impact of Pandita Ramabai and Amy Carmichael, I have put forth a case for social apologetics (social action as apologetics) as a more efficient model of apologetics in contemporary mission practice.

Although 1 Peter 3:15b is understood to be the staple Bible verse for conducting argumentative apologetics, a brief analysis of 1 Peter 3:13–16 makes clear the social and ethical dimension of Peter's apologetic mandate, prompting us to imagine social apologetics. In social apologetics, Christians who are living out their Christian lives in an ethical and social dimension will become apologists. Through their social engagement, they consciously or unconsciously provide a defense for their faith by their "salting effect upon the earth" (Henry 2003, 84).

It is often this salting effect that draws people and persuades them to consider the good news of Jesus Christ. This is the manner in which Ramabai and Carmichael lived out their Christianity in the midst of injustices in India. Their lives became the salt and light for the young women whom they rescued from temple prostitution and taught, eventually leading them to Jesus Christ. Ramabai and Carmichael made sure that they communicated (ministry of evangelism) the revelation and redemption of Jesus Christ to those they touched through social action. Ultimately, they sought eternal salvation for all the young girls they impacted.

Even though I have hinted that social apologetics can be relevant for the American evangelical church, it could be made relevant wherever the church exists in the midst of injustices. Ultimately, Christian social apologetics acknowledges our neighbors' unjust realities as we engage in Christian witness, demand action, and advocate for a better solution for injustices in light of the gospel and biblical framework. Collectively, it offers a persuasive effect for the character of Christianity.

Most contemporary books on apologetics have ignored Christianity's global expansion, as its center—because of large increases in the number of Christians in Asia, Africa, and Latin America—has moved from Global North to Global South. James Beilby acknowledges this reality and sees the lack of engagement as a "challenge for Christian apologetics in the coming century" (2011, 85). Thus far, most apologetics models have been developed and practiced by and large by Christians in the Western world. As a possible remedy for this problem, I have argued that social apologetics built upon Scripture and the biographies of Pandita Ramabai and Amy Carmichael provide a more efficient model for apologetics in the current global setting.

References Cited

Adhav, S. M. 1979. *Pandita Ramabai*. Madras, India: The Christian Literature Society.

Anandhi, S. 1991. "Representing Devadasis: 'Dasigal Mosavalai' as a Radical Text." *Economic and Political Weekly* 26 (11/12): 739–46.

Anderson, Allan H. 2006. "Pandita Ramabai, the Mukti Revival and Global Pentecostalism." *Transformation* 23 (1): 37–48.

Anyabwile, Thabiti. 2019. "An Evangel AND an Ethic." *The Gospel Coalition*, August 12, https://www.thegospelcoalition.org/blogs/thabiti-anyabwile/an-evangel-and-an-ethic/.

Beilby, James K. 2011. *Thinking about Christian Apologetics*. Downers Grove, IL: IVP Academic.

Blumhofer, Edith L. 2003. "From India's Coral Strand: Pandita Ramabai and U.S. Support for Foreign Missions." In *The Foreign Missionary Enterprise at Home: Explorations in North American Cultural History*, edited by Daniel H. Bays and Grant Wacker, 152–70. Tuscaloosa, AL: University of Alabama Press.

Brooks, Christopher. 2014. *Urban Apologetics*. Grand Rapids: Kregel.

Campbell-Jack, W. C., and Gavin McGrath, eds. 2006. *New Dictionary of Christian Apologetics*. Downers Grove, IL: IVP Academic.

Carmichael, Amy. 1905. *Things as They Are*. Pantianos Classics.

———. 1912. *Lotus Buds*. London: Morgan and Scott.

———. 1933. *Gold Cord*. London: SPCK.

Cho, Nancy Jiwon. 2009. "Prophylactic, Anti-Paedophile Hymn-Writing in Colonial India: An Introduction to Amy Carmichael (1867–1951) and Her Missionary Writings." *The Modern Language Review* 104 (2): 353–74.

Daughrity, Dyron B. 2008. "A Dissonant Mission: Stephen Neill, Amy Carmichael, and Missionary Conflict in South India." *International Review of Mission* 97 (384–385): 103–15.

Dulles, Avery Robert. 2005. *A History of Apologetics*. San Francisco: Ignatius Press.

Elliot, Elisabeth. 1970. *A Chance to Die: The Life and Legacy of Amy Carmichael*. Westwood, NJ: Fleming H. Revell Company.

Fredericks, James L. 1998. "Interreligious Friendship: A New Theological Virtue." *Journal of Ecumenical Studies* 35 (2): 159–74.

Henry, Carl F. H. 2003. *The Uneasy Conscience of Modern Fundamentalism*. Grand Rapids: Eerdmans.

Houghton, Frank. 1955. *Amy Carmichael of Dohnavur*. London: SPCK.

Hovey, Craig. 2012. "Christian Ethics as Good News." In *Imaginative Apologetics*, edited by Andrew Davison, 98–112. Grand Rapids: Baker.

Ireland, Jerry M. 2015. *Evangelism and Social Concern in the Theology of Carl F. H. Henry*. Eugene, OR: Pickwick Publications.

———. 2019. "Carl F. H. Henry's Regenerational Model of Evangelism and Social Concern and the Promise of an Evangelical Consensus." *Perichoresis: The Theological Journal of Emanuel University* 17 (3): 25–42.

Jeyaraj, Daniel. 2005. "Amy Carmichael: The Child-Rescuing 'Amma.'" *American Baptist Quarterly* 24 (3): 220–41.

Kosambi, Meera. 1992. "Indian Response to Christianity, Church and Colonialism: Case of Pandita Ramabai." *Economic and Political Weekly* 27 (43/44): 61–71.

———. 2000. *Pandita Ramabai through Her Own Words*. Oxford: Oxford University Press.

———. 2004. "Tracing the Voice: Pandita Ramabai's Life through Her Landmark Texts." *Australian Feminist Studies* 19 (43): 20–28.

Longman, Tremper, and David E. Garland. 2006. *The Expositor's Bible Commentary*. Volume 13. Grand Rapids: Zondervan.

McCarthy, Annie. 2014. "Agency and Salvation in Christian Child Rescue in Colonial India: Preena and Amy Carmichael." In *Divine Domesticities: Christian Paradoxes in Asia and the Pacific*, edited by Hyaeweol Choi and Margaret Jolly, 227–46. Canberra, Australia: ANU Press.

Metzger, Paul Louis. 2012. *Connecting Christ: How to Discuss Jesus in a World of Diverse Paths*. Nashville: Thomas Nelson.

Michaels, J. Ramsey. 1988. *Word Biblical Commentary: 1 Peter*. Volume 49. Waco, TX: Word Books.

Miller, Timothy E. 2017. "The Use of 1 Peter 3:13–17 for Christian Apologetics." *Bibliotheca Sacra* 174 (694): 193–209.

Neumann, Mikel. 2004. "The Incarnational Ministry of Jesus: An Alternative to Traditional Apologetic Approaches." In *Encountering New Religious Movements: A Holistic Evangelical Approach*, edited by Irving Hexham, Stephen Rost, and John Morehead, 25–41. Grand Rapids: Kregel.

Ramabai, Pandita. 1901. *The High Caste Hindu Women*. New York: Fleming H. Revell Company.

———. 2000. *Pandita Ramabai through Her Own Words: Selected Works*. Compiled, translated, and edited by Meera Kosambi. New Delhi, India: Oxford University Press.

Rosas, L. Joseph, III. 1989. "Evangelism and Apologetics." In *Evangelism in the Twenty-First Century: The Critical Issues*, edited by Thom S. Rainer, 113–20. Wheaton, IL: Harold Shaw Publishers.

Sharpe, Eric J. 1996. "The Legacy of Amy Carmichael." *International Bulletin of Missionary Research* 20 (3): 121–25.

Shetty, Parinitha. 2012. "Christianity, Reform, and the Reconstruction of Gender: The Case of Pandita Mary Ramabai. *Journal of Feminist Studies in Religion* 28 (1): 25–41.

Stackhouse, John G. 2002. *Humble Apologetics*. Oxford: Oxford University Press.

Suarsana, Yan. 2014. "Inventing Pentecostalism: Pandita Ramabai and the Mukti Revival from a Post-Colonial Perspective." *PentecoStudies* 13 (2): 173–96.

Tizon, Al. 2010. "Precursors and Tensions in Holistic Mission: An Historical Overview." In *Holistic Mission: God's Plan for God's People*, edited by Brian E. Woolnough and Wonsuk Ma, 61–75. Oxford: Regnum Books International.

Tucker, Ruth. 1999. "Biography as Missiology: Mining the Lives of Missionaries for Cross-Cultural Effectiveness." *Missiology* 27 (4): 429–40.

Van Rensburg, Fika, and Steve Moyise. 2002. "Isaiah in 1 Peter 3:13–17: Applying Intertextuality to the Study of the Old Testament in the New." *Scriptura* 80: 275–86.

White, Keith J. 2005. "Jesus Was Her Guru." *Christian History & Biography* 87: 12–18.

PART 3

Moving Forward
Missiological Models
for Missions in the Future

CHAPTER 11

Old Questions, New Answers:
Tensions of Continuity and Change in Approaches to the *Missio Dei*

ANNETTE R. HARRISON

Christians around the world are working out their participation in the *missio Dei* in innovative ways. This is not unprecedented. David Bosch described six different paradigms which have shaped church theology and mission practice throughout its history. Recent gatherings of mission practitioners have enunciated themes of change within the church's approach to the *missio Dei*—for example, "the challenge of developing adequate mission practice in and from contexts of complexity, uncertainty and change; and the reality of multiple approaches to mission and its practice" (Borthwick 2012, 107). Also, as we consider how to train up the next generation, we meet an increasing list of competencies and skills for missionaries in our current global context. Finally, the faces of the missionary sending force have been changing in recent years because of the global shift of world Christianity.

These are all types of change in the participation of the worldwide church in the *missio Dei*. How substantial are these changes? Are we facing another paradigm shift in church theology and mission practice?

Some elements of the church's approach to the *missio Dei* remain constant despite changes through church ages, global contexts, methods of access, and the identity of the missionaries. These include communicating and living out the Good News of salvation through Christ, urging reconciliation with God, celebrating regeneration by the power of the Holy Spirit, and living in obedience in a new community. Meet the paradox expressed in the French saying, "The more things change, the more they stay the same."

Bosch insisted that "the mission of the church needs constantly to be renewed and re-conceived" (1991, 519), while recognizing that even paradigm shifts may not mean complete abandonment of one set of elements for another: "A paradigm shift always means both continuity and change, both faithfulness to the past and boldness to engage the future, both constancy and contingency, both tradition and transformation" (Bosch 1991, 366). Apparent opposites must be held in "creative tension" (Bosch 1991, 367) as we work toward a renewed and recreated paradigm of (the theology of) mission.

What is being held in "creative tension" at present? This chapter represents a discussion of six constant tensions in how Christians have worked out their participation in the *missio Dei* in their time and contexts. I am presenting each of these tensions in the form of a question, followed by what implications may be apparent for current and future mission practice.[1]

What Kind of Gospel Are We Sharing?

While the concept of sharing the gospel initially appears straightforward, not all Christians in all ages and traditions have interpreted what is being shared in the same way. Even the writers of the four Gospels did not present the ministry or even the identity of Jesus Christ in precisely the same way. Is the gospel good news for the poor and freedom for the captives, as in Luke's Gospel, or is it an announcement of the kingdom of God among us, as in Matthew's Gospel? Do we share a gospel of power and action, as depicted in Mark's Gospel, or of the incarnate *Logos*, as in John's Gospel?

Contemporary scholars, such as David Hesselgrave (2005), have argued for the priority of the proclamation of the gospel over a holistic approach. In contrast, Bosch noted that evangelicals have tended to focus so much on Christ's death on the cross that they have isolated that fact from Christ's life and resurrection (1991, 512–18). Ralph Winter described the attention to social issues, as well as personal salvation, by "First-Inheritance Evangelicals," and later, after the world wars of the twentieth century, the narrowing of focus to only personal salvation in "Second-Inheritance Evangelicalism" (2007, 6–7). Don Richardson went farther

---

1 There are a number of terms that have been used to refer to the church that grew out of European historical contexts and the church in Asia, Africa, and South America. For some, terminological preference seems to depend upon relative positioning on the globe. For example, Alexander Chow has stated a preference for "East" and "West" from the perspective of the church in Asia, while Ruth Padilla Deborst finds "Global South" to be salient for Christians in her context of Central and South America (Stinton 2021). Because a sub-theme for this discussion includes the impact of the global shift of the church, I have chosen to use "Majority" and "Minority" (Borthwick 2012). Other terms include "Post-western" and "Western" (Sanneh 2012), "Global South(ern)" and "Global North(ern) (Jenkins 2002).

to explain that modern evangelicals have also isolated the New Testament gospel message from the Abrahamic Covenant in the Old Testament (2006). Finally, the vibrant spread of Pentecostalism demonstrates that for the Majority Church, the gospel must include the actions of the Holy Spirit (Center for the Study of Global Christianity 2020).

Rather than insist that the gospel only consist of the set of features of God's salvation that are dearest to us and our cultural and denominational context, we would do well to understand and be open to various aspects of the gospel message.

The "relatively simple" concept of sharing the gospel has been a point of tension for Christians through centuries, across denominations, and around the world. The particular opportunities and starting points, and what counts as "Good News" in a given community, may not always look the same, although the same God will be offering the same salvation as he has throughout time. Rather than insist that the gospel only consist of the set of features of God's salvation that are dearest to us and our cultural and denominational context, we would do well to understand and be open to various aspects of the gospel message. It must remain relevant and straightforward to the receptors so that it will be adopted and spread like leaven through the lump of dough (Matt 13:33; Luke 13:20–21), or the announcement by the Samaritan woman to the people of her town, "Come, see a man who told me everything I ever did" (cf. John 4:29 NIV), or the proclamation of mercy and healing by the formerly demon-possessed man (Mark 5:19–20).

For refugees, the gospel may be a welcome and safe haven; for the materially wealthy, the gospel may be the self-sacrifice that brings spiritual riches. In a world of increasingly diverse and divergent, yet interconnected contexts and people, the gospel message must remain locally relevant and easily reproducible (Kraft 1991; Payne 2013, 168–69). It cannot become a theological abstraction. The rapidly growing Majority Church is overwhelmingly poor, and in many places it is emerging in situations of religious persecution and political upheaval. Those contexts make Jesus' words very real and very relevant, as opposed to the comfortable theologies of the prosperous, comfortable Minority Church (Jenkins 2002, 214–20).

As the church becomes more diverse, so too will the gospel aspects that are shared (Sanneh 2013). As Lamin Sanneh has argued, the great missionary strength of the Christian message is that it is translatable (Sanneh 1989). We can be sure that in future mission contexts the gospel will be shared in "life translations" that are unknown today. These ideas will be taken up again in the question of the center of orthodoxy of the church.[2]

2 By "orthodoxy," I mean the points of theological doctrine and biblical interpretation that have been most widely agreed upon and accepted by church leaders through history and tradition.

How Do We Share the Gospel?

Jews want miracles for proof, and Greeks look for wisdom. As for us, we proclaim the crucified Christ, a message that is offensive to the Jews and nonsense to the Gentiles; but for those whom God has called, both Jews and Gentiles, this message is Christ, who is the power of God and the wisdom of God. (1 Cor 1:22–24 GNT)

These verses resonate through time to the current global state of Christianity in which the Minority Church prefers cognitive reasoning and clear explanation of orthodoxy, while the Majority Church seems to respond most to signs and wonders (cf. Jenkins 2002, 8, 67). Despite the theological importance of a well-reasoned presentation based on intellectual evidence, it seems that many people in the world today want living proof more than rhetorical proof. This was demonstrated for me in a discussion with students from the Minority and Majority Churches concerning what we look for in an authentic Christian. The Americans listed preferences associated with orthodox belief—a preference for cognitive reasoning—while students from Papua, Indonesia, preferred evidence in lifestyle as a demonstration of Christian identity.

Even so, at the beginning of 1 Corinthians, chapter 2, the Apostle Paul seems to confirm that to demonstrate God's all-surpassing greatness, the form of our testimony should not be the culturally comfortable one (i.e., reasoned arguments the Corinthians were accustomed to), but the most spiritually powerful one (as in verse 4, NIV: "but with a demonstration of the Spirit's power").

The tension first appears to be whether we share the gospel through reasoning or through signs, but it also reflects further differences among Christians worldwide. For example, the cognitive, reasoned approach to Christianity requires specialized training from professionals, often assuming literacy and written materials. Reliance on signs and wonders does not preclude professionals or written materials, but it may free the Christian message in ways that benefit primarily oral audiences. These audiences also tend to be poor and powerless, and therefore they are often interested in what spiritual power is available and effective to answer their pressing questions and needs.

Another reason I have been thinking about this tension in how to share the gospel is a disagreement I recently witnessed between a Muslim-background believer and a missionary engaged in a Muslim people group. The missionary advocated a kind of contextualization, while the Muslim-background believer perceived this approach as ineffective and even blasphemous, preferring instead a clear use of apologetic argument in ministry to Muslims.

The Enlightenment was not the first age in which Christians argued for their faith, as demonstrated through the Apostle Paul's experiences (e.g., Acts 17) and writings, though the Enlightenment has been held responsible for our current Western commitment to logical points of argument in sharing the gospel. In Bosch's description of a post-Enlightenment paradigm, he mentions the emergence of "narrative theology" and "theology as story" as a potential resolution and a trend toward the introduction of metaphor as a valid approach to expressing and teaching theological concepts (Bosch 1991, 352–54).

Reason and signs of power both have their place, as do metaphor, parable, and narrative. What is easily reproducible by the receptors is the appropriate method. The *missio Dei* does not rely on one way to share the gospel. Instead, we may choose to emphasize one at the expense of the other in certain contexts and at certain times.

One direction in which the "How" question is already being answered is through the emphasis on orality and on narrative. Narrative is one of the most common discourse genres in any culture, especially narrative that speaks to both self-identity and group-identity (cf. Box 2014). Narrative theology is part of the future direction in methods of sharing the gospel (Bosch 1991, 352–54).

Where Do We Share the Gospel?

This question concerns how broad or narrow the task may be. Christ told his disciples that they would be his witnesses "in Jerusalem, and in all Judea and Samaria, and to the ends of the earth" (Acts 1:8 NIV). Although Peter and John were at the forefront of announcing the gospel to the Jews, Samaritans, and Gentiles (Acts 2, 3, 4, 5, 6, 16), they seem to have continually oriented themselves toward Jerusalem. It took the strong motivation of persecution to convince the apostles to leave Jerusalem, and they apparently did not remain in exile for long. Only a few early Christians who are named—Philip, Barnabas, Paul, John Mark—maintained longer periods of time away from the center of Christianity, venturing farther into Gentile territory and away from Israel. Barrett and Reapsome (1988) have calculated that there have been close to 800 "global plans" to reach the entire world (cited in Bosch 1991, 419), yet the church continues to concentrate most manpower and funding in areas of the world where receptors are most similar to the senders and live in cultures affected by Judeo-Christian thinking, and/or where missionaries have been at work for a very long time.

The reluctance to cross geographic and cultural boundaries was also present at the beginning of the modern missions era with William Carey. The church in England and in the United States was very concerned about the social welfare of the poor and marginalized and had little motivation to make the arduous investment of traveling to the "heathen" to announce the gospel.[3] Even so, when missionaries were sent out, they were often sent to colonies or trading posts, thus contributing to the three Cs of their era: Commerce, Civilization, and Christianity. Relatively few broke away from coastal Africa or Asia to travel inland, and then only after decades of work on the coast. Very few left the comforts of colonial style to adopt the dress and lifestyle of those they served—as Hudson Taylor did, for example.

We know more today than previous generations did about the remaining task and about the blocks of people who remain resistant to the gospel or who have no opportunity to even observe a Christian neighbor. The current ease and accessibility of modes of safe and comfortable travel do not even compare with the difficulties faced by people in previous eras. We live in a context like those of epochs before us, in which one nation's or empire's world dominance facilitates access to people (Roman Empire in early Christianity; British Empire in Carey's time; the United States today). My US citizenship allows my visa to be approved for many countries because of the extensive web of treaties and agreements my nation has with other nations of the world. Granted, while access to enter a nation or to travel within a nation may still require courage, creativity, and perseverance, it cannot be considered a serious obstacle.

Some estimate that one-quarter of the world's population are "frontier peoples" (see Lewis 2018); they have no opportunity to meet a Christian (cf. see InterserveUSA.org). I believe the point of the "Jerusalem, Judea, Samaria, and to the ends of the earth" proclamation is that we must go where Christ's gospel has yet to be proclaimed. And we must maintain both centripetal and centrifugal forces (Bosch 1980); the church must remain visible and welcoming, as well as going to places where people have not had the opportunity to hear (Rom 10:14–15).

Cities may be those places in today's world. Urbanization is one of the great demographic shifts of our time. As people leave the restraints of their rural, often religiously conservative home area for urban areas, they come into contact with more ideas and values, and have more freedom to seek out new belief systems (Jenkins 2002, 73–74; Payne 2013, 95–111). Concepts such as the homogeneous unit principle and people groups do not lead to strategies that fit urban settings very well. There are too many populations who mix and mingle. The UN projects that 68 percent of the world's population will live in urban areas by 2050 (United Nations Department of Economic and Social Affairs 2018). The "Status of Global Christianity, 2020" (Center for the Study of Global Christianity at Gordon-Conwell Theological Seminary 2020) summary shows that while the global urban population grew by 2.14% in the last twenty years, the pace of the Christian

---

3 Recall the (in)famous utterance of the older minister: "Sit down, young man. When it pleases God to convert the heathen, he will do it without your help or mine!"

urban population did not keep up at only 1.58% growth. This indicates that more and more Christians are needed in cities to reach the world for Christ.

The final aspect of the question of "Where" we share the gospel concerns generational differences. In so many areas of the world, where Hinduism, Buddhism, and Islam are the dominant religions, the population is young. The presence of a church today does not guarantee a church in the next generation. This is borne out by the striking fact that trends in urbanization and "globalization" seem to affect younger people in the area of religious belief more than they affect older people. The Pew Forum's data show that in Westernized countries such as Canada, Denmark, Australia, and Germany, and in industrialized Asian giants like Japan and South Korea, young people are more likely to be "nones" than to adopt the faith of their parents and grandparents (Pew Research Center 2018). Each generation must be reached.

Someone has said, "All the easy places have been taken." It will take considerable perseverance and ingenuity to reach the large blocs of unreached and unengaged Muslims and Hindus (Lewis 2018) who will most likely live in cities in the near future, many of them young and secular. The "Where" question must now be edited to read, "In what places, to which audiences" so that it captures, in addition to a geographic (and implied ethnolinguistic) dimension, the religious, demographic, and generational dimensions that guide where we share the gospel.

Who Shares the Gospel?

Who is called to share the gospel? Is it necessary to receive a special call or anointing, or is every Christian a missionary? There is evidence that the early church did not consider everyone to be a missionary. A distinction was made between those who ministered the word of God and those who waited on tables (Acts 6:2). William Carey assumed that anyone who became a minister was also potentially a missionary (Walls 1996, 160–61). Hudson Taylor and Charles Spurgeon both made forceful comments in describing the necessity of a passion for the lost (Sills 2015, 301). In our era, John Piper has emphasized that all Christians are goers, senders, or disobedient (Piper and Steller 1996).

Short-term missions may be the one confounding phenomenon: Do participants in short visits count as missionaries? Many short-term teams are not equipped linguistically or culturally to share the gospel appropriately, so instead are limited to performing "good works" in the name of Christ. Even so, some ministries have attempted to harness the enthusiasm and cultural and linguistic capital of Americans to generate contacts and interest for long-term people to follow up with. These efforts point to Paul's one body, many parts metaphor: Each Christian may be able to participate in some way. This raises the additional question of what may be most popular and attractive versus what may be most helpful, strategic, and beneficial to the spread of the gospel. We will return to this question below.

The Center for Global Christianity lists 44,800 denominations and 5,500 sending agencies involved in the *missio Dei* of 2020.[4] As we consider what is helpful, strategic, and beneficial in the spread of the gospel, it is important to realize that the diversity of the worldwide Christian movement means that some Christian groups will believe that others of different theologies and backgrounds still need to be confronted with the gospel. The tension here is what priority to give to Christians sharing the gospel with others who may already consider themselves part of the worldwide family of God. A contentious example includes a consideration of several streams of Christianity: Catholic, Orthodox, Evangelical, and Pentecostal, and how participants in these streams may seek out people from another stream to convert them. An adequate discussion of this important issue is beyond the scope and topic of this chapter, despite its crucial relevance to the "Who" and "Where" questions.

The "Who" and "Where" questions are closely connected. Frank Laubach's strategy of "Each One Teach One" echoes Christ's inclusive "you," as in "You will be my witnesses (Acts 1:8). It also brings to mind Christ's parables of masters who give servants resources to invest (cf. parable of the talents, Matt 25:14–30 and Luke 19:12–27). Each of us, as Christ's servants, has been given talents to invest. The point is that we can each do something as we are able and equipped.

Minority-World Christians, who are willing and able, receive specialized training and raise partners to be sent out through an agency. The rise in "Business as Mission" and other creative access strategies reveals some changes to that paradigm. But the real shift is taking place among Majority-World Christians who are leading the way by going as economic migrants to find opportunities in the midst of daily life in places as diverse as the Middle East and the United States (Borthwick 2012, 89–95). This is a method similar to that used by Moravian missionaries who even attempted to sell themselves as slaves in order to minister Christ in everyday contexts among slaves in the New World (Oldendorp 1982).

As suggested earlier, a complex world calls for creative strategies to access the "Who" and "Where" in order to make the Good News known and available. The movement toward creative access strategies among Minority-World Christians, and a resurgence of the economic migrant method (the original tentmaking model!), in addition to the short-term missions movement, will all continue to be used for the foreseeable future.

---

4 Center for the Study of Global Christianity at Gordon-Conwell Theological Seminary. 2020 "Status of Global Christianity 2020." www.gordonconwell.edu/center-for-global-christianity/wp-content/uploads/sites/13/ 2020/01/Status-of-Global-Christianity-2020.pdf.

There are two important implications here. First, missionaries seem to be relying more on secular training and skills than on theological and cross-cultural training. And, secondly, the growth in the missionary force has been, and will most likely continue to be, among lay persons rather than ordained ministers. The rise in the lay movement has implications for where the center of Christian orthodoxy may lie in the future.

Who Are the Models of Christian Orthodoxy?

Christianity as an historical movement has known a number of splits or schisms due to grave theological disagreements. For example, the Eastern Church separated from the Western Church, and Protestants separated from Catholics (cf. Bosch 1991; Jenkins 2002). Behind the question of Christian orthodoxy is the question of whether the global shift of the church from Minority to Majority may be propelling Christians toward points of friction that may result in another schism. As discussed above, Minority and Majority Christians already demonstrate a preference for different kinds of gospel presentations. These preferences have also shown themselves in theological divergences that are foundational for our missiological views and priorities—for example, the church as bearer of a message of salvation or illustration of God's reign on earth (Bosch 1991, 381); or the church for the edification of Christ's body; or the church for the sake of those who are not (yet) part of the body (cf. Bonhoeffer 1971, cited in Bosch 1991, 375).

The question seems to be how many divergent aspects of Christianity can coexist, and at what level, before some larger division will take place. In the context of global Christianity, there are numerous denominations which differentiate themselves from each other on various points. Do enough commonalities remain to hold the global church together as a movement oriented to a common agreement on orthodoxy and the forms it may take?

The "translatable" (Sanneh 1989) and "essentially contextual nature" of the Christian faith means that deviations from an established form and doctrine may be viewed as heterodoxy, or more often as heresy (Bosch 1991, 421). Furthermore, while we recognize that we are "pilgrims in a strange land" and "not of this world," we are also conditioned by particular features of the "strange land"—the time, place, family, group, society, culture (Walls 1996, 7; see also Jenkins 2002, 44–52). This means that there will continue to be different looking theologies and practices within global Christianity. Walls insists that no one has the right to impose understandings from one context on to those in a different context (Walls 1996, 8), although this has not stopped people from doing exactly that.

In addition to the influences mentioned by Walls (1996), Christians are influenced by religious pluralism and secularism. While the church has always existed in a religiously plural context, religious diversity is increasing within many countries and regions (Bellofatto and Johnson 2013, 158). On one hand, this means that Christians are surrounded by more people who need to hear the gospel. On the other, it means that Christians will begin to have difficulty distinguishing their religious forms and doctrines from those of other religions. One example is the increase in the use of the vocabulary and concept of "mindfulness"; for example, see the Facebook page entitled "Mindful Christianity Today." While a similar idea has existed in Christian traditions as self-examination and meditation, "mindfulness" is a Buddhist concept (Nguyen 2017). The answer to this sort of dilemma is not to backtrack into thinking that the theological traditions and interpretations of Europe and the United States are untainted by other religions. In that arena, scientific secular materialism has had an adverse effect (cf. Jenkins 2002, 202; Wilkens and Sanford 2009, 100–120).

The question of a universal set of orthodox Christian faith statements is an old question; consider the Apostolic Creed and the Nicene Creed, which spurred deliberations and disputes. These creeds were developed in the midst of tumultuous changes to Christianity as a movement in religiously pluralistic and politically fraught contexts (cf. Holland 2019). In current and future contexts, will another creed be enunciated? But this raises yet another question.

In addition to the challenge of maintaining a firm foundation of orthodox faith is the question of where the center of the church is located: Who calls the shots? As soon as Greeks became Christians, there was a "majority" church (Hebrews) and a "minority" church (Greeks) in early Christianity (Acts 6). Likewise, the dominance of Christianity in Europe, and later in "Anglo-Saxon" colonies (America, Canada, Australia), created a "majority" church that remained until relatively recently. Now we are living in a time when Christianity has again shifted, and again the previously "majority" church has become the "minority" church. Those who are the models of Christian orthodoxy will have a lot of influence on the answers to the "What kind of gospel?" "Who?" and "Where?" questions.

As the center of orthodoxy shifts, it may become more and more apparent how much the Minority-World church needs renewal and revival of orthodox Christian beliefs. Indeed, this is already happening to some extent in Europe because of the influx of migrants and refugees from the Majority World, many of whom are free to encounter Christianity for the first time. Nevertheless, the Minority World will continue to influence theological training, and thus Christian orthodoxy, simply because so many of the training institutions are in the Minority World and staffed either by Minority-World theologians or by Majority-World theologians who were trained by Minority-World theologians.

A pertinent illustration is the *African Bible Commentary* (Adeyemo 2006), published in French and English versions. Though a very accessible, valuable, and much-needed resource for pastors in Africa, most of the contributors were trained by European or American theological institutions. The actual theology of the commentary seems to be Minority-World orthodoxy expressed by African theologians. We can expect this to change. With the shift in the global church, a number of writers have noted that the Minority Church will soon cease to be the center of Christian orthodoxy (cf. Jenkins 2002).

As a final point, the emphasis placed on cross-cultural servanthood by writers such as Elmer (2006) and Borthwick (2012) highlights another point of tension between Majority-World and Minority-World Christians. It concerns what could be called devotional strength. How much are we willing to commit and sacrifice in our obedience to Christ and in our participation in the *missio Dei*? Themes such as poverty and wealth, generosity and sacrifice, safety and persecution, are lived out very differently in the two churches. At what point will the relative wealth, ease, and paternalistic pride of the Minority Church make our theologies and practices irrelevant to the Majority Church? Borthwick seems to argue that we are already at that point of irrelevance (Borthwick 2012, 107, 109; see also Sanneh 2013).

These tensions between the Majority and Minority Church shape our respective theologies and practices, directly impacting how we participate in the *missio Dei*.

How Do We Maintain Faithfulness, Integrity, and Truth in Our Witness?

The five tensions discussed so far have all concerned aspects of participation in the *missio Dei* in the world. This last question is much more personal. Who are *we*? Are we witnesses whose commitment and devotion are adequate for faithful integrity and truth in the various contexts, approaches, and methods of ministry? How do we navigate the dynamic of being "in the world, but not of the world" (cf. John 17:14–19; Rom 12:2; 1 John 2:15–17).[5]

The first temptation may be to measure our own strength and achievement, as was King David's experience (2 Sam 24; 1 Chron 21). The danger of counting and measuring goes beyond human pride to mistaking quantity and "effectiveness" for quality and deep change. Justin Taylor cites Luis Bush's differentiation between "transactional things versus transformational things" (Taylor 1997, 22). In our time, it is tempting to default to pragmatic business models and practices, not only in the measurement of programs and progress "on the field," but also in how we treat each other, how we allocate resources and efforts, and how our sending organizations are constituted.

The role and the effects of technology in the *missio Dei* provide a good case study for the dangers of pragmatic, transactional approaches which might sabotage

---

5 Darrell Bock's recent book about cultural intelligence (2020) encourages attention to the tone of our engagement as well as our theological foundations. His discussion is pertinent and relevant to the "cross-cultural" nature of being "in the world, but not of the world."

the goals of qualitative personal transformation. While technological innovations in radio, cell phones, and the Internet allow more virtual contact between people than ever before, several dangers remain. First, we must consider disparities between those who have access to more advanced or complex technology and those who do not (cf. Kraft 1996, 177–79). Another consideration is whether existing or new technology and its limits strengthens the sustainability of a new message or other innovation within a community (cf. Myers 2011, 326–29). Finally, it is crucial to consider the tendency of technological contact to become transactional and impersonal rather than relational and transformational.[6] As mission organizations pivot to accommodate the restrictions imposed as a result of the COVID-19 pandemic, social media apps and platforms will be put to good use. But virtual contact may not come with all of the relational and communicational connections and scope. And it will take dedication and commitment to maintain these long-distance relationships via new technologies and to reach transformational goals.

Another challenge concerns the relative speed, ease, and convenience of ministry strategies. Are we willing to do the hard things today, in faith that there will be fruit in the future? Further, are we able to maintain the centripetal force of faithful witness? Our witness to the world is tainted by moral failings, both in deed and in word. The numerous scandals involving child molestation in the Catholic Church and Protestant mission agencies are one example. Another example comes from a recent survey of church youth groups on the topic of God's requirements for his people. Responses indicate that many teens believe that all God wants from them is to "avoid sex and bring a friend [to church or youth group]." The sentiment in these circles is that "Christianity is not a big deal… . God requires little, and the church is a helpful social institution filled with nice people focused primarily on 'folks like us'" (Kenda Creasy Dean, cited in Reid 2017, section 3). Our faithfulness, our obedience, our belief in Christ, is our principal centripetal witness (Brogden 2014, 92). These are the hard things that bear fruit.

Finally, the short-term missions movement may provide a cautionary tale concerning the maintenance, preservation, and practice of the essential transformational character, the crucial centripetal witness, and the application of faith and belief for future fruit. As mentioned above, there are positive aspects of short-term teams, such as the enthusiasm and some documented evidence of at least momentary reengagement in the local church through volunteering and giving—along with negative aspects, such as the participants not being adequately prepared for cross-cultural witness. Moreover, several scholars and practitioners have documented evidence that involvement in short-term missions does not

---

6 An encouraging counter-example: Embassy, a ministry of the Crescent Project, offers training and support to people willing to cultivate relationships through social media and other connecting technology, such as Voice over Internet applications.

actually serve to increase the number of committed, long-term missionaries (Howell 2012; Priest 2012; Trenda 2018).

Based on these findings, short-term missions in general appear to be essentially transactional in nature. Those moved to travel and volunteer across cultures tend to complete the transaction and then move on to the next one. In other words, there are serious limitations to effective centripetal witness in a short-term missions model (Corbett and Fikkert 2014; Priest 2012). The short-term mission phenomenon in its worst elements may be a demonstration of how much the American church has been infected by the individualism, safety, and comfort adored in our surrounding culture—a reminder for us to be more vigilant in the way we are "in the world, but not of the world." On the other hand, short-term missions, in its best elements, demonstrate the desire for interdependent connection with God's faithful people around the world—a necessary pushback against modern Enlightenment thinking (Bosch 1991, 362). The direction of the short-term mission phenomenon is something to watch in the years ahead; it may provide more telling revelations of the faithfulness, integrity, and truth in our witness.

Conclusion

Are we in line for another paradigm shift in how we participate in the *missio Dei*? Have our new answers to the old questions revealed radical differences? When we wonder what kind of gospel is being shared, we can be fairly certain that the increasing diversity of the church will result in fellow Christians describing and responding to different aspects of the gospel.

When we wonder how to share the gospel, we will continue to meet the tension of head versus heart—of abstract, logical reasoning versus the need for the tangible evidence of signs and wonders in daily life. And narrative will continue to be at the heart of how the gospel takes root and is reproduced in diverse communities.

The question of where we share the gospel retains its geographic and ethnolinguistic parameters, as well as the generational, demographic, and religious dimensions. It is crucial that sharing the gospel remains urgent, whether with frontier peoples or with the next generation at home.

For those who require creative access and long-term residence in another country, specialized training will continue to be appropriate, as well as a mark of difference between the sending practices of the Minority Church and the Majority Church. The point is that each one participates in the *missio Dei* according to his or her ability.

The first four points of tension also show points of continuity, largely because the God of salvation and his plans to glorify himself and redeem the world have not changed. The external variables of sociopolitics, economics, and religious

Are we in line for another paradigm shift in how we participate in the *missio Dei*?

contexts affect to a much smaller extent the choices of the kind of gospel, how it is shared, and to whom and by whom.

Yet, how we carry out effective witness in mission reflects the contexts, values, and priorities of the senders and go-ers. This is why the fifth and sixth points of tension concern faithfulness in doctrine, as well as in character. The changes ahead will reflect the nature of the participants in the *missio Dei*. Christians come from more backgrounds and countries than ever before—the most diverse church and the most diverse missionary force in history. Some aspects of that diversity are wonderful to see: we have more opportunity to learn about and experience God and his kingdom in ways that our own social and cultural contexts have not allowed us to see. Christians around the world are most likely sharing the impact of Christ in their lives in many ways, and in more places, and in more religious contexts than ever before. The strategies of access that have gained the most popularity in recent decades rely as much or more on secular training than they do on theological training. Thus, the missionary force is gaining more laypeople than vocational ministers.

More unsettling is a divergence between the Majority and Minority Churches, which appears to be between the relevant and the irrelevant. Will the relative wealth, ease of life, and available formal training of the Minority Church make those missionary efforts irrelevant to the poverty, difficulties, and practiced faith of people in the Majority World? The lives and witness of the Minority Church have grown easy, while many in the Majority Church have sacrificed and suffered for the sake of the gospel. The authority of their faith and witness will count when it comes to questions of orthodoxy.

The changes in the *missio Dei* reflect a translatable, contextualizing faith: While Christians may belong to a kingdom not of this world, we are nevertheless conditioned by our social and cultural surroundings. Bosch reminded us that the church—and I would say, those who are inextricably involved in the *missio Dei*—is always in the process of *becoming*. The current state of evangelical mission is "both the product of the past and the seed of the future" (Bosch 1991, 422). The old questions and new answers reflect the tensions of continuity and change in the *missio Dei* more than the potential for a paradigm shift.

References Cited

Adeyemo, Tokunboh. 2006. *Africa Bible Commentary*. Nairobi, Kenya: WordAlive Publishers/Zondervan.

Bellofatto, Gina A., and Todd M. Johnson. 2013. "Key Findings of Christianity in Its Global Context, 1970–2020." *International Bulletin of Missionary Research* 37 (3): 157–64.

Bock, Darrell. 2020. *Cultural Intelligence: Living for God in a Diverse, Pluralistic World*. Nashville: B&H Academic.

Borthwick, Paul. 2012. *Western Christians in Global Mission: What's the Role of the North American Church?* Downers Grove, IL: IVP.

Bosch, David J. 1980. *Witness to the World*. New York: Harper Collins Publishers.

———. 1991. *Transforming Mission: Paradigm Shifts in Theology of Mission*. Maryknoll, NY: Orbis.

Box, Harry. 2014. *Don't Throw the Book at Them: Communicating the Christian Message to People Who Don't Read*. Pasadena, CA: William Carey Library.

Brogden, Dick. 2014. *Live|Dead: Joy: 365 Days of Living and Dying with Jesus*. Live Dead.

Center for the Study of Global Christianity at Gordon-Conwell Theological Seminary. 2020. "Status of Global Christianity, 2020." www.gordonconwell.edu/center-for-global-christianity/wp-content/uploads/sites/13/2020/01/Status-of-Global-Christianity-2020.pdf.

Corbett, Steve, and Brian Fikkert. 2014. *When Helping Hurts: How to Alleviate Poverty Without Hurting the Poor … and Yourself*. Chicago: Moody.

Elmer, Duane. 2006. *Cross-cultural Servanthood: Serving the World in Christlike Humility*. Downers Grove, IL: IVP.

Hesselgrave, David. 2005. *Paradigms in Conflict: 10 Key Questions in Christian Mission Today*. Grand Rapids: Kregel.

Holland, Tom. 2019. *Dominion: How the Christian Revolution Remade the World*. New York: Basic Books.

Howell, Brian M. 2012. *Short-Term Mission: An Ethnography of Christian Travel Narrative and Experience*. Downers Grove, IL: IVP.

Jenkins, Philip. 2002. *The Next Christendom: The Coming of Global Christianity*. Oxford: Oxford University Press.

Joshua Project. n.d. "How Many People Groups Are There?" https://joshuaproject.net/resources/articles/how_many_people_groups_are_there.

Kraft, Charles H. 1991. *Communication Theory for Christian Witness*. Maryknoll, NY: Orbis.

———. 1996. *Anthropology for Christian Witness*. Maryknoll, NY: Orbis.

Lewis, Rebecca. 2018. "The Frontier Peoples: Still Waiting to Hear About Jesus." *Mission Frontiers* 40 (6): 6–11.

———. 2020. "Patterns in Long-Lasting Movements." *Mission Frontiers* 42 (2): 8–10.

Livermore, David. 2009. *Cultural Intelligence: Improving Your CQ to Engage Our Multicultural World*. Grand Rapids: Baker.

Müller, Retief. 2013. "The 'Indigenizing' and 'Pilgrim' Principles of Andrew F. Walls Reassessed from a South African Perspective." *Theology Today* 70 (3): 311–22.

Myers, Bryant L. 2011. *Walking with the Poor: Principles and Practices of Transformational Development.* Rev. ed. Maryknoll, NY: Orbis.

Nguyen, Tin. 2017. "The Challenge of Buddhism." Paper presented at Mission Connexion. January, Portland, OR.

Oldendorp, Christian Georg Andreas. 1982. "Missionaries Against Terrible Odds." *Christian History Institute.* https://christianhistoryinstitute.org/magazine/article/missionaries-against-terrible-odds.

Payne, J. D. 2013. *Pressure Points: Twelve Global Issues Shaping the Face of the Church.* Nashville: Thomas Nelson.

Pew Research Center. 2018. "The Age Gap in Religion Around the World." June 13, https://www.pewforum.org/2018/06/13/the-age-gap-in-religion-around-the-world/.

Piper, John, and Tom Steller. 1996. "Driving Convictions Behind Foreign Missions." *Desiring God Ministries*, https://www.desiringgod.org/articles/driving-convictions-behind-foreign-missions.

Priest, Robert, ed. 2012. *Effective Engagement in Short-term Missions: Doing It Right!* Pasadena, CA: William Carey Library.

Reid, Alvin. 2017. "Reaching the Next Generation." *The Exchange Blog* at *Christianity Today*, June 5, https://www.christianitytoday.com/edstetzer/2017/june/reaching-next-generation.html.

Richardson, Don. 2006. *Eternity in Their Hearts*, 3rd ed. Grand Rapids: Bethany House.

Saint, Steve. 2007. "Social Action and Evangelism Don't Compete, They Complement." *Mission Frontiers* 29 (5): 16–18.

Sanneh, Lamin. 1989. *Translating the Message: The Missionary Impact on Culture.* American Society of Missiology. Mary Knoll, NY: Orbis.

———. 2012. *Summoned from the Margin: Homecoming of an African.* Grand Rapids: Eerdmans.

———. 2013. "The Last Great Frontier: Currents in Resurgence, Convergence and Divergence of Religion." *International Bulletin of Missionary Research* 37 (2): 67–72.

Sills, M. David. 2015. "Missionary Call and Service." In *Missiology: An Introduction to the Foundations, History and Strategies of World Missions.* 2nd ed., edited by John Mark Terry, 297–308. Nashville: B&H Academic.

Stinton, Diane. 2021. "The Southern Cross: Navigating New Horizons in 21st Century Global Evangelicalism." A streamed event at Regent College, Feb. 19, in Vancouver, Canada. https://youtu.be/zU5UrExPhQM.

Taylor, Justin. 2010. "Two Essential Gospel Impulses: The Indigenizing Principle and the Pilgrim Principle." *The Gospel Coalition Blog*, October 26, https://www.thegospelcoalition.org/blogs/justin-taylor/two-essential-gospel-impulses-the-indigenizing-principle-and-the-pilgrim-principle/.

Taylor, William. 1997. "The Kingdom Forcefully Advances: What the Future Holds for the Indigenous Movements." In *Supporting Indigenous Ministries*, edited by Daniel Rickett and Dotsey Welliver, 15–23. The Billy Graham Center.

Travis, John Jay. 2015. "The C1-C6 Spectrum After Fifteen Years." *Evangelical Missions Quarterly* 51 (4): 358–65.

Trenda, Corey. 2018. *After the Trip: Unpacking Your Cross-cultural Experience*. Downers Grove, IL: IVP.

United Nations Department of Economic and Social Affairs. 2018. "68% of the World Population Projected to Live in Urban Areas by 2050, says UN," May 16, https://www.un.org/development/desa/en/news/population/2018-revision-of-world-urbanization-prospects.html.

Walls, Andrew. 1996. *The Missionary Movement in Christian History: Studies in the Transmission of Faith*. Maryknoll, NY: Orbis.

Wilkens, Steve, and Mark L. Sanford. 2009. *Hidden Worldviews: Eight Cultural Stories That Shape Our Lives*. Downers Grove, IL: IVP Academic.

Winter, Ralph. 2007. "The Future of Evangelicals in Missions: Will We Regain the Vision of our Forefathers in the Faith?" *Mission Frontiers* 29 (5): 6–15.

CHAPTER 12

Evangelical Mission in an Age of Global Christianity

TODD M. JOHNSON

The topic of this chapter is grounded in the lives of two of my mentors. In 1965, British Anglican missionary David B. Barrett founded, in Nairobi, the Unit of Research of the Church of the Province of East Africa. Barrett began studying the various kinds of Christians and how many there were: first in Kenya, then in Africa, and finally in the rest of the world. In 1982, he published the first edition of the *World Christian Encyclopedia* (Barrett 1982), presenting statistics on twenty thousand Christian denominations in 223 countries of the world. Barrett visited 212 countries in the 1960s and 1970s. In 1989, I joined Barrett in Richmond, Virginia, and we completed the second edition of the *World Christian Encyclopedia* in 2001 (Barrett, Kurian, and Johnson 2001). I moved to Gordon-Conwell in 2003, launching the Center for the Study of Global Christianity. Barrett passed away in August of 2011. In 2019, Dr. Gina Zurlo and I published the third edition of the *World Christian Encyclopedia*, documenting forty-five thousand denominations in 234 countries (Johnson and Zurlo 2019).

Then, in 1974, Ralph D. Winter, professor at Fuller Theological Seminary, gave a seminal talk at Billy Graham's gathering of evangelical leaders in Lausanne, Switzerland. Quite simply, he showed that if every Christian witnessed to his or her neighbor, then one-half of the world's population would not hear the gospel. This was because most neighbors of Christians were Christians and most non-Christians had no Christian neighbors. Consequently, four out of five non-Christians were beyond the reach of the gospel (Winter 1975). To address this shortfall, Ralph and Roberta Winter started the US Center for World Mission in 1976. The Winters then laid out their vision in an academic course and textbook, with dozens of

> Whereas evangelicals in the US tend to focus on issues related to sexuality, and especially to abortion, evangelicals globally are generally equally concerned with poverty, justice, immigration, and social welfare.

contributors, entitled *Perspectives on the World Christian Movement* (Winter and Hawthorne 1981). I took the course in 1981, and then married Ralph and Roberta's youngest daughter, Tricia, in 1983. I also began teaching units of the course, especially the history of the world Christian movement and the current status of global mission.

My reflections hearken back to 1981. That was the year, to the best of our calculations, that for the first time in over a thousand years a majority of Christians were in the Global South (Africa, Asia, Latin America, and Oceania) (Johnson and Ross 2009, 51). It was also the year the first edition of the *Perspectives* textbook presented a compelling case for a world where all peoples had access to the gospel. These well-known facts frame our discussion of evangelical mission today. If you are less than forty years old, your whole life has been lived in this global context.

The unprecedented slope of that 1981 graph guides questions we might ask about both the past and future of mission. Are you living in the past, when most Christians were White, or in the present—and future—when most Christians are people of color? And as we will see, Christianity continues to shift to the South, while many peoples still lack access to the gospel. This is why we can speak of "evangelical mission in an age of global Christianity."

As I mentioned, in 1981, after fourteen years of research, Barrett finished the *World Christian Encyclopedia*, and it was published early in 1982. *TIME* magazine called it a "Miracle from Nairobi" (Ostling 1982). It was the first time that all Christian denominations and traditions were described in the same book. By locating where Christians were living all over the world, the encyclopedia began to answer the question of where Christians were *not* living. Barrett's work intersected with the quest to locate peoples with little or no gospel access. And his ecumenical approach also avoided the problem that evangelicals created when they identified the British Royal Family (Anglicans) and the Norwegians (Lutherans) as unreached peoples.

After eight years of research, Barrett and I completed the second edition of the *World Christian Encyclopedia* in 2001. We identified thirty-three thousand Christian denominations. We also documented a wide range of issues, including martyrdom (half of all martyrs were killed in the twentieth century) and ecclesiastical crime (6 percent of all Christian funds are embezzled by those trusted to steward them).

In 2019, Dr. Gina Zurlo (who wrote her dissertation on Barrett) and I published the third edition. We managed to do a book launch at the Pew Research Center in Washington DC just before the COVID-19 shutdown. Most of what I am sharing in this chapter comes from the findings of this new volume. In addition, we are working on a ten-volume series, the *Edinburgh*

Companions to Global Christianity (born out of our *Atlas of Global Christianity* project). Unlike the *WCE*, these volumes contain essays—350 of them, by the time we are done—from indigenous scholars. The first four volumes, highlighting Africa and Asia, have been published. Producing these very different reference works at the same time has given me much to consider.

Before I share some findings, I will pause to say that the first question I am often asked is "Where do you get your numbers?" In answer to that question, we published *The World's Religions in Figures: An Introduction to International Religious Demography* (Johnson and Grim 2013). We followed this up with a yearbook series, which has recently become *The Journal of Religion and Demography*, a semiannual, peer-reviewed journal. In this line of scholarship, we are paying close attention to source and method.

Global Christianity

Where do Christians find themselves today? In one sense, there isn't much to report since Christians of all kinds have represented about a third of the world's population over the past 120 years. But this doesn't tell the whole story. In 1900, 82 percent of all Christians lived in the Global North, in the historic areas of "Christendom" in Europe and Northern America. During the twentieth century, Christian affiliation decreased in the North and simultaneously increased substantially in the South. In 2020, the Global South represented 67 percent of all Christians in the world, projected to reach 77 percent by 2050. The Global South also has a much larger overall population than the North: over 6.2 billion versus nearly 1.1 billion (Johnson and Zurlo 2019, 8). Momentous change! Needless to say, many of our challenges in mission lie precisely in the shift, because, to oversimplify, although we are no longer a White, European religion, we often act like it.

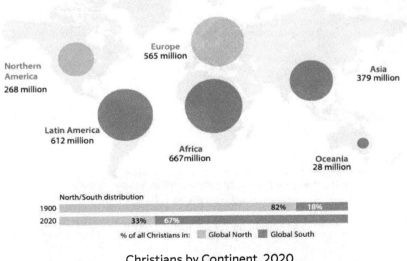

Christians by Continent, 2020

Another way to think about the shift is to look at it on a map. We can chart the southern shift of the statistical center of gravity of Christianity over the past 120 years. This is the point on the earth where there are an equal number of Christians to the north, south, east, and west. Note that it moved steadily southwest through 1950 and then continues southeast after that. This is due to the growth of Christianity in Asia in the latter part of the twentieth century. These points are the results of the relative weight of Christians in 234 countries. The center of gravity today is near Timbuktu, Mali. (Johnson and Ross 2009, 53). I have a colleague who used to there, and when she saw this map she offered to drive a stake in the ground with the sign, "This Is the Center of Christianity." But I told her she would have to get up every morning and move the stake 150 yards toward Nigeria.

For self-identified evangelicals, the shift has been even more profound. In 1900, 92 percent of all evangelicals lived in the Global North, leaving only 8 percent of evangelicals in the Global South. This fell precipitously to only 23 percent by 2020. So fully 77 percent of all evangelicals today are in the Global South (Johnson and Zurlo 2019, 25). This reality runs against the popular perception in the Global North that the United States is the "home" of contemporary evangelicalism, where evangelicalism is largely a White, politically conservative movement. However, the social and theological concerns of most White evangelicals in the US are unlike those of the majority of evangelicals worldwide. Whereas evangelicals in the US tend to focus on issues related to sexuality, and especially to abortion, evangelicals globally are generally equally concerned with poverty, justice, immigration, and social welfare. Evangelicals have shifted more significantly than Christians as a whole. In 2020, nine of the ten countries with the most evangelicals were in the Global South. The United States, the country with the most evangelicals, is the only country in the Global North on the list.

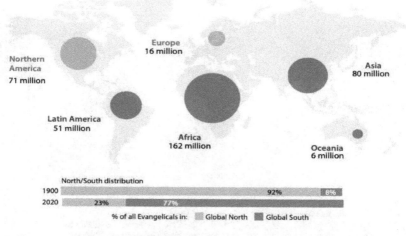

Evangelicals by Continent, 2020

Pentecostals/Charismatics are even more proportionately present in the Global South (86 percent). Depending on how one counts, one-third to one-half of all evangelicals are Pentecostals or Charis-matics, but they are underrepresented in most conferences, consultations, and books. Yet Pentecostals are the best positioned for mission to those currently without access to the gospel. And research has shown that they are deeply engaged in social justice around the world (Johnson and Zurlo 2019, 26).

One of the first questions for us to ask is "How does the shift of Christianity (or evangelicalism) to the Global South impact North American evangelical mission work?" There are a number of ways to consider this question. First, superficially, there are now more Global South evangelicals to recruit for Global North plans. This indeed has been the case for several organizations in the past forty years or so. In technical terms, this is what might be referred to as an "international approach" in which the resources and authority reside in the Global North while the activities take place all around the world. At a deeper level, Christians in Africa, Asia, Latin America, and Oceania are creating their own agencies and plans. The Global North could accept criticism from the Global South about Global North plans and join as equals in new plans. In this case, we are looking at what could be called a "global" approach in which there is no one center, but many cultural expressions with equal authority (Gundling, et. al. 2011, 79–80). This is the polycentric approach—the way forward in an age of global Christianity.

Allow me to illustrate this further. I was at an evangelical conference in Wittenberg, Germany, in 2017 to celebrate the anniversary of five hundred years of the Protestant Reformation. I presented our research, showing that over 40 percent of all Protestants are Africans (Johnson and Zurlo 2019, 24). Out of the hundred people or so at the meeting, only a few were Africans. I was sitting next to a leader from Ghana, when someone from the stage said that Africans were welcome at the table in this evangelical movement. My colleague quietly recounted a Ghanaian proverb to us: "It is good if you invite me to your table, but it is far better if you invite me into the kitchen."

What would it mean to have Africans in the kitchen? Why are Christians from the Global South invited to a Global North table when they should be found with everyone else in the kitchen? Unfortunately, our own global assessment shows Global North dominance in theology, mission, music, and many other aspects of the Christian life. Needless to say, the shift of Christianity to the South should be accompanied by a shift in vision and leadership.

Languages of Christians

The shift of Christianity to the Global South is nowhere more apparent than in the languages Christians speak. Since the mid-twentieth century, Spanish has been the number-one mother tongue of Christians worldwide—not because of Spain but because of Latin America. Number two is English (which includes the British Royal Family!). Third is Portuguese, not because of Portugal but because of Brazil. Fourth is Russian, largely because of the post-Communist resurgence of the Orthodox Church. Fifth is Mandarin Chinese. Christians are mother-tongue speakers of 82 percent of the world's languages, compared with Muslims, the next highest, speaking 25 percent of the world's languages. Tagalog, from the Philippines, is now seventh, having recently passed Polish and German, and almost certainly will pass French soon. In languages eleven to twenty, one finds Amharic (Ethiopia), Korean, Yoruba and Igbo (Nigeria), Cebuano (Philippines), and Tamil and Malayalam (India) (Johnson and Zurlo 2019, 939).

But are indigenous languages and cultures honored in the realm of worship, theology, and biblical studies? Not always, as I discovered when I visited Mongolia in 2018. The church there is barely thirty years old. The Mongolian leadership of the Bible society told me that they know from the Scriptures that their culture and language is valued, but almost everything they sing or read is translated either from the West or from Korea. I met one Mongolian who is writing indigenous hymns, but these face stiff competition from European hymns and Australian choruses. As one of my Korean colleagues told me, "There is no market for indigenous music."

Global Religions

The twenty-first century began with two major unexpected trends in relation to the world's religions. First, despite the predictions of the collapse of religion by leading academics fifty years ago, the world is becoming increasingly religious. In 1970, 81 percent of the world professed a religion. This was the high point of the nonreligious in the twentieth century, just before the collapse of Communism in the Soviet Union. In 2020, 89 percent professed a religion (Johnson and Zurlo 2019, 28). The demographic pivot was the collapse of Communism in the late twentieth century and the opening of China to the rest of the world. China, the world's largest country, has experienced a resurgence of religions of all kinds since the end of the Cultural Revolution (1976). Russia has reclaimed its Orthodox heritage, as have other former Soviet republics in Eastern Europe. Many other countries have experienced a resurgence of religion in the last twenty years, including Albania (formerly the world's only official atheistic country) and Cuba.

Second, the world is becoming more religiously diverse, particularly when measured at the national level. This is especially true in Asia—which has always been the most religiously diverse continent—and beyond, where migration has transformed previously homogeneous societies into more diverse communities. Singapore, home to seven religions that each make up more than 1 percent of the nation's population, remained the world's most diverse country in 2020. In light of these changes in religious demographics, it is also significant to note that Christians and Muslims together represented only 33 percent of the world's population in 1800. Now this is about 57 percent, and is expected to surpass 66 percent sometime before 2100 (Johnson and Zurlo 2019, 28). Consequently, Christian-Muslim relations will increasingly be an important issue in local, national, and international contexts.

Unfortunately, Global North theology was developed in the context of Christendom. Gordon-Conwell Theological Seminary president, Scott Sunquist, points out that both theology and ecclesiology (primarily Protestant) developed as in-house discussions, arriving at a definition of church as an institution among Christians, not as a movement for non-Christians. This is ironic in light of the fact that the Christian faith was born in the context of Christian mission, first in the context of the Roman Empire and then along the Silk Road as far as China. Much of the serious theological work was done where Christians lived as a minority in multireligious contexts (Sunquist 2013, 278).

Asbury Seminary president, Timothy Tennent, is concerned that Western systematic theology textbooks seem tidy and organized and comprehensive, but when carried overseas they have glaring weaknesses, shocking silences, and embarrassing gaps. He writes,

> The basic problem is that Western systematic theologies are still written with a Christendom mind-set, assuming the absence of rival theistic claims as well as rival texts. They tend to be overly preoccupied with philosophical objections to the Christian message, rather than with religious objections based on sacred texts or major social traditions that contradict the claims of Scripture. (Tennent 2007, 256–57)

The Western approach to Christian faith and mission tends to dominate and does not encourage indigenous theological reflection. In our *Edinburgh Companions* series, we are hearing this refrain over and over again. For example, Isaias Paulo Titoce concludes his article,

> The churches in Mozambique are still passing through a transitional period, in which they operate by default on the basis of the legacy left by the missionaries. They need visionary leaders to shape their vision and mission. Their biggest challenge is to achieve a shift from being churches that receive and implement

policies fashioned in the West to being churches that engage in proactive ways with the dynamics of popular culture. Such a shift is needed in order to ground Christianity in the hearts of the people for the benefit of coming generations. (Titoce 2017, 73)

In addition, Christians in the Global North generally are not adept at interacting with people of other religions; yet, with their resource base, they have the most to say about it. A recent study in Singapore found that nine out of ten Singaporeans are comfortable living and working with people of different ethnicities or religions (Wy 2017). In the Global North, similar surveys find results closer to one or two in ten. But it is Christians in the Global North who write most of the books about how people in different religions can get along! Xenophobia and anti-Semitism is also increasing in North America and Europe. Christians in Asia, who are used to living in multireligious contexts, should be leading the way in how to love and interact with people of other religions.

Personal Contact
In relation to world religions, another finding relates to personal contact—focusing on the importance of friendship across religious boundaries. Broadly speaking, Buddhists, Hindus, and Muslims have relatively little contact with Christians, and this has not changed much in the last two decades. An estimated 87 percent of Buddhists, Hindus, and Muslims do not personally know a Christian (Johnson and Zurlo 2019, 29). Hearkening back to Winter's talk in 1974, this finding reinforces the fact that Christians are still separated from those furthest from the gospel.

Do Christians reflect the human tendency to isolate oneself from cultural groups that are different? In the Global North, increasing diversity often brings increasing cultural isolation. The same can be said of the Global South, where people can be isolated by tribe, cultural group, religion, and/or language. Breaking free of this isolation—and perhaps of fear—is essential to the future of mission. If non-Christian peoples are to hear of Christ, Christians must be willing to cross cultures, learn languages, build friendships, and become religiously aware.

Finally, do Christian ministries rely too heavily on non-personal methods of evangelism? The importance of incarnation in a biblical theology of evangelism suggests that the positive contributions of media and technology in evangelism cannot be utilized at the expense of personal contact. Among Muslims, Hindus, and Buddhists, Christians must emphasize placing personal contact alongside appropriate use of non-personal methods of evangelism. One potential consequence of a lack of personal contact is a plateau in the percentage of the world's population that has access to the gospel. We published a graph in *Christianity Today* in 2015 that showed a lack of progress in the future of evangelization, when we were becoming more aware of higher birth rates in peoples who have little or no access to the gospel. Our work on the *World Christian Encyclopedia* has confirmed this suspicion. Christian ministries have much work ahead.

Women

Surveying Christian activities around the world for the *World Christian Encyclopedia*, we were reminded over and over again of the phenomenal contributions of women. Ranging from ordained pastoral leadership to health care and education, women play a vital role in churches around the world. The American missionary movement was majority female in the nineteenth and early twentieth centuries, and female missionaries often performed all the tasks of their male counterparts except to administer sacraments and serve as permanent pastors of churches. Bible women were preachers in their own right and key to the twentieth-century spread of Christianity in the Global South. Women were at the forefront of Pentecostal revivals in India and Chile and served as apostles during the Azusa Street Revival in Los Angeles, helping the early spread of Pentecostalism. It is estimated that the majority of missionaries today, as well as those who actively support them, are women. In short, there is no world Christianity to speak of without the contributions of women (Johnson and Zurlo 2019, 27).

What role will women play in global evangelical leadership? There is strong evidence that the COVID pandemic has been better navigated by women leaders than by men (Taub 2020). Some believe this is because societies that are comfortable electing women to top positions are also more likely to listen to varying points of view. Yet, despite this reality, the vast majority of leaders in evangelical mission are men. Understanding the global Christian context means overcoming this limitation and favoring the voices of women to truly represent what is happening in our communities. By representing the world's cultures, especially those of the Global South, and highlighting the contributions of women, we can begin to comprehend a truly global Christian perspective. Maybe it's time to start asking women for directions!

Integral Mission

Two streams flow from the 1974 Lausanne meeting: a call to address the unreached peoples of the world and a call to minister to the poor and advocate for social justice. The Scriptures, when read in the Global South, are clear in regard to the need for integral mission. Many wealthy people in the Global North read the same Scriptures and see only a need to proclaim the gospel. Evangelicals may diverge in opinion on the place of social activism, but the Scriptures are clear that concern for the poor, the refugee, and the stranger is not optional. Social concern recognizes the inherent value of all humanity based on the concept of *all created in the image of God.* As image-bearers and vicarious representatives of God, the actions of Christians toward others are then to be viewed as actions on

Scriptures are clear that concern for the poor, the refugee, and the stranger is not optional.

behalf of God himself. Doing justice is multidimensional and holistic, and this is pervasive in Scripture.

Christians from the Global South seem to have a more intuitive sense of integral mission. South African Bishop Desmond Tutu said,

> I don't preach a social gospel; I preach the gospel, period. The gospel of our Lord Jesus Christ is concerned for the whole person. When people were hungry, Jesus didn't say, "Now is that political or social?" He said, "I feed you." Because the good news to the hungry person is bread. (Claiborne, et. al. 2010, 71).

Consequently, our assessment of Christianity worldwide documents Christian care for refugees and strangers, for the education of children, especially girls, for health care, especially for those who have little or no access to it, for the alleviation of poverty, for other Christians, and for humanity as a whole, and finally, for care of the earth, especially the impact of climate change in the Pacific islands.

Global Leadership

These findings suggest that a global approach is sorely needed for evangelical mission. In global Christianity, everyone is equal, and everyone is welcome in the kitchen. We belong to a worldwide family, which requires the decentering of Global North ideas (no longer making them the standard) while giving equal status to ideas from around the world. That is more difficult than it sounds, especially when it relates to leadership. In fact, most of the time when you hear the phrase "global leadership," it refers to Global North leadership taught around the world. While Global North leadership texts, translated and distributed abroad, offer helpful information, they cannot represent a truly *global* leadership. We have to recognize the liabilities of leadership concepts that are culture-bound with respect to a world that is all-encompassing, multidirectional, interlinked, and complex.

Global North institutions, seeing these wider realities as an inconvenience, tend to underscore similarities while underestimating differences. For instance, this mindset is manifested in questions such as …

"Aren't we all basically the same?"

"Aren't others becoming more like us?"

"Isn't the world converging toward common standards?"

In other words, most Global North leaders assume—either directly or by default—that leading a global organization is not very different than leading a local or regional organization: that the same approaches apply to securing resources, building and motivating teams, creating and applying new models, understanding and serving different situations, and so on. What Global North leaders don't realize is that the Global North position is not neutral in a global context. It can actually cause harm.

BBC polling seems to suggest that a majority in Global North countries are less interested in considering themselves as global citizens, while those in most Global South countries are embracing this identity (Grimley 2016). Christianity is a global religion, so it makes sense for Christians to embrace a global identity. And, as I'm suggesting, it is critical for the future of mission. But rising nationalism in the Global North might be moving us in the wrong direction.

White nationalism, in particular, has a toxic impact. Christians in the United States have a legacy of mistreatment of Blacks and of Native Americans, whose cultures were usually seen as inferior and not worthy of Christianity. Slaves and Native Americans were often beaten when they sang or spoke in their mother tongues. This is the antithesis of good missiology—and even more so, of the Christian gospel. Recent research, such as Robert P. Jones' new book, *White Too Long*, has shown, unequivocally, that the residual effect of this White supremacy still exists in structural racism in the United States. Despite some improvements, people of color and Native Americans are severely disadvantaged. Nonetheless, seven out of ten White evangelicals believe that Whites are just as disadvantaged as Blacks (Jones 2020, 155–66). Such poor intercultural awareness would seem to be a disqualification for providing leadership for a global missionary enterprise.

Reading While White

One of our Gordon-Conwell graduates, Esau McCaulley, recently published a book entitled *Reading While Black: African American Biblical Interpretation as an Exercise in Hope*. Esau's book revealed to me that what I have been doing all these years when I read the Bible is "Reading While White" (although one would have to look long and hard to find a book with that title). I remember my surprise when, after reading the Bible through many times as a teenager, I discovered that I treated the English word *you* as a singular pronoun—referring to *me*—when, in fact, nearly all uses in the Hebrew and Greek are as plural pronouns. Yet it is assumed that "Reading While White" is normative, and that "other groups" read with their own perspective. Esau diagnoses the problem when he states that "everybody has been reading the Bible from their locations, but we are honest about it" (McCaulley 2020, 20).

Do we really want our missiology to be based on the dishonesty behind the myth of a race-less, contextual-less, correct reading of Scripture? I, for one, am grateful for Richards' and O'Brien's *Misreading Scripture with Western Eyes*, which offers specific examples of the hazards of "Reading While White."

While this is certainly a crisis for White evangelicals in the United States, it has also become a global problem. In *Rediscipling the White Church*, author David

Swanson says that White Christians cannot simply add diversity to their churches (or mission agencies) to become global. Instead, they have to admit that there is such a thing as White Christianity; and because it is tied to wealth, power, and privilege, they need to relearn their faith in humility in order to work as equals with the rest of the world's Christians (Swanson 2020). This is very likely the path that we will need to take in order to be *global* (representing the various cultural perspectives of evangelical faith) instead of *international* (promoting Western evangelicalism around the world).

Conclusion

Global approaches respond in a manner that is both biblically faithful and culturally relevant. Global leadership recognizes the complexity of serving in a cross-national, cross-cultural context. A new set of skills is required to navigate today's complex world. Global leaders can identify and call on different individuals who together possess all the pieces necessary to make the vision a reality. In the context of a truly global Christianity, evangelical leadership training must value indigenous perspectives, as opposed to parroting those of the Global North.

While the Global North (a minority of Christians) still speaks with the loudest voice, Christians of the Global South (the majority of Christians) are producing new and exciting perspectives on leadership, delving into different cultures and connecting them to address the world's most pressing issues. These perspectives differentiate a global organization, one that is polycentric in its decision-making, from an international organization, which radiates its leadership from its home country. Which is your style of leadership? Global leaders and their organizations will be the ones that show the way to mutuality and solidarity in our endeavors.

Nigerian theologian Victor Ezigbo captures this well when he writes,

> Christianity is not truly global by its mere presence in many countries of the world. It is truly global when two criteria are met. First, the local communities of the world's nations are given the freedom to rethink and re-express Christianity's teaching about God's relationship with the world through Jesus Christ. And second, the local communities see themselves as equals, conversing and critiquing each other and contributing theologically to Christianity's long tradition. (Ezigbo 2014, 88)

These two criteria are precisely what evangelical mission needs in order to navigate a global future. We need to learn from the global church and from indigenous and diaspora Christians. Only a global approach will lead us into the future so clearly shown in the Scriptures—where all peoples worship in their own languages and Christians work together for the alleviation of human suffering, giving special attention to the poor. That is a future that we can embrace together.

References Cited

Barrett, David B. 1982. *World Christian Encyclopedia: A Comparative Survey of Churches and Religions in the Modern World.* First ed., New York: Oxford University Press.

Barrett, David B., George T. Kurian, and Todd M. Johnson. 2001. *World Christian Encyclopedia: A Comparative Survey of Churches and Religions in the Modern World.* Second ed., New York: Oxford University Press.

Claiborne, Shane, Jonathan Wilson-Hartgrove, and Enuma Okoro, eds. 2010. *Common Prayer: A Liturgy for Ordinary Radicals.* Grand Rapids: Zondervan.

Ezigbo, Victor Ifeanyi, and Reggie L. Williams. 2014. "Converting a Colonialist Christ: Toward an African Postcolonial Christology." In *Evangelical Postcolonial Conversations: Global Awakenings in Theology and Praxis,* edited by Kay Higuera Smith, Jayachitra Lalitha, and L. Daniel Hawk, 88–104. Downers Grove, IL: InterVarsity Press Academic.

Grimley, Naomi. 2016. "Identity 2016: 'Global Citizenship' Rising, Poll Suggests." *BBC News* April 28, https://www.bbc.com/news/world-36139904.

Gundling, Ernest, Terry Hogan, and Karen Cvitkovich. 2011. *What Is Global Leadership? Ten Key Behaviors That Define Great Global Leaders.* Boston: Nicholas Brealey.

Johnson, Todd M., and Brian J. Grim. 2013. *The World's Religions in Figures: An Introduction to International Religious Demography.* Oxford: Wiley-Blackwell.

Johnson, Todd M., and Kenneth R. Ross, eds. 2009. *Atlas of Global Christianity.* Edinburgh: Edinburgh University Press.

Johnson, Todd M., and Gina A. Zurlo. 2019. *World Christian Encyclopedia.* Third ed., Edinburgh: Edinburgh University Press.

Jones, Robert P. 2020. *White Too Long: The Legacy of White Supremacy in America.* New York: Simon & Schuster.

McCaulley, Esau. 2020. *Reading While Black: African American Biblical Interpretation as an Exercise in Hope.* Downers Grove, IL: InterVarsity Press.

Ostling, Richard, and Alistair Matheson. 1982. "Counting Every Soul on Earth: Miracle from Nairobi: The First Census of All Religions." *TIME* Magazine, May 3.

Richards, E. Randolph, and Brandon J. O'Brien. 2012. *Misreading Scripture with Western Eyes: Removing Cultural Blinders to Better Understand the Bible.* Downers Grove, IL: InterVarsity Press.

Ross, Kenneth R., and Todd M. Johnson, series eds. 2017–2025 (projected). *Edinburgh Companions to Global Christianity,* 10 volumes. Edinburgh: Edinburgh University Press.

Sunquist, Scott W. 2013. *Understanding Christian Mission: Participation in Suffering and Glory.* Grand Rapids: Baker Academic.

Swanson, David W. 2020. *Rediscipling the White Church: From Cheap Diversity to True Solidarity.* Downers Grove, IL: InterVarsity Press.

Taub, Amanda. 2020. "Why Are Women-Led Nations Doing Better with Covid-19?" *New York Times,* May 15.

Tennent, Timothy C. 2007. *Theology in the Context of World Christianity: How the Global Church Is Influencing the Way We Think About and Discuss Theology.* Grand Rapids: Zondervan.

Titoce, Isaias Paulo. 2017. "Mozambique." In *Christianity in Sub-Saharan Africa*, vol. 1, *Edinburgh Companions to Global Christianity*, edited by Kenneth R. Ross, J. Kwabena Asamoah-Gyadu, and Todd M. Johnson, 67–73. Edinburgh: Edinburgh University Press.

Winter, Ralph D. 1975. "The Highest Priority: Cross-Cultural Evangelism." In *Let the Earth Hear His Voice*, edited by J. D. Douglas. Minneapolis: World Wide Publications.

Winter, Ralph D., and Steven Hawthorne, eds. 1981. *Perspectives on the World Christian Movement*. First ed. Pasadena, CA: William Carey Library.

Wy, Abigail Ng. 2017. "Building Bridges to Greater Interfaith Understanding." *Straits Times*, April 1.

APPENDIX

Lessons in Mission Strategy from the Last Fifty Years:
Thirty Mission Trends, Movements, and Models

Luis K. Bush and Tom Steffen

Mission models sometimes produce movements that have impacted the cause of Christ. This appendix reviews some of the models that have resulted in thirty mission trends over the past fifty years. These trends are demonstrable by patterns of growth in diverse places over at least one decade. Habakkuk's inspired prophecy anticipates the day when "the earth will be filled with the knowledge of the glory of the Lord, as the waters cover the sea" (Hab 2:14 NIV). As God's servants, we follow his prophet's mandate to look, see, and wonder as we consider his workings in and through his people in recent times.

We recognize that biblical missiology informs these trends while remaining "surrendered to Scripture to maintain its distinctive contribution" (Steffen 2003, 131). We are indebted to respected missiologists who evaluated each major mission trend to ensure they met the criteria for inclusion. Other mission trends fit the selection criteria, but were not included for security reasons. The mission trends are listed sequentially by date, with a brief accompanying explanation.

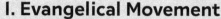

I. Evangelical Movement

Evangelicalism arose during the First Great Awakening, in the eighteenth century, as pastors and church leaders emphasized personal salvation rather than ritual and tradition. Evangelicalism inspired the rise of missionary societies in the nineteenth century. In the twentieth century, evangelicals turned their attention to applying gospel principles to social, political, and economic issues.

Evangelicalism, whose adherents have tripled in the last fifty years is defined by Bebbington (1989) as including four characteristics: conversionism, activism, biblicism, and cricicentrism. "Evangelicals," notes Patrick Johnstone, "were only just beginning to emerge from a half-century of marginalization; but from then on Evangelicalism became the most dynamic belief system in the world and its fast-growing numbers put it at the center of global Christianity" (Johnstone 2011, 130).

2. Pentecostal & Charismatic Movement

Pentecostalism has roots in the nineteenth-century Holiness Movement, which promoted personal piety. Within the Pentecostal movement, Christians sought direct personal experience with God through the baptism with, or in, the Holy Spirit. Charles Fox Parham was instrumental in the formation of Pentecostalism.

Pentecostal-type revivals broke out in Korea and India and beyond at about the same time as the 1906 Azusa Street Revival in Los Angeles. Pentecostal and charismatic Christians together make up about 26 percent of all Christians and more than 8 percent of the world's total population (Zurlo et al. 2019).

In the 1980s, Pentecostals surpassed all other Protestant groups to become the largest Christian body globally, with more than one out of four Christians and almost one out of ten of the world's total population.

3. Church Growth Movement

The Church Growth Movement, started by Donald McGavran, postulates that effective evangelism starts (not ends) with a homogeneous unit (a social-cultural division of a people group) and results in people movements.

Donald McGavran launched the School of World Mission and Institute of Church Growth at Fuller Theological Seminary in 1965, focusing on methodology. He claimed, notably, that "the great obstacles to conversion are social, not theological. . . . People like to become Christians without crossing racial, linguistic or class barriers" (McGavran and Wagner 1990, 156, 163).

McGavran, known as the "father of the church growth movement," wrote two classics. First, his book *The Bridges of God* (1955) laid the foundation for the movement. He posited that the theological foundations for church growth is the task of finding the lost and making disciples. He explained that the ethical criteria for the movement should be whether it produces church growth. And he established the missiological basis for the movement in the behavioral sciences, because they provide understanding for how people become Christians, i.e., through family "bridges" and kinship ties ("homogeneous units").

McGavran's *magnum opus* was *Understanding Church Growth* (1970). Here he laid out the principles of church growth, adding a plethora of new terms—e.g., conversion growth, quality growth. His protégé, C. P. Wagner, opened the door to US pastors and expanded the curricula to include prayer and spiritual warfare.

4. Lausanne Movement

The Lausanne Movement mobilizes evangelical leaders, connecting influencers and ideas to collaborate for world evangelization with a vision of the whole church taking the whole gospel to the entire world.

In the aftermath of Edinburgh 1910, Billy Graham pioneered a form of grassroots cooperation in evangelism that bolstered ties with evangelical leaders worldwide, thereby providing support for global undertakings. With those relationships, he was able to catalyze global support for the Lausanne Committee for World Evangelization (LCWE) in 1974. There Graham called for clarification of the relationship between evangelism and social responsibility. He expected the congress to reaffirm that witness included word and works. The seeds of the Lausanne Movement had just been planted.

Lausanne '74 broadened the meaning of the term *mission* previously articulated by John Stott. Stott's position had changed since Berlin '66; he now believed that the Great Commission included social and evangelistic responsibility, as both are inextricably linked.

The Lausanne Covenant reads, "World evangelization requires the whole Church to take the whole gospel to the whole world" (Stott 1974, para. 6). This led to the Consultation on the Relationship Between Evangelism and Social Responsibility, cosponsored by the LCWE and World Evangelical Fellowship (WEF) in 1982.

5. People Group Model

The People Group Model primarily focuses on the "10/40 Window" of the world within which most unreached people groups live. The Lausanne Committee for World Evangelization defines a people group as "the largest group within which the gospel can spread as a church planting movement without encountering barriers of understanding or acceptance" (Johnson 2001, 91).

Ralph Winter introduced the concept of "unreached people groups" at the 1974 Lausanne International Congress on World Evangelism. He spoke of the overwhelming need of the gospel to be preached to unreached people groups, since no indigenous church existed to evangelize them.

Winter highlighted that out of the estimated 24,000 people groups in the world, 17,000 remained unreached. This shocked many Christians.

Winter's revelation launched a new era of missions (Snodderly and Moreau 2011) focused on the dual concepts of:

- viewing the earth's inhabitants in terms of people groups instead of nation states, and
- recognizing that a different kind of cross-cultural evangelism was required to reach them.

A paradigm shift within mission strategy reawakened the world mission movement. Completing the Great Commission's task became the most significant assignment of the world church. For Winter's contribution to missions, *TIME* magazine selected him as one of the 25 Most Influential Evangelicals in 2005. The complexities of humanity have challenged the UPG paradigm.[1]

6. Integral Mission Model

The Integral Mission Model incarnates the values of the kingdom of God and witnesses the love and justice revealed in Jesus Christ through the power of the Spirit for the transformation of human life in all its dimensions, individually and communally.

At Lausanne '74, Samuel Escobar and Rene Padilla introduced the concept of "integral mission" in their plenary sessions titled "Evangelism and Man's Search for Freedom, Justice, and Fulfillment" and "Evangelism and the World." The congress would take a definitive step in affirming an integral mission as the church's mission.

---

1 See *EMQ,* 56 (4) 2020.

Integral Mission, also called holistic mission, references the task of bringing the whole of life under Jesus' lordship. This affirmed that no biblical dichotomy exists between evangelistic and social responsibility. Integral mission is expressed in *shalom*, enjoying harmony with God and one's neighbor and God's creation (Padilla 2004).

Prerequisites that qualify a church to practice integral mission include:

1. Commitment to Jesus Christ as Lord of everything and everyone;
2. Every member of the church is called to discipleship as a missionary lifestyle;
3. The church confesses Jesus Christ as Lord and lives in the light of that confession; and
4. The church commits to the use of spiritual gifts to fulfill its vocation.

7. International Orality Movement

The International Orality Movement (ION), launched by the International Orality Network, is an affiliation of agencies and organizations partnering to make Scripture available to oral communicators in culturally appropriate ways that produce church-planting movements.

The modern-day orality movement debuted in 1981 in Pattaya, with New Tribes Mission (NTM). Trevor McIlwain spoke daily about Chronological Bible Teaching, an evangelism-discipleship church-planting model focused on Bible stories.

One result of the NTM conference was the highly viewed EE-Taow video (1989). Jim Slack, researcher with the International Mission Board (IMB) in the Philippines, heard of the model and had McIlwain introduce it to IMB in 1983. Slack and J. O. Terry (IMB) then propelled the model into a movement within IMB and beyond.[2]

In 2001, Avery Willis and Paul Eshleman helped initiate the Oral Bible Network (OBN), comprised of fifteen agencies. In 2004, the Lausanne Committee for World Evangelization organized the Issues Forum in Pattaya, Thailand, resulting in "Making Disciples of Oral Learners" (Issue Group 2004). The rural movement had now reached urban settings.

The Making Disciples of Oral Learners Working Group merged with OBN in 2005 to become the International Orality Network (ION), offering training and materials for those reaching oralists (by situation or choice).

---

2 For an historical overview of the orality movement, see Steffen (2018) and ION (n.d.).

8. The COMIBAM Movement

The COMIBAM Movement serves the Ibero-American missionary movement, representing more than 27,000 missionaries from Latin America, Portugal, and Spain, in collaboration with other alliances, churches, and agencies worldwide.

"From a mission field to a mission force" was the rallying cry of Ibero-Americans taking their place among the world harvesters (Bush 1997). After years of receiving missionaries, God was transforming Latin America into a mission base from which thousands would be sent to the world's unreached peoples. In 1987, in São Paulo, Brazil, some three thousand Latin American leaders decided to be a light to the nations. COngresso Missionera IBeroAMericana (COMIBAM) was launched.

In 2017, COMIBAM celebrated its fourth congress. About 1,800 mission leaders met in Bogota, Colombia, to evaluate the fruit of the missionaries to better equip and serve them. They agreed to:

1. Strengthen the missiological foundations of the Ibero-American mission community through biblical reflection and research;
2. Discuss challenges facing the missionaries and senders, and consider ways to grow and modify mission practice;
3. Present mission opportunities and the need to increase mission participation with increased effectiveness; and
4. Encourage deepening relationships to increase unity and collaboration in the regional and global mission movement.

9. The AD2000 Movement

The AD2000 Movement is a global, informal network of Christian missionary agencies, denominations, churches, and individuals committed to world evangelism, with the goal of a church for every people and the gospel for every person by the year 2000.

At Lausanne II in 1989, John Stott, noting that the year 2000 had become a challenging milestone, asked, "Can we commit ourselves to evangelize the world during the last decade of this millennium? There is nothing magical about the date, yet should we not do our best to reach this goal?" (Lausanne Movement 1989). Denominational leaders at the summit agreed to work together to evangelize the world by AD2000.

The AD2000 Movement served as a Great Commission catalyst to focus on the unreached (Bush, AD2000 as a Great Commission Catalyst). It incorporated the following operating principles: 1) seeking to listen carefully to what God is saying to us, 2) thinking outside the box, 3) a pioneer spirit with new ideas, 4) respond to the responders, 5) based primarily on relationships, 6) grassroots, bottom up, and 7) own and control nothing.

As the movement extended beyond 2000, Ralph Winter called the AD2000 & Beyond Movement *"the largest, most pervasive global evangelical network ever to exist"* (Winter 1993, para. 4; italics in original). The AD2000 & Beyond Movement is a movement of God for the people of God.

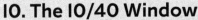

10. The 10/40 Window

The 10/40 Window puts the spotlight on regions of the Eastern Hemisphere, plus the European and African part of the Western Hemisphere, located between 10 and 40 degrees north of the equator, an area with the highest level of socioeconomic challenges and least access to the Christian message and Christian resources on the planet. More than five billion people, representing more than two-thirds of the world's population, live in the so-called 10/40 Window.

The 10/40 Window mission focus came about in the early 1990s, as missions leaders recognized that the least evangelized people and countries worldwide live there. These people have the lowest quality of life in terms of life expectancy, infant mortality, poverty, and literacy. Eighty-four percent of all the unreached people groups live in the Window. More than ninety percent of the frontier groups, which are less than one percent Christian, make their home in the 10/40 Window (Bush 1998). Jesus said, "From everyone to whom much has been given, much will be required" (Luke 12:48 NRSV).

11. Joshua Project Model

Joshua Project helps define the unfinished task of fulfilling the Great Commission by encouraging the global missions movement to focus on unreached people groups.

Inspired by the Unreached People Group Movement, Joshua Project began in the mid-1990s with a partial listing of about 1,750 of the largest unreached people groups.

In the early 2000s, the Joshua Project list was expanded to become a comprehensive global people group list. Many new unreached people groups were documented for the first time. Today the list has 17,400 people groups, 7,400 of which are still considered unreached.

The dual concepts of 1) viewing the earth's inhabitants in terms of people groups instead of nation states, and 2) recognizing that a different kind of cross-cultural evangelism was needed to reach them, represented a paradigm shift within mission strategy that has been unparalleled in the twentieth century and beyond.

Increased gathering and analysis of data has brought greater clarity to the unfinished task. For the last twenty-five years, Joshua Project has helped the global missions movement focus on unreached people groups.

12. The Saturation Church Planting Movement
The Saturation Church Planting Movement works nationally to involve most Jesus followers working together for the purpose of multiplying churches in all of that nation's geographic, ethnic, and cultural spaces.

When Discipling a Whole Nation (DAWN) launched in Europe in the 1990s, excitement and skepticism reigned. There was great excitement about the whole church being mobilized for saturation church planting, using best practices learned from DAWN. And there was great skepticism about the strategy's adaptability on a secular continent.

Twenty years later, DAWN no longer existed on Europe's radar, much less the world's. It came, and landed, but failed to conquer the old continent. Or did it?

In 2010, church leaders met in Oslo to discuss current national church-planting processes in their respective nations. France, for example, planned to plant one church for every ten thousand inhabitants. But how? A similar national strategy had already been in place in Norway. Norway, then, was able to help France advance the ball. That gathering produced a framework to help develop National Church Planting Processes (NC2P) across Europe (NC2P n.d.). As of 2020, twenty nations are involved. One can only wonder … Is NC2P a revised DAWN?

13. Women in Mission Leadership
Today more than 60 percent of Western missionaries are women. Many, like Sharon Mumper of Magazine Training Institute, are founders of mission organizations.

Mary Vijayam, seeing the challenges women faced in a stratified Indian society, cofounded TENT (Training in Evangelism Needs and Technology). Simultaneously, she saw the potential Christian women have in the church, missions, and community. Mary began a program exclusively for women at TENT, named Indian Women in the Lord's Labor (IWILL), where women receive training in witnessing for Christ to bring spiritual, social, and economic transformation. Through IWILL, Mary trained more than 1,200 grassroots-level women and 450 undergraduate-level women from India and Nepal.

From Kenya, Judy Mbugua became a successful manager in a large insurance company in Nairobi, even with five children. On the side, she started Home Care, inspiring thousands of Christian women to pray for their unsaved husbands.

14. MANI—Mobilizing African National Initiatives

The Movement for African National Initiatives (MANI) is a grassroots movement committed to catalyzing the African body of Christ to strategically partner to disciple the nations and to send Africans in mission around the world.

MANI was birthed when 320 delegates from thirty-six African nations met in Jerusalem for the African Millennial Consultation in 2001. Building upon the AD2000 & Beyond Movement, these African leaders affirmed God's mighty work across the continent and committed to accelerating the gospel's advance through networking and collaboration.

Participants shared the divine conviction that Africa's hour had come to take primary responsibility for the final gospel thrust in Africa and beyond. Recognizing that the AD2000 & Beyond Movement was disbanding, the delegates determined to establish a continuing African movement. They therefore unanimously adopted the "Jerusalem Declaration," affirming their commitment to carry the torch for national and global evangelization.

MANI's purpose is to affirm, motivate, mobilize, and network Christian leaders and churches by inspiring them with the vision of reaching the unreached and least-evangelized in Africa, and beyond.

15. Majority-World Mission Movements

Majority-World Mission Movements demand more interconnectedness and interdependence to advance God's kingdom in our generation.

Patrick Johnstone wrote, "The whole paradigm of missions has now changed. The old, Western ways of forming relationships and strategies and working in the field will no longer do now that missionaries are being sent out from all over the world. Increasingly, everyone will need to deal with multiple initiatives aimed at the same populations; agencies and networks will have to cooperate across cultures, and multicultural teams will become the norm" (Johnstone 2011, 228). The West began to notice this movement around the 1970s.[3]

---

3 Larry Keyes and Larry Pate, "Two-Thirds Missions: The Next One Hundred Years," *Missiology: An International Review* 21 (1993): 187–206. Larry Keyes and Larry Pate discovered that by the early 70s over two hundred Majority-World agencies existed with over three thousand missionaries. And those numbers continue to climb. For a more recent resource, see Enoch Wan and Michael Pocock, eds., *Missions from the Majority World: Progress, Challenges, and Case Studies*. Pasadena, CA: William Carey Library, 2009.

16. Acceleration of Bible Translation
The Acceleration of Bible Translation began with the 1999 Wycliffe Bible Translator's international convention "Vision 2025" that called for a Bible translated in every language group that needed one.

During the 1990s, God's Word and Literature Resource Network, led by Lars Dunberg and Dick Eastman, proposed the following: "Mobilize and encourage networking among Bible societies, Bible translation agencies, media, literature, and related ministries committed to evangelizing and discipling the unreached to systematically provide all people access to God's Word in their language" (Bush 1993, 56).

At the Wycliffe Bible Translators International's convention in 1999, delegates boldly called for "Vision 2025." "Motivated by the pressing need for all peoples to have access to the Word of God in a language that speaks to their hearts, and reaffirming our historical values and our trust in God to accomplish the impossible; we embrace the vision that by the year 2025 a Bible translation project will be in progress for every language that needs it" (Cornelius and Niemandt 2013).

Bible Translation is on pace to be completed in 2042. With new translation methodology, crowd-sourcing, and technology speeding up the process, with Para Text software's emergence, non-copyrighted translations were forthcoming faster than previously. We are the first generation that can genuinely say the Word of God may be available in every language that needs it.

17. Praying Through the Window Movement
The Praying Through the Window Movement promotes worldwide prayer initiatives to galvanize God's people to engage in fervent, focused prayer for people living in countries with the highest socioeconomic challenges and least access to the gospel and Christian resources.

"Praying Through the 10/40 Window" began in 1991. A year later, a group met at Every Home for Christ in Colorado Springs to discuss ways to organize a global prayer movement to penetrate the 10/40 Window. Bev Pegues, interceding in the room next door, organized the first Praying Through the Window.

In 1995, the AD2000 United Prayer Track networked with others to develop Praying Through the Window II, focused on the one hundred "Gateway Cities" of the 10/40 Window. More than 35 million intercessors participated. In 1997, Praying Through the Window III focused on unreached people groups, with nearly 27 million intercessors from 121 nations. In 1999, Praying Through the Window IV returned to its roots to pray for Window countries.

The Praying Through the Window emphasis of focusing intercession on the 10/40 Window and sending prayer journey teams proved to be an effective means of motivating churches to preach the gospel everywhere until every nation knows the glory of Christ's love.

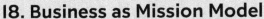

18. Business as Mission Model

The Business and Professional Network was launched at Global Consultation on World Evangelization (GCOWE) '97. One model that emerged was BAM, which seeks to fulfill the creation mandate as both medium and message. BAM demonstrates love and righteousness through the development of God-given capacities, encouraging Great Commission companies, developing kingdom entrepreneurs, and celebrating business for blessing.

Paul's tentmaker role regained popularity in the late 1990s through Business as Mission (BAM). BAM models are diverse. Addressing multiple needs, they

- provide lay businesspeople a frontline missions role;
- provide holistic hope for the least-reached peoples;
- provide new ways to create sustainable wealth (see Deut 8:18);
- create jobs, rather than take or fake them;
- move beyond gaining family riches to kingdom-expansion wealth;
- move beyond microenterprise to the macro, providing stronger income sources;
- fund missions at home and abroad;
- train expatriates and locals in sustainable, profit-making BAM; and
- transform societies through establishing God's reign within and without the workplace (Steffen 2017, 13)

BAM has become an international movement, with different tributaries, as the Lord has moved the hearts of businesspeople. Closed mission fields have opened to business in this season of globalization.

19. Global Cities/Urban Mission Models

Global Cities and Urban Mission Models increasingly frame our missional calling as a primary field of missions, with more than one-half of the world's population living in cities. Cities have rapidly increased in importance to global missions in the last fifty years, due to the population growth from 650 million to 2.58 billion. The percentage of urban population has also increased significantly, from 36.6 to 56.2 percent. The number of cities of over one million population has risen from 145 to 579 (Zurlo et al. 2019).

Today, we are more likely to minister in a city than a rural setting. In the 1980s, Ray Bakke developed a theology of the city that reoriented missions.

Cities are both "collection points," providing missionaries the opportunity to reach people from many different ethnicities in one place, and "launching points," from which servants of God return to their peoples.

In a collaborative initiative with Transform World Movement in 2009, Tim Keller hosted engaged Christian leaders from the world's seventy most-influential cities. Providing a Global South perspective of the urban mission's challenge, Atul Aghamkar, based in India, wrote *From Periphery to the Center: Re-conceptualizing Urban Mission in India* (Aghamkar n.d.).

20. Bi-Vocational Mission Movements
Bi-Vocational Mission Movements are growing, with the recognition that the whole church is vital to God's missional work globally.

A Barna report, produced in partnership with the International Mission Board, lists three ways mission work is changing:
1. what constitutes success for a missionary;
2. the losing appeal of donations; and,
3. the redefined role of the missionary. Missions like OM and IMB are increasingly engaging in bi-vocational missions (Barna Group 2020).

Who better to model this vital message on the mission field than bi-vocational workers? Informed by this data, agencies and assemblies will be better equipped to select and train personnel for the future of missions as they seek to make disciples of all nations.

2l. Finishing the Task (FTT) Coalition Model
Finishing the Task Coalition seeks to fulfill the Great Commission, based on Matthew 28:19, determined by an autonomous, flourishing, reproducing church-planting movement, that no longer needs outside help, in every people group by the year 2030.

Finishing the Task (FTT) is a movement of 1,600 churches and organizations to reach the Unengaged, Unreached People Groups (UUPGs) with no Bible access to believers. FTT defines the fulfillment of the Great Commission of Matthew 28:19 as a self-sustaining, flourishing, reproducing church-planting movement in every ethnos (people group).

The mission of FTT is to form a global network of local churches, denominations, church planters, and mission agencies that are willing to work together in partnership to see church-planting initiatives launched among the remaining Unengaged, Unreached People Groups (UUPG).

When Paul Eshleman assumed FTT leadership from Marcus Vegh in 2007, he established the first finish line for FTT to accomplish, sending full-time workers in every people group.

Rick Warren now leads FTT. We are entering a new era in the movement—one of a broader vision and greater partnership, where we reach toward the goal of Bibles, believers, and bodies of Christ for everyone, everywhere.

22. World Inquiry Listening Model

World Inquiry Listening Model seeks to discern what God's people are saying regarding the challenges, current realities, obstacles, and opportunities to advance God's kingdom purposes where they reside.

As the AD2000 Movement drew down, the question arose, "Where do we go from here in world evangelization?" By examining Scripture, theology, missiology, church history (including global conferences), and Christian leadership, catalytic impulses were observed, resulting in a God-given purpose (Bush 2003b).

The World Inquiry took place from 2002 to 2004, involving almost seven thousand Christian leaders from 850 cities representing many countries. Sponsored by Fuller Seminary in collaboration with the Lausanne Committee, the results were presented at the Lausanne Issues Forum in Pattaya in 2004 (Bush 2002).

The findings of the three-year inquiry were presented at the World Evangelization Issues Forum in Pattaya in 2004:

1. our world is changing radically: demographically, economically, politically, and religiously;
2. the winds of change are intensity swirling around the Christian world; and
3. emerging streams are converging in movements.[4]

The World Inquiry signaled the emergence of a new paradigm—transformation, which led to the Transform World Movement from 2005 to 2011 and the Transform World 2020 Handbook (Transform World n.d.).

---

4 See India Inquiry 2020-2021 and India Inquiry Report 1.0 2020-2021.

23. The Transform World Movement: 2005–2020

The Transform World Movement calls God's servants to act as catalysts on a mission of transformation as a unifying, converging, committed core in response to the challenges of regional cultural influences.

Six months after meeting in London, where the mission mandate became "catalyze and connect God's servants to work together in mission as transformation by sharing people resources, by consultations, prayer efforts, communication materials and case studies of models of transformation," the first global Transform World took place in Jakarta in 2005.

Phase I (2005–2011) of Transform World Connections (TWC) mission was to connect people and nations who shared the transformation vision. The basic idea was that more could be done together than separately, as the participants sought to express Jesus' lordship over all of life.

Phase II (2012–2020) of the Transform World Movement, led by Daniel Kim, furthered Phase I. Each of the challenges continued: Islam; the family; orphans; poverty, justice; Christ's missional and celebration challenges. Respective Transform World 2020 catalysts focused on their geographical regions as they facilitated generational transformation among the nations.

24. The 4/14 Movement

The 4/14 Movement commits to reach, rescue, root, and release this generation of 4/14ers into the dream of God for their lives. Motivated by the love of Jesus, Christian leaders worldwide committed themselves to reach, rescue, root, and release children from ages 4 to 14.

Participants in the New York launch in 2009 resulted in national 4/14 initiatives worldwide, with the commitment to speak up for those who cannot speak for themselves (see Prov 31:8). Their challenge is to raise a new generation from the 4/14 Window to transform the world.

Various strategic tracks helped develop strategies to mobilize 4/14ers as full partners. They developed concrete plans for their colleagues in their nations across the world to raise a new generation to transform the world. As Jesus said, "Let the little children come to me, do not hinder them, for the kingdom of God belongs to such as these" (Luke 18:16 Berean Study Bible).

25. World Without Orphans

The World Without Orphans Movement (WWO) exists for every child to grow up in a safe and loving family and reach their God-given potential. It calls and equips national leaders and churches to collaborate to solve their own country's children crisis.

Starting in Ukraine in 2010, it became a global movement, with initiatives as of 2020 in thirty-eight countries with forty-seven emerging partners. In 2010, Ukrainian leaders committed to a nation without orphans. The vision spawned multiple grassroots initiatives to spread to other countries.

In 2016, WWO organized its first Global Forum in Thailand, with 480 participants from 69 countries. A second forum followed in 2019, with more than 500 participants from 80 countries. Through broad-scale collaboration, a comprehensive tool resourced WWO's vision—"Roadmap: Foundations for Active Engagement." In 2020, WWO joined with others in response to the Parenting for Lifelong Health initiative.

26. The Honor-Shame Movement

Honor-Shame Movements recognize that this moral value is a dominant theme in Scripture and for most people globally, whether in rural or urban settings. Participants, therefore, attempt to view the Bible, live, relate, and communicate with honor and shame in mind, without minimizing other moral values that may be within a given culture.

While the moral values of honor-shame dot the landscape of Scripture and societies, for most Western missionaries these values remained off the radar screen till around 2000. Blinded by the strong legal language of innocence-guilt, the relational language of honor-shame tended to be overlooked. This resulted in evangelism, discipleship, leadership, theology, prayer, counseling, business, and music models that failed to highly impact strong honor-shame societies.

Jason Georges (pseudonym) helped change this oversight by starting HonorShame.com, which offers numerous helpful resources. In 2017, the first Honor-Shame Conference was held at Wheaton College, with around 285 attending. This resulted in *Honor, Shame, and the Gospel: Rethinking Our Message and Ministry*. COVID-19 cancelled a second conference.

Christian mission must account for the predominance of strong honor-shame cultures in Scripture and today's world. Uncovering, living, and utilizing these core moral values will do much among the nations to make "his story" their story—and the story of their family and friends. The global church is being called to live and articulate a theology that equips all Christians to follow Jesus in their sociocultural context. That includes honor-shame realities.

27. China Mission 2030
Model and Back to Jerusalem Movement
A new China envisions a new church and a new world with a China Mission 2030 and Back to Jerusalem Movement.

A twenty-year spiritual harvest described as "the greatest revival in history" (Bush et al. 2013, 3) followed China's Cultural Revolution. Since opening up to the outside world in 1979, China has been transformed from an isolated land populated primarily by peasant families to a veritable economic powerhouse. By the end of 2011, more than half of China's people lived in urban areas for the first time in the nation's long history. Not only are these urban migrants building the infrastructure of today's and tomorrow's cities, they have also become integral to the very functioning of urban life.

The Back to Jerusalem movement evangelizes the unreached in China and beyond as the journey westward to Jerusalem is made. It has been a journey of learning, adjusting, and seeing Satan's kingdom give way to God's kingdom.

28. The 35/45 Turkic World Gateway Model
The 35/45 Turkic Window is a gateway model to the Muslim world and experienced the highest geographic response rate to the gospel in the 1990s.

The Silk Road draws a band across the heart of the modern Turkic World. Almost 90 percent of the world's estimated 145 million Turkic speakers live along the Silk Road, between the 35th and 45th parallels of the so-called 35/45 Turkic Window.

The Turkic church grew at over 40 percent per year during the 1990s, adding over 43,000 Christians (Casper 2020). Since 1990, annual meetings have birthed more than a dozen Turkic partnerships. These partnerships draw representatives from more than one hundred agencies, churches, and organizations, and provide an essential forum for communication, prayer, and fellowship. They tend to integrate cooperative initiatives in church planting, Bible teaching, and teaching (Bush 2003a).

29. Disciple Making Movements
and Church Planting Movements
The emphasis on Disciple Making Movements (DMMs) leads to the rapid multiplication of church planting movements (CPMs).

Some define Disciple Making Movements (DMMs) as distinct from Church Planting Movements (CPMs), while others see them as synonymous. A DMM refers to disciples making disciples who multiply discipleship groups (DMMs Frontier Missions n.d.), while a CPM is defined by David Garrison as "a rapid multiplication of indigenous churches that sweep through a people group or population segment" (Garrison 2004, 21). Following 2 Timothy 2:2, four generations of new believers have to be in place for a movement to be considered a CPM.

Victor John tells the compelling account of exponential growth among the 100 million Bhojpuri people of North India that represents one of many DMMs/CPMs (Coles and John 2019, 16–18). After beginning ministry in 1992 without a blueprint, a breakthrough occurred in 1998. That was when the New Testament debuted. The result was small house churches that didn't require a paid staff, making them easily reproducible yet less likely to invite attention and persecution. The goal was to have every generation start a new church. Victor John notes that they don't count believers, but rather churches or generations. And the movement now consists of over one hundred generations!

30. The Yes Effect Model
The Yes Effect Model seeks to unite the old and young to dream together in pursuit of the fullness of God.

The Yes Effect calls young and old to unite in one vision for God's coming kingdom and for his will to be done on earth. The maximized Yes Effect occurs when old and young unite to pursue the *fullness* of God (Joel 2:28; Acts 2:17).

The Yes Effect generates generational goals with dreams and visions surrounding the expansion of God's kingdom. Joel's prophetic word is fulfilled as the Holy Spirit anoints every believer. The atmosphere incorporates the social, spiritual, and relational factors that influence what individuals think and do.

It is the *final* time. It is time for *fullness*. It is time for old and young to unite to reach *all* with the gospel. Let us join together on his mission, for "No eye has seen, no ear has heard, and no mind has imagined what God has prepared for those who love him" (1 Cor 2:9 NLT).

Conclusion

The major trends in missions over the past fifty years reveal the DNA of dynamic models and catalytic impulses of Christian mission movements (Pierson 2006). These include renewal movements; affirmation of the priesthood of every believer; lowering barriers, including race, class, gender, clergy, crises—whether moral, political, economic, social, or spiritual; reform of the broader church, mission activity on the periphery of the church, emerging streams from the Global South; and new leadership emergence. From God's revelation in the book of Habakkuk, we have assurance that the gospel we carry to the nations will be victorious over evil, and that Jesus will reign forever. Amen!

References Cited

Aghamkar, Atul Y. n.d. "Migration, Change, and Christian Mission Among Migrants," https://documentcloud.adobe.com/link/review?uri=urn%3Aaaid%3Ascds%3AUS %3Acf20bea4-37db-4491-ba5f-9d03b3b23354#pageNum=1.

Barna Group. 2020. "The Future of Missions: 10 Questions About Global Ministry the Church Must Answer with the Next Generation." A Barna Report produced in Partnership with the International Mission Board, https://documentcloud.adobe. com/link/track?uri=urn:aaid:scds:US:bcd7aaff-c097-4654-a438-edcf49e06e3c.

Bebbington, D. 1989. *Evangelicalism in Modern Britain: A History from the 1730s to the 1930s.* London: Unwin Hyman.

Bush, Luis K. 1993. *AD2000 & Beyond Handbook,* https://documentcloud.adobe.com/ link/review?uri=urn%3Aaaid%3Ascds%3AUS%3Ad6339699-affb-4e6b-9ff6-09a4629bd331.

———. 1997. COMIBAM 97: "An Assessment of the Latin American Missions Movement." http://www.ad2000.org/re71216.htm.

———. 1998. "Global Trends, with a Special Focus on the 10/40 Window." https:// documentcloud.adobe.com/link/review?uri=urn:aaid:scds:US:d81c8130-6a0f-4e5c-a886-0fbae2adf78a.

———. 2000. "The 35/45 Turkic Window: A Gateway to the Muslim World." AD 2000 & Beyond and Joshua Project 2000.

———. 2002. "Catalysts of World Evangelization." PhD diss., Fuller Theological Seminary. https://documentcloud.adobe.com/link/track?uri=urn%3Aaaid%3Ascds %3AUS%3Ae2a5ecf-cce8-499b-81e3-15af5167c350#pageNum=1.

———. 2003a. "The Bases for a Missiological Decision Making Framework." https:// documentcloud.adobe.com/link/review?uri=urn%3Aaaid%3Ascds%3AUS%3A56f ed266-1a12-4720-a14e-09815303824c.

https://drive.google.com/drive/folders/1Z0SSbqHI6iP0OCKvNzjPRn9-ToAivlQV.

———. 2018. "Transform World 2020 (TW2020) Report on Challenge Response Factors as of November 2018." *Transform World,* https://documentcloud.adobe. com/link/track?uri=urn%3Aaaid%3Ascds%3AUS%3A275158ba-bf2f-4852-aec7-73b903954545.

———. n.d. *The 35/45 Turkic Window Booklet.* https://drive.google.com/drive/ folders/1Z0SSbqHI6iP0OCKvNzjPRn9-ToAivlQV.

———. AD2000 as a Great Commission Catalyst. https://documentcloud.adobe.com/ link/review?uri=urn%3Aaaid%3Ascds%3AUS%3A1e944f59-8e7e-44c4-9309-0decf86408bd.

Bush, Luis; Brent Fulton, and A Christian Worker in China. 2013. *China's Next Generation: New China, New Church, New World.* https://documentcloud.adobe. com/link/review?uri=urn%3Aaaid%3Ascds%3AUS%3A050ddfd6-2e66-435d-9be8-acdff4af1cb1#pageNum=1.

Casper, Jayson. 2020. "Researchers Find Christians in Iran Approaching 1 Million." *Christianity Today,* September 3, https://www.christianitytoday.com/news/2020/ september/iran-christian-conversions-gamaan-religion-survey.html.

Coles, Dave, and Victor John. 2019. "A Still Thriving Middle-Aged Movement." *Mission Frontiers* 41:16–18. http://www.missionfrontiers.org/issue/article/a-still-thriving-middle-aged-movement.

Cornelius, Kirk J. Franklin, and J. P. Niemandt. 2013. "Vision 2025 and the Bible Translation Movement." *HTS Theological Studies* 69 (1). http://www.scielo.org.za/scielo.php?script=sci_arttext&pid=S0259-94222013000100048.

DMMs Frontier Missions. n.d. "What Is a DMM?" https://www.dmmsfrontiermissions.com/disciple-making-movement-what-defined/.

Garrison, David. 2004. *Church Planting Movements*. Midlothian, VA: WIGTake Resources.

ION. n.d. "How We Began." International Orality Network. https://orality.net/about/ion-history/how-we-began/.

Issue Group. 2004. "Making Disciples of Oral Learners." Lausanne Occasional Paper No. 54. https://lausanne.org/content/lop/making-disciples-oral-learners-lop-54

Johnson, Alan. 2001. "Part II: Major Concepts of the Frontier Mission Movement." *International Journal of Frontier Missions* 18: 89–97, https://www.ijfm.org/PDFs_IJFM/18_2_PDFs/AJmajor.pdf.

Johnstone, Patrick. 2011. *The Future of the Global Church*. Colorado Springs: Global Mapping International.

———. 2013. "Catching up with the Global Church." *Christianity Today*, January 14. https://www.christianitytoday.com/pastors/2013/winter/catching-up-with-global-church.html.

Lausanne Movement. 1989. "The Manila Manifesto." https://www.lausanne.org/content/manifesto/the-manila-manifesto.

McGavran, Donald A., and C. Peter Wagner. 1990. *Understanding Church Growth*. Grand Rapids: Eerdmans.

NC2P. n.d. "Reaching Your Nation through Church Planting." http://nc2p.org.

Padilla, C. Rene. 2004. *Transforming Church and Mission*. Publisher Unknown. https://documentcloud.adobe.com/link/review?uri=urn%3Aaaid%3Ascds%3AUS%3Ac9f623dd-a8e3-49ec-b1f8-974f2317e95c.

Pierson, Paul. 2006. "Factors in Revival and Renewal Movements." MovementsEverywhereRant, October 2. https://movementseverywhererant.wordpress.com/2006/10/02/factors-in-revival-and-renewal-movements-by-dr-paul-pierson/.

Snodderly, Beth, and A. Scott Moreau, eds. 2011. *Evangelical and Frontier Mission Perspectives on the Global Progress of the Gospel*. Oxford: Regnum Books. https://documentcloud.adobe.com/link/review?uri=urn%3Aaaid%3Ascds%3AUS%3Aa255270c-d910-4655-99dd-4053e51a272f.

Steffen, Tom. 2003. "Missiology's Journey for Acceptance in the Educational World." *Missiology: An International Review* 31 (2): 131–53.

———. 2017. "BAM 101." *Evangelical Missions Quarterly* 4: 12–15.

———. 2018. *Worldview-Based Storying: The Integration of Symbol, Story, and Ritual in the Orality Movement*. Richmond, VA: Orality Resources International.

Stott, John. 1974. "The Lausanne Covenant." https://www.lausanne.org/content/covenant/lausanne-covenant#cov.

Transform World. n.d. "TW2020: Thy Kingdom Come." https://documentcloud.adobe.com/link/track?uri=urn%3Aaaid%3Ascds%3AUS%3Abef74480-7c3d-424e-b018-10d667b56372#pageNum=4.

Winter, Ralph D. 1993. Editorial Comment. *Mission Frontiers*, March 1. http://www.missionfrontiers.org/issue/article/editorial-comment82.

Zurlo, Gina A., Todd M. Johnson, and Peter F. Crossing. 2019. "World Christianity and Mission 2020: Ongoing Shift to the South." *International Bulletin of Mission Research* 44 (1). https://journals.sagepub.com/doi/10.1177/2396939319880074

About the Contributors and Editors

AMINTA ARRINGTON (PhD, Biola University) is an associate professor of intercultural studies at John Brown University in Siloam Springs, Arkansas. Aminta is the author of *Songs of the Lisu Hills: Practicing Christianity in Southwest China.*

KEN BAKER (ThM Dallas Theological Seminary, DMiss Trinity Evangelical Divinity School) spent twenty-four years church planting with SIM in three West African countries—in five, primarily Muslim, contexts. After that, Ken was national director of Culture ConneXions, a ministry that coaches churches in intercultural life and ministry. Currently Ken is the global team training lead for SIM International.

LUIS BUSH (PhD Fuller Theological Seminary), born and raised in Latin America, is married to Doris, with whom he has four children, twenty grandchildren, and one great grandchild. He is a servant catalyst on God's missional movements, including COMIBAM—a Latin American cross-cultural missions movement; AD2000 & Beyond Movement; toward a church for every people and the gospel for every person; 10/40 Window—focusing on the region of the world with the greatest human suffering, combined with the least exposure to the gospel; Joshua Project—bringing definition to the unfinished task; Praying Through the Window—mobilizing prayer for the peoples of the 10/40 Window; North India Harvest Network; MANI—Mobilizing African National Initiatives; 35/45 Turkic Window; Evangelizing Our World Inquiry; Transform World Movement—connecting God's agents of transformation; 4/14 Window Movement—raising up a new generation of children to transform the world; Transform World 2020—responding to seven mega challenges, through seven spheres of cultural influence in ten regions of the world; WWO—World Without Orphans; equipping servant-leaders in China and North Korea for the advancement of God's kingdom purposes; and B2J—Back to Jerusalem Movement.

MICHAEL D. CRANE (PhD, Malaysia Baptist Theological Seminary) serves as a professor of urban missiology for two different seminaries and codirects an urban research think tank called Radius Global Cities Network. He was raised in several Asian urban centers by missionary parents and has served for sixteen years teaching and church planting in Asian cities. He has written a number of articles and books on urban missiology, as well as Asian church history, including *City Shaped Churches: Planting Churches in the Global Era* (Urban Loft).

XENIA LING-YEE CHAN is a doctoral student at Wycliffe College (Toronto School of Theology), specializing in Old Testament. Of Hong Kong diaspora descent, Xenia is currently church-planting in a diaspora-dominant city just north of Toronto. Her previous work experience includes journalism, government, and parachurch and church ministries.

ROBERT L. GALLAGHER (PhD, Fuller Theological Seminary) is professor emeritus of intercultural studies at Wheaton College Graduate School in Chicago, where he has taught since 1998. He has served as the president of the Midwest Mission Study Fellowship (2019–20) and the American Society of Missiology (2010–11). Earlier Robert served as an executive pastor in Australia (1979– 90). His publications include coediting *Mission in Acts: Ancient Narratives in Contemporary Context* (Orbis 2004), *Landmark Essays in Mission and World Christianity* (Orbis 2009), *Footprints of God: A Narrative Theology of Mission* (Wipf & Stock 2011), and *Contemporary Mission Theology: Engaging the Nations* (Orbis 2017), as well as coauthoring *Encountering the History of Missions: From the Early Church to Today* (Baker Academic 2017) and *Breaking through the Boundaries: God's Mission from the Outside In* (Orbis 2019).

ANNETTE R. HARRISON (PhD, UC Santa Barbara) is a Third Culture Kid who has lived, learned, and worked on four continents. She and her husband served with Wycliffe Bible Translators for twenty-three years, participating in Bible translation needs assessment through research, consulting, and training in Francophone Africa. Since 2012, Annette has taught courses in intercultural communication, applied linguistics, sociology, and anthropology at Corban University in Salem, Oregon. As associate professor of intercultural studies, she is a researcher, teacher, and mentor to her students.

TODD M. JOHNSON (PhD, William Carey International University) is the Eva B. and Paul E. Toms Distinguished Professor of Mission and Global Christianity and codirector of the Center for the Study of Global Christianity at Gordon-Conwell Theological Seminary. He is coauthor of the *World Christian Encyclopedia* (second and third editions), coeditor of the *Atlas of Global Christianity*, and series editor (with Ken Ross) of the ten-volume *Edinburgh Companions to Global Christianity* series.

KENNETH NEHRBASS (PhD, Biola University) has taught missiology at Liberty University, Biola University, and Belhaven University. He is an anthropology and translation consultant for the Summer Institute of Linguistics in the Pacific Area. He has authored or edited over sixty missiological publications, including *Advanced Missiology* (Cascade), *God's Image and Global Cultures* (Cascade), and *Christianity and Animism in Melanesia* (William Carey Library Press).

LISA PAK (MDiv, Gordon-Conwell Theological Seminary) currently serves as the global strategist for Finishing The Task (FTT). Her previous experience includes serving as the regional director for Ontario and Nunavut at the Canadian Bible Society, in addition to fourteen years of pastoral ministry and church experience in South Korea, Singapore, and Canada, with a particular focus among the Korean-diaspora community. Lisa is a second-generation Korean-Canadian and Toronto native, and is passionate about diaspora communities and mobilizing the young generation for the gospel.

MARTIN RODRIGUEZ (PhD, Fuller Theological Seminary) is assistant professor of practical theology at Azusa Pacific University. Martin was born in Modesto, California, and raised on the mission field in Puebla, Mexico. Like many bicultural Latinx individuals, he has learned to thrive in the liminal space between cultural narratives. Before obtaining his PhD at Fuller, Martin's love for God and the global church led him to five years of mission work among emerging Christian leaders in East Asia. Martin has seventeen years of leadership experience in intercultural faith communities. Currently, Martin's research interests lie at the intersection of postcolonial hybridity theory and late-modern leadership theories. He is especially interested in exploring missional leadership practices that honor God's agency and the agency of cultural others in the midst of cultural pluralism and power asymmetries.

NARRY SANTOS (PhD, Dallas Theological Seminary; PhD, University of the Philippines) is assistant professor of practical theology and intercultural leadership at the seminary of Tyndale University, Toronto, Canada. His books include *Slave of All* (Sheffield Academic Press), *Turning Our Shame into Honor* (Life-Change), and *Family Relations in the Gospel of Mark* (Peter Lang).

LINDA P. SAUNDERS (PhD, Columbia International University) has served as a career missionary in South America for more than seventeen years (Linda and her family lived in Venezuela for almost 15 years). Her passion is to equip and involve African Americans (especially young adults) in global missions. Linda has published several articles with the Evangelical Missiological Society (EMS) where she serves on the leadership team. She is an adjunct faculty member at CIU and an adjunct professor at Liberty University. She is also a multicultural consultant for Wellspring of Hope, LLC in Lynchburg, Virginia and Community Faith Partners of Ithaca, NY. Linda and her husband reside in Virginia and love spending family time with their children and grandchildren.

ROCHELLE SCHEUERMANN (PhD, Trinity Evangelical Divinity School) is associate professor of evangelism and leadership and program director for three master's programs at Wheaton College. She is an ordained minister, a former church planter, and has been in education for ten years. Her books include *Preaching in the Contemporary World* and *Controversies in Mission*. She served for five years as the North Central Regional VP and is currently the VP of Membership for EMS.

TOM STEFFEN (PhD, Biola University) is professor emeritus of intercultural studies at the Cook School of Intercultural Studies, Biola University. He specializes in church multiplication, orality, honor and shame, and business as mission.

ALLAN VARGHESE is a PhD student in intercultural studies at Asbury Theological Seminary and researches on the intersection of Pentecostalism, interreligious encounters, and missional social engagement. He comes with cross-cultural social work experience, especially working with churches and nongovernmental organizations in Bangalore, London, and Durham, North Carolina. He holds a MSW (Christ University, Bangalore), MA in Integrative Psychotherapy (London School of Theology), and MTS (Duke University) and is a graduate of Oxford Center for Christian Apologetics.

EMMA WILD-WOOD (PhD, University of Edinburgh) is co-director of the Centre for the Study of World Christianity and Senior Lecturer in African Christianity and African Indigenous Religions at the University of Edinburgh. She has taught in Cambridge, UK, Uganda, and Congo. Her most recent books are *The Mission of Apolo Kivebulaya: Religious Encounter and Social Change in the Great Lakes (c.1865-1935)* (2020) and, edited with Alex Chow, *Ecumenism and Independency in World Christianity: Historical Studies in Honour of Brian Stanley* (2020).

MATTHEW WINSLOW is a faculty member at the East Asia School of Theology in Singapore, where he enjoys teaching courses in church history and in systematic theology. He is also currently a PhD candidate at Trinity Evangelical Divinity School, where he is researching the impacts of the 1908 Manchurian Revival on the growth of the church in China. Matthew is married to Sze Chieh, and they have three kids and a dog.